# crazy about
# chocolate

# crazy about
# chocolate

More than 200 Delicious Recipes
to Enjoy and Share

**Krystina Castella**

STERLING
New York

**STERLING**
New York

An Imprint of Sterling Publishing
387 Park Avenue South
New York, NY 10016

ISBN 978-1-4027-9884-9

Library of Congress Cataloging-in-Publication Data

Castella, Krystina.
  Crazy about chocolate : more than 2000 delicious recipes to enjoy and share / Krystina Castella.
    pages cm
  Includes index.
  ISBN 978-1-4027-9884-9
  1. Cooking (Chocolate) I. Title.
  TX767.C5C37 2013
  641.6'374--dc23
                                2013004182

Distributed in Canada by Sterling Publishing
c/o Canadian Manda Group, 165 Dufferin Street
Toronto, Ontario, Canada M6K 3H6
Distributed in the United Kingdom by GMC Distribution Services
Castle Place, 166 High Street, Lewes, East Sussex, England BN7 1XU
Distributed in Australia by Capricorn Link (Australia) Pty. Ltd.
P.O. Box 704, Windsor, NSW 2756, Australia

For information about custom editions, special sales, and premium and corporate purchases,
please contact Sterling Special Sales at 800-805-5489 or specialsales@sterlingpublishing.com.

Manufactured in China

2  4  6  8  10  9  7  5  3  1

www.sterlingpublishing.com

*For Dawn, Vince, and Madison Fiore.*

*Here's to a sweet life.*

**Acknowledgments**
Thank you to a great team:
Jennifer Williams, editor
Sasha Tropp, assistant editor
Kimberly Marini, production editor
Teri Lyn Fisher, photographer
Jennifer Park, food stylist
Larena Faretta, baking assistant
Rachel Maloney, design director
Elizabeth Mihaltse, cover art director
Jason Chow, cover designer

# Contents

# The Most Popular Flavor on Earth

When asked, "What do you want to be when you grow up?" kids know that some answers get a better response than others. I realized that "a doctor" or "a lawyer" received oohs and aahs, and I was a kid who liked positive feedback, so those were my standard answers even though I had my own secret ambition: to grow up and own a chocolate factory—one that boasted conveyer belts with truffles speeding by and big mixers whipping up vats of fudge, where chocolate candy bars were assembled layer by layer and packed with caramel. I would dip everything that was already great—including potato chips and fortune cookies—in chocolate, making it even better. At the chocolate factory I would toil happily all day in a chocolate-scented environment, and then, at the end of the workday, I would treat myself to a reward: a piece of free chocolate, whichever one I liked best.

I first got this idea from my role model at the time, Lucille Ball. She was funny and everyone loved her, and when it was time for her to get a job she knew how to choose a good one—one where you work side by side with your best friend and hide chocolate under your hat! I explored life in a chocolate factory further in the book *Charlie and the Chocolate Factory*, where I learned that there was more to it than simply making chocolate—there were golden tickets, chocolate rivers, and gigantic machines. And spy-like secrecy was very important (after all, chocolate is a serious subject, not to be discussed lightly). The movie *Willy Wonka & the Chocolate Factory*, which was based on the book, was even darker and scarier than I had imagined, but that did not change my mind. I knew I could be fearless enough to take on the job and whip the place into shape. At school, when everyone in my class chose to write their history papers on the United States, I opted to study the history of chocolate: its evolution from the Mayan and Aztec food of the gods to the socially popular European beverage to its current ubiquity as mass-consumed candy bars. To me, this was so much more interesting than other topics not affecting my daily life. Chocolate was important. I soon gained popularity as the go-to person for anything chocolate.

My sister, Dawn, and a group of girls on Genesee Avenue in Staten Island, New York, where I grew up, all agreed with everything I believed in regarding chocolate (i.e., that it was by far not only the best food but also the best thing on this planet). Being the oldest of the group, I would organize and lead our Saturday bike rides to the corner candy store, where we would buy our favorite chocolate bars and then hang out outside the store, eating and talking about whatever grade school girls talk about.

In the summer, my family would visit the New Jersey shore. Although I loved the ocean and the beach, what I loved even more were the old-fashioned boardwalk candy shops that sold homemade fudge, chocolate-covered apples, and caramel-and-pecan-filled turtles. Visiting these mini chocolate factories, where I got to see real people making chocolate by hand and even some of the machines in action, I realized I did not need a big factory with a chocolate river. Here by the seaside, I could focus on making the best chocolate in the world and play in the sand on my days off. I looked forward to these chocolate outings, which filled up the year between the "chocolate holidays."

Luckily for me, there are many holidays that involve chocolate big-time. On Valentine's Day, the first big one of the year, my sister and I would sit by the front door waiting for our dad to come home with a big box of crème- and cordial-filled chocolates for each of us. These were fancier than the candy bars we ate on Saturdays and were to be savored slowly. Easter was all about the chocolate bunnies waiting for me in my basket; Christmas had its peppermint bark. I would craft my own holiday sweets by melting chocolate in a mold, assembling the confections, and decorating with even more chocolate.

Out of all the chocolate holidays, I anticipated Halloween the most. I had trick-or-treating down to a science. My goal each year was to collect 365 pieces of candy, crossing my fingers that most of it was chocolate, with some candy corn and lollipops thrown in. As soon as school let out on Halloween day, I started going door-to-door, my trek lasting until about nine at night—a full six hours. I collected my loot in a plastic jack-o'-lantern that fit fifty to fifty-five pieces of candy. This meant about seven rounds of trick-or-treating. Every time my container filled up and I couldn't stuff another treat into it, I would return home, empty the contents onto my bed, and then head out in a different direction to start again. Once I finished my seven excursions, I sorted the candy by type into four large piles—pile 1: chocolate; pile 2: lollipops; pile 3: candy corn; pile 4: miscellaneous candy I considered "just okay." I then created packages of seven pieces, taking one or two from each pile and placing them into fifty-two separate plastsic bags. I put these in a box and stored them in a cool, dark place that only I knew about. Each week I removed one plastic bag from the box, hiding it in my sock drawer, and indulged in one treat a day per week. With my system, the plastic bags lasted the entire year until next Halloween. Any extra candy over the 365 mark (or 366 if it was a leap year) went to Grandma Lucarelli, who shared my love of chocolate and always visited from Brooklyn on Halloween to join the excitement. Little did I know then that my practice of enjoying one piece of candy a day taught me something very important: Eating chocolate every day is the secret to happiness. For more than twenty years, my husband, Brian, and I have each savored a one-ounce piece of dark chocolate after every dinner as the ultimate indulgence to end the day.

Around the age of eight I began experimenting in the kitchen and quickly realized that chocolate was not just a candy, but also an ingredient that could make just about anything fabulous—sweet *or* savory. At that point in my life every meal, from breakfast to lunch to dinner, had a bit of chocolate in it. No matter what I created— waffles, cupcakes, cookies, ice pops, pudding—everything always tasted its best with chocolate. Sometimes the more I added the better it was, and at other times just a few chips were enough to bring out delightful flavors. I loved candy crafting and the simplicity of melting and tempering chocolate, then forming it into the best shape for the occasion. I melted chocolate into lollipops to fill Easter baskets (page 194), decorated solid chocolate cakes for birthdays (pages 121–122), and created chocolate skulls for Halloween (page 217). I feel the same way today about chocolate as I did back then. Nothing has changed one bit.

So what happened to my dream of a chocolate factory? I'm working on it. I continue to play and create in the kitchen, and chocolate is my favorite ingredient. Recently I've been focusing my effort on developing these recipes to share with you. My lifetime of learning was brought into a tighter focus as I experimented with some of my favorite chocolate recipes, sweet and savory, perfecting them for this book. I used multiple processes—baking, freezing, melting, you name it—and thought long and hard about what to include in this collection. As part of my creative process, I observed the evolving chocolate trends, new flavor combinations, and modern lifestyles.

In the past, the word "chocolate" simply said it all. Today, we're aware that chocolate is not just a single ingredient but is made with various percentages of cacao to create different types of chocolate. The many varieties are commonly combined with new flavors, such as chili and salt, that ten years ago would have seemed exotic but have now become commonplace for snacking in homes and offices. In addition, chocolate is added to savory dishes more than ever before, and the newly discovered health benefits of dark chocolate make it the perfect indulgence for an after-workout treat. I used three criteria to help determine what to include in this collection of more than 200 delicious treats that capture what chocolate is about today: the search for the ultimate taste; crafting chocolate as an art form; and cultural and flavor trends.

## SEARCHING FOR THE ULTIMATE TASTE

If you're a chocolate lover, you know the flavor of quality chocolate cannot be matched. Chocolate can be an affordable luxury, so cost is often not an issue. With quality ingredients, the simplicity of these recipes shines. When unpretentious bold flavors, such as in the Caramel Mocha Ice Cream Cake (page 105) or Pumpkin Tart (page 224), meld with high-grade chocolate, the recipes become an approachable celebration of life's basic delights. Try to select cocoa bars and powder by aroma and texture—they should be smooth and crisp with a strong aroma—and buy the best you can afford. When purchasing chocolate, honor its cultural roots by keeping in mind the agricultural practices, business ethics, and sustainability policies of the company that makes it. As far as variety goes, healthy dark chocolate is well liked and currently all the rage, but milk chocolate is making a comeback. Combining dark and semisweet chocolate with fruits, as in the recipes for Chocolate-Dipped Dried and Candied Fruit (page 234), Chocolate Yogurt and Fruit Parfaits with Granola Topping (page 98), and Chewy Chocolate Fruit Bars (page 213), is a good way to promote wellness without sacrificing enjoyment.

## WORKING WITH CHOCOLATE AS AN ART FORM

A strong foundation in art and design has led me to approach food as a material to craft. Chocolate, especially, gives us permission to have fun— and I am not alone in this sentiment. There is a growing artisanal scene of confectioners and bakers who share my love of working with chocolate. Once you've learned a few simple techniques, including melting and tempering (page 29), making truffles (page 52), baking the perfect layer cake (page 56), and preparing the best homemade piecrust (page 241), chocolate holds no boundaries. Its ability to be molded (see Solid Chocolate Wedding Cakes, page 121), combined with other ingredients (see Florentines, page 65), and filled (see Filled Molded Chocolates, page 186) creates a seemingly endless variety of ways to have fun with chocolate. You're the artist—keep chocolate in your imagination.

## CULTURAL AND FLAVOR TRENDS

With my preference for the classic I don't typically pay attention to trends, but when it comes to food I follow what is new and hot because it's often experimental, and anything experimental is worth a try at least once. The proof is in the pudding, as they say (and there are several in this book), so a trend lasts with me only if it has some legs. I've listed some of the most recent food and chocolate movements that I believe are here to stay for a while, and which inspired many of the recipes for this book. Some I noticed evolving by myself; others I saw highlighted at chocolate festivals throughout the world.

UPDATES ON RETRO FOODS: Made simply, these recipes feature new, better ingredients and subtle flavor additions. Desserts inspired by the twentieth century, such as Bundt cakes (page 101), nougat (page 231), tapioca pudding (page 95), and fondue (page 166) are very popular, but these are not your grandma's recipes.

ANYTHING SWEET AND FRIED IS GOOD: We just can't give up splurging on something a little bad for us if it's hot and delicious. Doughnuts (page 129), fried sesame balls (page 179), and sweet potato fries with chocolate sauce (page 242) are all a must every now and then.

STATE FAIR FARE AND SEASIDE TREATS: Location, location, location inspired these recipes. Chocolate is no longer just a snack to munch on while meandering around booths, as state-fair-favorite chocolate-covered bacon makes the move to the breakfast plate when served alongside French Toast. Sweets typically found in seaside shops, such as turtles (page 46), fudge (page 48), and caramel apples (page 219), have been simplified for you to make at home for special occasions or everyday treats.

SAVORY CHOCOLATE: Chocolate can spice up brunch (page 137), dinner (page 155), cocktail parties (page 165), and barbecues (page 145). Although savory chocolate may be a new approach for some, have no fear—chocolate has been added to savory recipes for centuries.

MINI AND INDIVIDUAL DESSERTS: This trend, which seems to have no end in sight, started with the cupcake (pages 108–109) and continues in éclairs (page 132), cream puffs (page 132), brownie bites (page 169), and even burgers (page 150), all small enough to customize one (or more) of your very own.

A FLAVOR TWIST ON THE FAMILIAR: Old standbys find new life when updated with modern trends. No more plain hot chocolate when you have Spicy Hot Chocolate (page 217). Chocolate-coated caramel becomes salted chocolate and buttery caramel (page 43). Homemade frozen wonders, including ice cream (page 91), sorbet (page 85), ice cream cake (page 105), and ice cream pops (page 88), all add a refreshing chill to chocolate.

INTERNATIONAL INFLUENCES: Experiment with world cuisines; for example, swap out the traditional fillings in Asian desserts with chocolate. Inspirations include mochi (page 173), caramel sesame candy (page 178), bubble tea (page 181), pineapple moon cakes (page 174), and sesame balls (page 179). Italian recipes, such as the panforte (page 232), cranberry crostata (page 225), and torrone candy bars (page 231), reflect my heritage. French macarons (page 127) are an all-time favorite of mine for baby celebrations. Jewish traditions also receive an update with the addition of Chocolate Chip Challah (page 208).

## ABOUT THIS BOOK

I organized the recipes in this book into five chapters covering an array of chocolate recipes in all textures and flavors. In "Everyday Chocolate" you will find basic recipes for almost anything you can imagine— candy, cakes, cookies, breads, pies, ice creams, puddings . . . and the list goes on. These simple-to-make confections are perfect for spur-of-the-moment kitchen fun. "Chocolate for Special Occasions" contains treats to help us celebrate three of the most important occasions in our lives—birthdays, weddings, and baby celebrations. The "Party Chocolate" section chapter includes recipe suggestions for everything from a casual weekend brunch to a formal dinner. "Holiday Chocolate" offers chocolate recipes that have become synonymous with seasonal holidays, as well as new ideas that present a twist on tradition. Finally, the "Sauces, Crusts, and Toppings" chapter provides accompaniments to be used with recipes throughout the book, as well as supplemental flavorings that you can try mixing and matching to suit your own tastes.

If you want to learn more about the tools, techniques, ingredients, and how-to's of working with chocolate—including tips on choosing the right equipment, setting up your kitchen, and expanding your technical skills—take a look at the first chapter, "Chocolate in the Know," and sidebars throughout the book. I also offer troubleshooting solutions for the most common questions. The step-by-step techniques, recipes, and design ideas in this book are here for you to re-create in your kitchen or to use as a springboard for concepts of your own. Make your recipes as simple or complex as you like; follow the recipes exactly or experiment with them at will. Whatever approach you choose, I hope you have fun exploring all the possibilities that chocolate provides.

Now, let the chocolate loving begin. Enjoy!

# Chocolate in the Know

## THE CHOCOLATE MAKER'S TOOL KIT

Many of the recipes in this book can be made with common kitchen equipment and tools. Standard-size baking pans, pie and tart tins, baking sheets, muffin tins, and other kitchen tools are used throughout the recipes. In some cases specialized pans or tools are suggested to create unique designs or special presentations, such as an oval cake instead of the traditional round style or hexagonal mousse cakes. Those who have not experimented with candy making before may need to stock up on a few candy molds, a dipping tool, a candy thermometer, and accessories such as paper or foil liners and lollipop sticks.

### Basic Kitchen Setup

#### ENVIRONMENT

When you're making candy with chocolate, controlling the air temperature and humidity is more important than any piece of equipment in your kitchen. Humidity should be low so the chocolate doesn't sweat, and the ideal temperature is between 68°F and 70°F so the chocolate doesn't melt when you don't want it to. A cold environment works best for making pies and tarts, as the biggest challenge is keeping the crust cold while you're working with it. The same is true for rolled cookie dough. For cakes, puddings, and ice cream, maintaining a cold room temperature is most important when softening ingredients or decorating with whipped cream.

### MICROWAVE

A microwave oven can be used to quickly melt chocolate or butter or to thin honey. However, I am not a big fan of melting chocolate in the microwave—it's hard to keep a watchful eye on it. For information on how to melt chocolate in the microwave, see page 29.

### OVEN

Not all ovens actually maintain the temperature displayed on the controls, so be sure to use an oven thermometer before baking. Place the thermometer in the center of the oven, double-check the temperature for accuracy, and make adjustments as needed. The weather, time of day, and altitude can also affect oven temperature. Know your oven's hot and cool spots and always provide adequate circulation around the item you are cooking by using the center rack and leaving several inches of space around the pan.

### REFRIGERATOR AND FREEZER

Confectioners have mixed opinions on refrigerating chocolate to set it, although most people agree that when chocolate is allowed to set naturally, the time it takes for the cocoa butter to return to solid form is not forced, giving the chocolate a smoother mouthfeel and more consistent results. Refrigerating poorly tempered chocolate makes it more likely to bloom (see sidebar on page 35 for more on this), yet sometimes I think it's okay to refrigerate chocolate. If the chocolate is tempered properly, refrigerating sets it more quickly and allows molded chocolate to get harder than it would if it set at room temperature; harder chocolate is also somewhat easier to remove from the molds. In general, I leave this decision up to you, but in some recipes I specifically tell you to return the chocolate to room temperature by setting it out, and in others I suggest refrigerating it.

The refrigerator is also used to chill dough for cookies and piecrusts, set puddings quickly, and keep items cold while you're working with other recipe ingredients. The freezer can be used to make many frozen delights, from ice cream to ice pops to snow cones. It can also be used to chill cookie dough and piecrusts more quickly than the refrigerator. Keep in mind that you cannot set specific temperatures in the freezer, and the compressor continually turns on and off to maintain temperature. Allow plenty of time—patience is key—and keep the door closed as much as you can to retain temperature.

### STOVE TOP

When working with chocolate, you will be using your stove top continually, employing a double boiler to melt and temper the chocolate and a saucepan or double boiler to blend ingredients. A standard kitchen stove top works fine. In a pinch I have worked with chocolate on location with a hot plate. Choose a gas stove if you have the choice; it's easier to adjust for more precise temperatures.

### WORK SURFACE

You will need a smooth work surface for chopping and scoring chocolate, rolling out your cookie dough and piecrusts, and arranging decorations before placing them on your final masterpiece. A plastic or wood cutting board, marble or granite countertop, or really any flat, cool, clean kitchen surface will do. Professional shops use a stone countertop when working with chocolate to keep the environment cold. When dough needs to be chilled after being rolled out, it is best to work on a cutting board that can be easily wrapped and transferred from work surface to refrigerator.

## Equipment

### BOWLS

Start with three bowls: a 3-quart, a 2-quart, and a 1.5-quart bowl. You will use the larger bowls for whipping, creaming, and mixing ingredients and the smaller bowl for melting chocolate in the microwave and combining mix-ins such as chips, nuts, and dried fruits. An array of 1-cup bowls to hold chopped ingredients and other small mixtures is also handy. Plastic bowls are light, durable, nonreactive (some metal bowls react to some acidic ingredients, such as citrus fruits and tomato, and can impart a metallic taste), and relatively quiet when using a hand mixer. If you plan to microwave chocolate or butter, use a microwave-safe glass bowl such as Pyrex. Buy bowls with a spout for pouring.

## COOLING RACKS

Cooling racks are gridded metal racks that can be used for setting dipped chocolate out to harden. Cakes, pies, and cookies are often partially cooled in the pan and then transferred to a cooling rack, allowing the air to circulate around the baked good for even cooling. If you have a small kitchen, look for stackable cooling racks, since it is helpful to have more than one.

## ELECTRIC MIXERS

An electric mixer can be used to whip air into marshmallows and nougat, beat eggs to various stages of consistency, cream ingredients, and knead dough. Buy a handheld mixer that has a good range of power and speeds and both whisk-style and standard beater attachments. If you already own or are in the market for a stand mixer, you know that its main advantage is that you don't need to hold the mixer or the bowl, which locks in place. Stand mixers also come with many different attachments for everything from whisking to kneading dough to making ice cream. A 5-quart mixer with paddle, whip, and dough attachments is useful.

## FOOD PROCESSOR AND BLENDER

Food processors and blenders are great for chopping ingredients, grinding nuts, pureeing fruit, forming dough, and blending small amounts of sauces. A blender can sometimes be used as a food processor to whip or puree ingredients.

## SIFTER

Sifting gets rid of lumps in dry ingredients such as cocoa powder, flour, and confectioners' sugar that can cause clumps in your final product. When directed to, sift before measuring. If you don't have a sifter, you can use a handheld sieve. Small sifters also are good for dusting cakes with confectioners' sugar or cocoa powder.

# STORAGE CONTAINERS

- For storing cookies and bars, I recommend using tall, airtight glass or plastic containers (cookies and bars break less when stacked vertically). Store the treats with waxed or parchment paper between layers to prevent sticking.
- Use short, wide containers for storing candy since it keeps better when the pieces are stored side by side rather than stacked.
- If you plan on purchasing a new pie pan, buy one with a lid, which makes storing and transporting the pie easy. Cream and custard pies should always be stored in the refrigerator; nut and fruit pies can stay out on a counter for a day or two and then be transferred to the refrigerator to stay fresh longer.
- Cakes containing perishable ingredients, such as cream cheese, custard, or whipped cream, and cakes topped with frosting that contains raw eggs or milk should be refrigerated. Pound cakes, fruitcakes, scones, and muffins will stay fresh at room temperature in a cake keeper or covered with plastic wrap for two to three days. Fruitcakes soaked in alcohol last for several weeks. Cakes with moist ingredients and fresh fruits can lose their freshness quickly and should be placed in a cake keeper or covered in plastic wrap and stored in the refrigerator.
- Ice creams and sorbets should always be tightly packed in a container and stored in the freezer. Ice cream cakes should be covered in plastic wrap; ice pops should be stored in the molds that they were prepared in until ready to eat.
- Puddings should be covered and stored in the refrigerator.

## Cookware

### BAKING PANS

Numerous types of baking pans are used throughout the book. Candy can be a pretty sticky business, so make sure all the pans you use for candy are nonstick. The height of the sides should be 1½–2 inches. Bars and bread pudding are made in rectangular or square baking pans, and round, square, and oval baking pans can be used for cakes. You'll need a springform pan with a removable bottom for cheesecakes, a pie pan for pies, and tart pans with removable bottoms for tarts. Use muffin tins, commonly available in mini, medium, and large sizes, to make cupcakes. Although you can bake directly in the tin—and some recipes specify doing this—most people prefer to use paper, foil, or silicone liners so that the cupcakes are easy to remove and hold. Silicone pans work well to form mousse into shapes. If you will be storing a baked good, pans with lids are good choices.

### BAKING SHEETS

Baking sheets have multiple uses. They can be used for baking cookies, of course, but you can also place them under pie and cake pans in the oven to evenly distribute heat or put them under a cooling rack to gather drizzles of chocolate being used as coating. The best sheets are made from shiny aluminum; darker sheets absorb heat and may make baked goods too brown on the bottom. There are two types of baking sheets, flat and rimmed. Flat sheets have no lip on three sides and a raised, angled lip on the fourth side to make it easy to remove from the oven. Rimmed baking sheets, which have an edge all the way around the pan, can be set under a cooling rack and used to collect poured chocolate coatings. This chocolate can then be gathered and reused for additional coatings. Purchase baking sheets about 4 inches smaller than your oven, so heat can circulate around them—12 x 15½ inches is a good size. Line baking sheets with parchment paper to diffuse the heat and prevent sticking.

## CANDY MOLDS

You can find a full selection of plastic molds at every cake and candy supply store. These inexpensive, thin, rigid molds, which contain a few concave decorative shapes, are made to be used a few times and then tossed out. They crack easily and the plastic becomes brittle over time. Because of their low cost, they're a good choice for beginners. They also work well when you need to make candy for a specific event or occasion. Don't use them for hard candy lollipops, though, since the candy tends to stick to the molds. Silicone baking molds or heat-proof ice cube trays are another good choice for forming chocolate. If you decide you like working with chocolate, you should invest in professional candy molds created for long-term use. Made of metal, polycarbonate, plastic, or silicone, they are higher quality and have more cavities per mold than lower-quality versions.

## DOUBLE BOILER

A double boiler is the most important piece of cookware for working with chocolate. You'll need it for melting and tempering chocolate, blending delicate sauces, and preparing other ingredients that must be heated very slowly or gently over low heat. Look for a double boiler with a shallow top saucepan (about 3 inches high for a 2-quart saucepan). To use a double boiler, fill the bottom pan with water almost to the top, but do not let it touch the top pan; then put ingredients in the top pan as directed in the recipe. The steam from the hot water heats the top pan at a low temperature, which gives you good control over cooking or melting the ingredients. You can also fashion a double boiler by placing a large heatproof bowl over a slightly smaller saucepan filled with simmering water. Choose a glass bowl so you can monitor the water temperature and levels. Although you can also melt chocolate in the microwave, I prefer the double boiler method since it heats the chocolate more evenly. Actively stirring while melting ensures smooth results.

### SAUCEPANS
Saucepans are used often in these recipes to combine ingredients. You should have good-quality, nonreactive, heavy-bottomed, stainless steel 2-quart and 4-quart saucepans that distribute heat evenly.

### TEMPERING MACHINE
Tempering machines are specialized machines used to temper chocolate and keep it at the correct temperature for the recipe. If you find yourself addicted to making chocolate and not just eating it, and have a kitchen with enough storage space, a tempering machine is worth the investment.

## Measuring Tools

### MEASURING CUPS AND SPOONS
To achieve the most accurate measurements, use 2-cup glass measuring cups with spouts for liquids, and 2-quart measuring cups for dividing batter between pans. You'll need a measuring cup set that comes in graduated sizes—typically ¼, ⅓, ½, and 1 cup—for dry ingredients. Spoon the dry ingredients into the cups (do not scoop from the container) and remove any excess ingredients by running a knife over the top of the cup to level it. Household teaspoons and tablespoons usually are designed for aesthetics and are not accurate for cooking or baking. To be sure you have the correct volume, use a set of measuring spoons in graduated sizes.

### RULER
A clean ruler is good to have on hand for measuring chocolate pieces, marking a cake before cutting it into layers, and ensuring that decorations are evenly spaced.

## KITCHEN SCALE

Although culinary professionals in the United States measure ingredients by weight, home chefs tend to measure by volume. Therefore, the ingredients listed in this book are measured by volume, except solid chocolate, which is measured in ounces, making a digital household kitchen scale very helpful. Since most bars of chocolate come molded in 1-ounce squares or rectangles, they're easy to measure and break.

## THERMOMETERS

You'll need a thermometer to measure the temperature for both sugar and chocolate, so buy the best one you can find; it should very dependable, accurate, and easy to read. Test the thermometer by placing it in boiling water. It should read around 212°F (note that it will be lower at high altitudes). When measuring temperatures, never let the thermometer touch the pan or your results will be inaccurate. Below is a list of the different thermometers that you might encounter when working with chocolate. For the recipes in this book, the candy thermometer is the most important one to own.

> **Candy Thermometer**: Available in glass tube, dial, or digital probe styles and designed for high temperatures, a candy thermometer is used to measure sugar mixtures, sauces, and frostings at various stages of cooking.
>
> **Chocolate Thermometer**: Perfect for tempering chocolate, a chocolate thermometer reads much lower temperatures than a candy thermometer, ranging from 40°F to 130°F.
>
> **Deep-Fry Thermometer**: A deep-fry thermometer measures the temperature of oil for frying doughnuts and French fries. Some thermometers can be used for both candy making and deep-frying. Purchase one that clips onto the side of the saucepan.
>
> **Oven Thermometer**: Although your oven has a temperature gauge, rarely is it right on target. Place a portable oven thermometer in the center of the oven, double-check it for accuracy, and make adjustments as

needed. The weather, time of day, and altitude can all affect oven temperature. Know your oven's hot and cool spots and always provide adequate circulation around baking pans.

**TIMER**

Baking time is always going to be inexact, since it depends on the amount of moisture in the ingredients, the number of pans in the oven (and thus how much room there is for air to circulate), and the accuracy of your oven's temperature. Buy a kitchen timer and carry it with you while baking. You don't want the timer on your stove or oven to beep when you're too far away to hear it!

## CANDY STAGE CHART

| Stage | Temperature | Description | Usage |
|---|---|---|---|
| Thread | 223–235°F | The sugar syrup drips from a spoon and forms thin threads when drizzled in water or over a plate. | Candied fruits |
| Soft ball | 235–240°F | The syrup easily forms a ball when dropped in cold water but flattens once removed or pressed lightly with your fingers. | Fudge |
| Firm Ball | 245–250°F | The syrup forms into a stable ball but loses its round shape once pressed with your fingers. | Caramel candies |
| Hard ball | 250–266°F | The syrup holds its ball shape but remains sticky and pliable. | Marshmallows |
| Soft crack | 270–290°F | The syrup forms firm but pliable (not brittle) threads when dropped in water. | Nougat |
| Hard crack | 300–310°F | The syrup solidifies when dropped in water and cracks if you try to mold it. | Lollipops and brittle |
| Caramel | 320–350°F | The sugar syrup turns golden or dark reddish amber. | Caramel |

# Hand Tools

## COOKIE CUTTERS

If you are just starting a collection of cookie cutters, invest in good stainless steel sets of round ones and square ones with plain and fluted edges. You'll use these frequently to cut baked goods into shapes after baking, cut dough to make decorative crusts, and cut doughnuts into playful shapes. Once you have the standard cutters in your cabinet, then you can start splurging on common shapes such as gingerbread men, leaves, flowers, and an alphabet set, all of which I use very often. After that you can branch out and build your collection with butterflies or pumpkins or whatever you choose. Metal cutters are usually the sharpest, although if you're looking for a specific shape, plastic cookie cutters will also do if that's all you can find. Metal cutters rust if not dried properly, so be sure to place them in an oven on low heat (200°F) for 10 minutes to dry out after washing.

## DIPPING TOOLS

There are two types of tools designed for dipping fruit and centers into chocolate: rounded and forked. A rounded dipping tool holds fragile creamy centers or soft fruit in a basket-shaped spiral, while the prongs of the fork tool are pierced into more rigid centers. These tools make it easy to suspend the dipped piece in the chocolate and allow the chocolate to flow off. A standard fork is too big for most candy, but you can make your own dipping tool by using pliers to bend two prongs of an inexpensive fork about 45 degrees upward.

## DISPOSABLE GLOVES

Chocolate picks up imprints from the oils in our fingers. Since nobody likes to see fingerprints or smudges on their beautiful piece of chocolate, wear disposable gloves in the final stages of making truffles, molded chocolates, and other chocolate candies. You should also put on gloves when placing goodies in a box for gifting.

## DOUGH CUTTERS

Pizza or pastry cutters can be used after cookie or pie dough is rolled to create straight lines and free-form cuts.

## KITCHEN SHEARS

These specialized scissors are used to cut dough or trim the excess overhanging dough from the bottom and top crusts of pies. Paring knives also can be used.

## KNIVES

To chop chocolate into chunks, choose a large chef's knife with a long, broad blade and sharp edge. When you need a specific size or shape of chocolate, it should be scored first with a small paring knife and then broken along the score. For dividing and cutting cake layers, use a long serrated knife. A utility knife can cut straight edges with a ruler as a guide or can be used to make free-form shapes.

## LADLE

A ladle is the easiest tool to use when pouring chocolate into molds. Choose one with a spout to give you the best control over the pour.

## LONG-HANDLED TWEEZERS

Excellent for moving delicate chocolate to a cooling rack or into a box without fingerprint smudges, long-handled tweezers are also handy for precise placement of tiny toppings when decorating candy, cakes, and cookies.

## PASTRY BAGS AND TIPS

Pastry bags are cone-shaped bags used to extrude ("pipe") chocolate, whipped cream, and meringue through a plain circular tip. A device called a coupler holds the tip to the bag. When you want to drizzle chocolate or create small lines, you can cut off the tip of the bag to leave a hole in the desired size without adding a plastic or metal tip. Pastry bags are made out of either reusable or disposable materials, such as plastic, canvas, parchment paper, or nylon. For chocolate, smaller bags are better (about 6 inches); for whipped cream and frostings, bigger bags are better (10 inches and 12 inches are the most common sizes). It's convenient to have several pastry bags at your disposal so you can use several different colors or fillings on a single project without stopping to clean and refill.

Many stores carry disposable, ready-made tubes of icing and frosting with the piping tip built into the end. You can cut the tip to vary the line thickness and throw the tube away when finished. You can also use homemade tools, such as recycled squirt bottles and airtight plastic bags with a corner cut off, to pipe frosting (the latter is excellent for drizzling chocolate).

Large tips are good for thick mixtures like meringue and buttercream, small tips work well for chocolate and delicate writing, and medium-size tips are best for borders. Serrated tips extrude textured lines and are used to create stars, zigzags, textured borders, shells, ropes, and rosettes. To get started, you need just a few round and star-shaped tips in large, medium, and small sizes.

### PASTRY BRUSHES

Pastry brushes are used to paint chocolate into molds, distribute sauces and syrups evenly, and brush egg washes and glazes on top of crusts. Invest in tightly woven, natural boar-bristle or high-quality silicone brushes in small, medium, and large sizes. Both types of brushes are designed to hold liquids for easy coating. Boar-bristle brushes will give you more control when detail is required. Silicone brushes are odor resistant and easy to clean.

### ZESTERS, PEELERS, AND GRATERS

Used to remove the zest from citrus fruits, a zester or microplane grater allows you to remove just the thin outer layer of peel and not the bitter white pith. A box grater works for large ingredients like carrots, and many have a side with small holes for zesting as well. You can use the small side of the grater for shredding small chocolate pieces and the large side for creating curls. A vegetable peeler can also be used to make curls.

### ROLLING PIN

A rolling pin is the most important tool for flattening pie and cookie dough into an even thickness. My favorite is a heavy two-handled marble rolling pin. The weight makes it easy to roll out a very thin crust. The roller also stays cool, which is crucial when working with dough. A rolling pin can also be used as a form to shape chocolate into curls or cylindrical shapes before it sets. Wrap the rolling pin in parchment, and either pipe the chocolate using a pastry bag or spread it with an offset spatula to create curls and let set.

### SKEWERS AND TOOTHPICKS

Bamboo skewers can be used to poke holes for venting and to draw textures, indentations, and details (such as the veins of a leaf) on pie or cookie dough. Toothpicks serve the same purpose, but skewers are easier to work with because they're longer and therefore easier to hold.

### SPATULAS AND WOODEN SPOONS

Stock your tool kit with wooden spoons and spatulas of various sizes. Use whisks for mixing liquid ingredients, wooden spoons for combining mixtures and stirring hot ingredients, and rubber or silicone spatulas for scraping the bowl, folding ingredients, and blending frosting. There are three kinds of metal spatulas: straight, offset, and triangular. Use whichever type you find easiest to maneuver. I prefer the offset ones, as they are very helpful for lifting candy from a cooling rack and spreading smooth surfaces on the tops of filling. These stainless steel spatulas come in many sizes, but it's most important to have a small (4½-inch) one and a large (8–10-inch) one for icing cakes.

### WIRE WHISKS

Used to combine dry and liquid ingredients and to stir custards while thickening, whisks can also be used to whip heavy cream, although an electric mixer is usually quicker. If you hate to sift, wire whisks are the next best way to smooth out lumps while mixing dry ingredients. A large (12-inch) whisk (measured from top to bottom, including the handle), 2½ inches in diameter at its widest part, works very well.

## Wraps, Papers, and Silicone Mats

### ACETATE SHEETS

Shape or pipe chocolate designs onto clear sheets of acetate. The smooth surface of the plastic allows the chocolate to glide off easily.

## PLASTIC WRAP AND WAXED PAPER

Use plastic wrap whenever you want to retain moisture, for example, when chilling dough or setting pudding in the refrigerator. Waxed paper is used to keep pieces of stored chocolate from sticking to one another and to cover surfaces when rolling out dough. Don't place anything wrapped in plastic wrap or waxed paper in the oven.

## PARCHMENT PAPER

Since parchment paper is an insulator, line your pans with it to avoid sticking, encourage even baking, and prevent the bottoms of your baked goods from burning by absorbing and distributing the heat. Some people like to butter the paper before filling the pan with batter to further prevent sticking when using mixtures that are low in fat, but it's not necessary unless the recipe calls for it. You can also roll out dough between two pieces of floured parchment paper. Silicone-coated parchment paper allows you to pipe chocolate or decorations directly onto the parchment paper to let them harden before transferring to your final arrangement. Design templates can be drawn on parchment paper using a pencil. Parchment paper is available in both rolls and sheets. Large sheets can be folded into a double layer and then flipped over and repurposed for a new batch, and small sheets can be cut to the size of the baking sheet.

## SPECIALIZED CAKE-MAKING EQUIPMENT

**ICING SPATULA:** A flexible metal icing spatula with a thin, straight edge makes frostings and fillings so much easier to apply and helps to achieve a smooth finish. Choose a stainless steel spatula with a 6–8-inch blade with a rounded tip. For spreading icing with a more detailed pattern, such as swoops and waves, use an offset spatula.

**CARDBOARD "PLATTERS":** To make cleanup and presentation easier, instead of decorating a cake on the serving plate, decorate it on a very stiff piece of corrugated cardboard the same size as or slightly larger than the cake. Then carefully transfer the cake to a serving plate using a large spatula.

**CAKE LEVELER:** This adjustable tool cuts a cake horizontally into equal thicknesses. A sharp, long, serrated knife can also be used for creating layers.

**TURNTABLE:** Useful for rotating the cake while filling or topping it, a cake-decorating turntable elevates the cake, although a lazy Susan will work just fine.

## SILICONE MATS

These reusable mats can be used almost anywhere parchment paper is called for. They are excellent for baking cookies or as a surface for piping chocolate. However, their rigidity makes them harder to conform to a pan's shape when blind baking a piecrust, although they can be used for that purpose if necessary.

## Accessories

### STICKS

Paper lollipop sticks and basswood craft sticks make playful holders for lollipops, ice pops, and cake pops. These sticks come in many sizes, so be sure the ones you choose fit your lollipop molds (they should extend at least halfway into the lollipop treat's center). Wooden sticks work best for ice pops since the wood absorbs the liquid as the ice freezes, causing it to expand and securing the pop around it.

### PACKAGING MATERIALS

Candy labels, foil wrappers, ribbon, cellophane bags, tins, boxes, rice paper, and gold leaf can all be used to wrap candy for gifting or favors, as well as for personalization. They also prevent individual pieces from sticking to one another. Both rice paper and gold leaf are edible.

# INGREDIENTS

One does not need to do anything but sample a few bites to appreciate the differences between the quality of good chocolate and that of not-so-good chocolate. The methods, standards, and attention to detail in the growing and processing practices are the reasons why even the same type of chocolate (dark, for example) tastes different from brand to brand. Think of your part in these recipes as the final step in the processing—mixing the chocolate with other quality ingredients that complement the flavor to create a final masterpiece. Here I explain how various types of chocolate affect flavor. In most recipes I choose one type of chocolate or a combination of a cocoa powder and a solid chocolate. It is generally okay to customize the recipes and blend two types of chocolate together; keep in mind, however, that substituting 50 percent dark and 50 percent milk chocolate in a recipe that calls

for dark chocolate, for example, will yield a different flavor than if you used just the dark the recipe calls for. I also discuss the type of ingredients used throughout the book and how they will affect the caliber and flavor of whatever you choose to make.

# Types of Chocolate

## CHOCOLATE POWDERS

**Natural Unsweetened Cocoa Powder and Chocolate Liquor**: Although they are two very different forms, these are actually similar ingredients, as cocoa powder is just chocolate liquor that has most of the cocoa butter pressed out. Some varieties of powder contain more than 22 percent fat, while others contain less than 10 percent. Chocolate liquor, made from ground cocoa beans, is usually labeled as unsweetened chocolate. It can contain milk solids, has a cocoa butter content of 50–60 percent, and is added to recipes that require a deep chocolate taste without a lot of sweetness. Cocoa powder can be sifted or combined with a small amount of boiled water before it is added to a mixture.

**Dutch-Process Cocoa Powder**: This unsweetened cocoa has been treated with an alkali to neutralize its acids and minimize sour flavors. Because it is neutral and does not react with baking soda, it should only be used when recipes call for baking powder, unless large quantities of other acidic ingredients are present. Recipes requiring a more delicate flavor often specify Dutch-process cocoa powder. As it is dark in color (sometimes reddish in hue), foods made with Dutch-process cocoa have a blackish-brown color.

## SOLIDS

**Semisweet or Bittersweet (Dark) Chocolate**: Bittersweet, or dark, chocolate has a strong, sharp chocolate taste, while semisweet chocolate generally contains more sugar. I use these chocolates most often in my recipes since they bring out a sweet, robust chocolate taste. The best dark chocolate contains at least 65 percent chocolate liquor; the

## DEFINITIONS

**COCOA BEANS:** Cocoa beans are the seeds from the fruit pod of the cacao tree. All chocolate comes from the cocoa bean, except for white chocolate. Different methods of processing produce different types of chocolate.

**COCOA SOLIDS**: Cocoa solids, such as cocoa powder, are the low-fat components extracted from the cocoa bean.

**COCOA BUTTER:** The melt-in-your-mouth quality of chocolate comes from cocoa butter, which is the vegetable fat of the cocoa bean and contains no dairy. Although stable at room temperature, it melts at body temperature.

**CHOCOLATE LIQUOR:** The name is misleading; there is no alcohol in this ingredient. It's actually ground cocoa beans, with almost equal amounts of cocoa butter and dry cocoa solids.

**COCOA CONTENT:** This is the percentage of ingredients used from the cocoa bean.

higher the percentage, the more flavorful the chocolate. In the United States these chocolates may contain up to 12 percent milk solids and butterfat, although higher-quality chocolates don't include these ingredients. The most popular chocolate chips are made from semisweet chocolate and usually contain a low amount of cocoa butter so they retain their shape in baking. Use semisweet chocolate chips when a recipe calls for them, and try not to substitute chocolate chips for other types of chocolate since the viscosity will affect the results.

**Sweet Chocolate**: Sweet chocolate is, as expected, sweeter than semisweet chocolate and contains 15–34 percent cacao. It's typically comprised of milk solids and butterfat blended with chocolate liquor, sugar, cocoa, flavorings, and lecithin.

**Milk Chocolate**: This creamy chocolate, when made in the United States, may contain as little as 10 percent cacao and 90 percent sugar and milk solids. Ingredients include milk and sugar, usually either condensed milk or a milk and sugar mixture. Milk chocolate contains less chocolate liquor than bittersweet and semisweet chocolate. The better brands have more than 30 percent cacao, and dark milk chocolate usually contains between 40 and 65 percent cacao. The lower-percentage varieties have more of a milky taste, while the higher-percentage varieties are similar to dark chocolate with a slightly milky taste.

**White Chocolate**: Although it has been called chocolate for a very long time, only recently has white chocolate legally been identified and labeled as chocolate. Since it technically does not contain chocolate liquor, purists still say it is not true chocolate. White chocolate must contain at least 20 percent cocoa butter, 14 percent milk solids, 3.5 percent butterfat, and no more than 55 percent sugar. High-quality brands contain many of the ingredients found in chocolate, such as cocoa butter, sugar, milk solids, vanilla, and lecithin. As it is very delicate, always melt white chocolate over very low heat.

# LABELING

The FDA has developed legal standards for chocolate labels so that consumers know what is in the chocolate they purchase. Here is a list of the information you'll find on the packaging.

**PERCENTAGES**: Chocolate is labeled to show its components' percentages, including the amount of chocolate liquor and cocoa butter—in other words, anything that comes directly from the cacao tree. The percentage conveys the chocolate's relative sweetness but does not tell you anything about the quality, how well it melts, or the viscosity of the melted chocolate.

**GEOGRAPHIC ORIGIN:** Cacao originated in Mesoamerica, although it is now grown in tropical climates around the globe, between the twentieth parallels. The largest producers of cocoa beans are the Ivory Coast, Ghana, and Indonesia. Quality and flavor differ depending on where and how the beans were grown and processed. Only over the past twenty years has origin been considered in chocolate labeling. Before then chocolate was processed and blended using beans from around the world. Today there are single-origin chocolates from the same region of the world, the same farm, and even the same tree. Some say these are the finest-quality chocolates; others prefer the blend of complex flavors made by combining beans of different origins.

**VARIETY:** There are three types of cocoa beans grown for chocolate: criollo (the rarest, and considered the best quality), forastero (the most common cultivar, comprising most of the world's chocolate production), and trinitario (a natural hybrid of criollo and forastero). Manufacturers often specify the type of cocoa bean on the package label if criollo beans were used in order to promote their product as a delicacy.

**PROCESSING:** Sustainability and fair-trade practices have become increasingly important in cacao farming and processing, and small-batch and artisanal roasting are growing in popularity as well. After the cacao beans are harvested, they are roasted, and then the hull is separated from the nib using air pressure and gravity. The nibs are ground into tiny particles and aerated to further develop the chocolate's flavor profile and ensure that the chocolate flows well and has a smooth mouthfeel. Since most chocolate gets better with age, it is then properly stored and aged until the desired flavor is achieved. Some manufacturers temper their chocolate, while others don't. It's usually hard to tell whether chocolate is tempered, since most brands don't state this on their labels. To be safe, temper it again.

**Baking or Unsweetened Solid Chocolate**: This is 100 percent cocoa in its rawest form with no added sugar. It has a strong bitter taste that is sweetened by the sugar in baked goods.

**Couverture Chocolate**: A high-quality chocolate found in specialty stores, couverture chocolate adheres to European legal standards and is typically used for coating. It must include 35 percent cacao and 31 percent fat. When tempered, the chocolate develops a smooth finish and sheen.

**Compound Coating or Confectionery Coating**: A chocolate substitute that uses vegetable fat instead of cocoa butter and contains little or no cocoa butter, this ingredient was created for those who do not want to fuss with tempering chocolate for dipping and molding. Although it does not taste as good as real chocolate, it is an okay substitute. Some brands are

## CHOCOLATE SUBSTITUTIONS

| Type | Original Amount | Substitution |
|---|---|---|
| Bittersweet Chocolate | 1 ounce | 1 ounce semisweet chocolate* |
| | ½ ounce | ½ ounce unsweetened baking chocolate plus 1 tablespoon granulated sugar |
| Semisweet Chocolate | 1 ounce | 1 ounce unsweetened baking chocolate plus 1 table-spoon granulated sugar |
| | 1 ounce | 3 tablespoons cocoa powder, 3 tablespoons sugar, and 1 tablespoon butter |
| Sweet Baking Chocolate | 1 ounce | 3 tablespoons cocoa powder, 4 tablespoons sugar, and 1 tablespoon butter |
| Unsweetened Chocolate | 1 ounce | 3 tablespoons cocoa powder plus 1 tablespoon butter |
| | 1 ounce | 1 ounce bittersweet or semisweet chocolate plus ½ tablespoon granulated sugar |
| | 1 ounce | 1 ounce milk chocolate |
| Dutch-Process Cocoa Powder | 1 ounce | 3 tablespoons natural unsweetened cocoa powder plus ⅛ teaspoon baking soda |
| | 1 ounce | 1 ounce unsweetened chocolate plus ⅛ teaspoon baking soda; reduce fat in recipe by 1 tablespoon |
| Natural Unsweetened Cocoa Powder | 3 tablespoons | 3 tablespoons Dutch-process cocoa powder plus ⅛ teaspoon cream of tartar, freshly squeezed lemon juice, or white vinegar |
| Mexican Chocolate | 1 ounce | 1 ounce semisweet chocolate plus ½ teaspoon ground cinnamon |
| Milk Chocolate | 1 ounce | 1 ounce bittersweet or semisweet chocolate, 1 table-spoon granulated sugar, and 1 tablespoon butter |
| | 1 ounce | 1 ounce white chocolate |

*Although bittersweet and semisweet chocolates may be used interchangeably at a 1:1 ratio, there may be slight differences in flavor and texture.
· Do not substitute chocolate syrup for melted chocolate.
· Do not substitute cocoa powder for flour in a recipe without adding sugar and fat.

## MEASURING CHOCOLATE

Chocolate is typically measured in ounces. Here are some convenient conversions.

| Solid Chocolates | |
| --- | --- |
| 6 ounces | 1 cup, chopped ½-inch pieces |
| 8 ounces | 1½ cups, chopped ½-inch pieces |
| 12 ounces | 2 cups, chopped ½-inch pieces |
| 16 ounces | 3 cups, chopped ½-inch pieces |
| 6 ounces | ⅔ cup, melted |
| 8 ounces | ¾ cup, melted |
| 12 ounces | 1 cup, melted |
| 16 ounces | 1½ cups, melted |
| 6 ounces | 1⅓ cups, grated |
| 8 ounces | 1¾ cups, grated |
| 12 ounces | 2⅔ cups, grated |
| 16 ounces | 3½ cups, grated |

| Cocoa Powder | |
| --- | --- |
| 3 ounces | ½ cup |
| 6 ounces | 1 cup |
| 8 ounces | 2 cups |
| 12 ounces | 3 cups |
| 16 ounces | 4 cups |

better than others. You can find it in dozens of colors when using small amounts, which I find to be a real plus.

**Mexican Chocolate:** Sweet chocolate with a blend of spices (typically cinnamon, nutmeg, and allspice), Mexican chocolate is used mostly for making hot cocoa and mole sauce.

## Storing Chocolate

When properly stored, chocolate has a long shelf life. Dark chocolate typically lasts 12 months; milk and white chocolate last around 6 months. Store in airtight containers in a dry, dark, cool place (around 65°F, at a humidity of less than 50 percent). Chocolate is easily affected by the aromas of other foods, so store it separately. For long-term storage, vacuum-seal the chocolate. Try to avoid refrigerating chocolate for a long period of time since it will pick up moisture, possibly causing it to bloom (meaning it turns white on the surface). However, on a hot day you may need to refrigerate it to avoid melting. Avoid humidity whenever possible. If the chocolate has bloomed while in storage, melt and temper it to restore it.

Baked goods with toppings and fillings made of perishable ingredients such as butter, eggs, milk, and cream cheese should be refrigerated for safety. Wrap tightly in plastic wrap or store in a cake keeper to preserve moisture, since baked goods dry out when refrigerated. Unfrosted or unfilled cakes or those with nonperishable toppings and fillings can be kept at room temperature.

## Sweeteners

**Agave Nectar**: Rapidly becoming the sweetener of choice for those who want to lower their intake of foods high on the glycemic index, agave nectar is a good substitute for honey, maple syrup, corn syrup, granulated sugar, and brown sugar. Agave nectar, which adds moisture to fillings as a liquid sweetener, has a more neutral flavor than honey or maple syrup, and, like corn syrup, it will not crystallize. It's best to use agave nectar to replace other liquid sugars, but you can use it to replace sugar granules if you reduce the other liquids in the recipe.

**Artificial Sweeteners**: Although you can purchase confections made with artificial sweeteners, it is very difficult to develop great-tasting sweets with them at home, and I do not recommend using them.

**Blackstrap and Golden Molasses**: These sweeteners are syrups removed from sugar during the refining process, each at a different stage. Blackstrap molasses is dark and rich, while golden molasses is lighter in color and flavor.

**Brown Sugar**: Combining white sugar with molasses creates brown sugar. It is available in both dark and light varieties; choose either depending on how much molasses flavor you want. Always pack brown sugar firmly into the measuring cup to get an accurate measurement.

**Confectioners' (Powdered) Sugar**: This is sugar that is ground to a light powder and combined with cornstarch. Although sometimes used for baking to achieve an extremely fine texture, it is more often used in icings to produce a silky-smooth surface.

**Crystal (Coarse) Sugar:** Used for decorating, this sugar has extra-large granules and is available in many colors.

**Granulated and Superfine Sugars:** Granulated sugar is standard white table sugar, which has a medium-grain texture and is a good all-purpose sugar for cakes, cookies, pies, candy, ice cream, and puddings. Superfine sugar, also known as caster sugar, has fine-grain crystals and dissolves more easily than granulated sugar, making it good for delicate cakes and meringues.

## SWEETENER SUBSTITUTIONS

| Ingredient | Substitution | Ratio | Notes |
| --- | --- | --- | --- |
| Granulated sugar | Brown Sugar | 1:1 | |
| | Honey | 1:$\frac{7}{8}$ | Use $\frac{7}{8}$ cup honey for 1 cup of granulated sugar and decrease other liquids in the recipe by about 3 tablespoons |
| | Maple syrup | 1:$\frac{3}{4}$ | Use $\frac{3}{4}$ cup maple syrup for 1 cup granulated sugar and decrease other liquids in the recipe by about 3 tablespoons |
| Brown sugar | Agave nectar | 1:$\frac{2}{3}$ | Use $\frac{2}{3}$ cup agave nectar for 1 cup brown sugar and decrease other liquids in the recipe by $\frac{1}{4}$–$\frac{1}{3}$ cup |
| | Granulated sugar | 1:1 | Add 4 tablespoons unsulfured molasses per cup of granulated sugar and decrease other liquids in the recipe by about 3 tablespoons |
| | Honey and molasses | 1:$\frac{3}{4}$ | Use $\frac{1}{2}$ cup honey and $\frac{1}{4}$ cup unsulfured molasses |
| Molasses | Agave nectar | 1:$\frac{2}{3}$ | Use $\frac{2}{3}$ cup agave nectar for 1 cup molasses and decrease other liquids in the recipe by $\frac{1}{4}$–$\frac{1}{3}$ cup |
| | Honey | 1:1 | |

**Honey:** If you are staying away from processed sugars, all-natural honey is perfect as both a flavoring and a preservative. Clover honey is the most common type, although other varieties such as lavender and orange blossom are also available.

**Light Corn Syrup:** This processed sugar syrup, derived from cornstarch, often gets a bad rap. But it prevents sugar from crystallizing when you're making candy, which is a good thing, so some recipes in this book utilize light corn syrup.

## Dairy and Animal Products

**Butter:** Butter adds to the creamy texture and flavor of chocolate baked goods and candy. I prefer butter to other shortenings since I think it contributes the most flavor, and I use unsalted instead of salted butter so I can control the amount of salt in a recipe. All the recipes in this book call for unsalted butter.

**Cream Cheese:** The most common type of cheese used in baking, cream cheese is soft and smooth and gives cheesecake its wonderful texture. Always use softened blocks of cream cheese, not the whipped variety.

**Creams:** Heavy cream and heavy whipping cream are more or less the same thing. Both contain at least 36 percent milk fat, double in volume when whipped, and are a key ingredient in making ganache. Regular whipping cream and light whipping cream, which have between 30 and 36 percent milk fat, can also be whipped. When piped, heavy cream and heavy whipping cream hold shapes better than lighter, lower-fat whipping creams. Always use cold cream and chill the bowl and beaters to achieve the thickest cream.

**Eggs:** Whole eggs are used to bind fats in cakes, cookies, puddings, and ice creams, while egg whites are used to aerate nougat, make meringue, and glaze piecrusts for a golden glow. All the recipes in this book use cooked egg whites for food safety.

**Milk:** I developed the recipes in this book using whole milk (when required) in order to obtain the richest flavor. Some recipes call for buttermilk to add a deep, tangy, buttery flavor to baked goods, although when buttermilk is specified, whole milk can be substituted.

**Processed Milks:** Evaporated, or dehydrated, milk has had about 60 percent of its water removed, making it very dense and giving it a strong and somewhat processed flavor. Sweetened condensed milk, a heavy, creamy milk with added sugar, is often used in cake sauces and candies for a thick, smooth consistency.

**Sour Cream and Yogurt:** Sour cream and yogurt have unique flavors that add tanginess to chocolate baked goods.

**Vegetable Shortening:** Vegetable shortening is sometimes used to thin chocolate and to make it easier to coat dipped fruits or other items.

## Flours, Meals, and Oats

**All-Purpose Flour:** Most of the recipes in this book use unbleached all-purpose flour, a high-protein gluten flour good for creating dense cakes, cookie dough, and piecrusts. Many people look for opportunities to add whole grains to their diet for health reasons, so you can substitute whole wheat flour for up to half the flour in recipes that call for all-purpose.

**Cake Flour:** Because it contains less protein than the all-purpose variety, cake flour makes baked goods softer, lighter, and more airy. It is available in bleached and unbleached forms, which can be used interchangeably. Bleached flour produces a cake that's brighter in color but is more processed than unbleached flour.

**Cornmeal:** Ground from yellow, white, or blue corn, cornmeal comes in different textures, including fine, medium, and coarse. I usually prefer to use fine- or medium-ground cornmeal.

**Oats:** When making cookies and granola, it's best to use uncooked old-fashioned rolled oats, not instant ones, which produce mushy results. Steel-cut oats can also be used, but they are less absorbent and give cakes a crunchy texture.

**Whole Wheat All-Purpose Flour and Whole Wheat Pastry Flour:** Whole wheat flour lends cakes an earthy flavor. Pastry flour, a softer and finer form, works well in cakes and pastries and is preferable for baking, although the two can be used interchangeably in these recipes. Just make sure to sieve whole wheat flour to soften it a bit before baking. You can substitute up to half the quantity of all-purpose flour for whole wheat flour in a recipe.

## Binders

**Cornstarch**: One tablespoon of cornstarch, a common thickener in pies and sauces, thickens 1 cup of liquid to a smooth sauce consistency.

**Gelatin**: Gelatin is a thickener used in mousse to stabilize the form and create a creamy texture.

**Tapioca**: Tapioca is a starch that comes from the yucca, or cassava, root. It thickens at a lower temperature than cornstarch, is stable when frozen, and gives fruit fillings in pies a glossy sheen. The recipes in this book call for instant tapioca since it is readily available, but you must grind it in a food processor first to avoid lumps. Tapioca starch is more finely ground than instant tapioca and will give you a smoother texture. Tapioca is also processed into balls, or pearls, that range from 1–8 millimeters in diameter, with 2–3 millimeters being the most common. The pearls must be rehydrated in water until they expand to twice their volume and have become leathery and swollen.

## Flavorings

**Coffee and Tea**: When flavoring with coffee, tea, wine, or other ingredients that contain a lot of water, boil them to reduce their water content by half to one-quarter to increase their strength. Instant espresso or espresso brewed at double strength works best. You could also use straight ground coffee if you're fine with a grainy texture, or instant coffee powder if you're looking for a smoother mouthfeel. Brew tea leaves with cream or milk to infuse them with a variety of tea flavors. Green tea powder, or matcha, provides a pleasing flavor complement to chocolate and can be found in high-quality teashops. Store it in the refrigerator because it is perishable.

**Extracts**: Found in many chocolate recipes to enhance flavor, vanilla can be used either straight from the bean or in extract form. When heating liquids for a long period of time, I steep vanilla beans in the liquid to release their flavor. The steeping process takes too long for most of these recipes, however, so I typically use pure vanilla extract (try to avoid the artificial stuff).

**Herbs**: Herbs such as mint, lavender, rosemary, and lemongrass can be used to instill flavor in chocolate. Try experimenting with these in ganache fillings by infusing the herbs into the milk while it's heating and then straining them from the liquid.

**Liqueurs**: Sweet alcoholic liqueurs pack a rich taste, and many of them go very well with chocolate. Throughout this book I use fruit-, nut-, and coffee-based varieties to flavor chocolate and baked goods. Note that it is not illegal for children under the age of twenty-one to consume chocolate with liqueurs due to the minimal alcohol content.

**Salt**: Although I add it only in small amounts here, salt is very important as a flavor enhancer when making sweets. Most of the recipes use table salt, although I call for coarse sea salt in recipes that feature salt as a decorative element, as in Hand-Dipped Salted Caramels (page 43).

**Spices**: Invest in range of spices, but because they lose their potency quickly, I recommend buying only a little more than the quantity you need. Grind your own in a miniature food processor for the freshest flavor.

## Fruits, Nuts, and Seeds

**Dried and Candied Fruit**: Dried fruits such as raisins, cranberries, cherries, and apricots add intense flavor and a chewy texture to chocolate treats. Candied fruits, such as pineapple and cherries, have been heated in a sugar syrup and are much sweeter and a bit softer than dried fruits. Larger dried or candied fruits like apricots are often chopped when added to recipes.

**Fresh Fruit**: Fresh fruits add flavor and texture to cakes, pies, and many other baked goods and are delicious dipped in chocolate. Due to their high water content, they are rarely used in candy making, except occasionally in puree form, such as in the Raspberry Cream Truffles (page 52). Oranges, strawberries, raspberries, blueberries, and cherries are my favorite fruits to pair with chocolate.

**Nuts and Seeds**: The most popular flavor complement to chocolate, nuts can be mixed into the batter or filling of cakes,

---

### MEASURING NUTS AND DRIED FRUITS

Always measure nuts and dried fruits according to the format listed in the recipe. For example, when I call for "1 cup chopped walnuts," the nuts should already be chopped when you measure them, but when I call for "1 cup walnuts, chopped," you should measure out 1 cup of walnut halves and then chop them. You will use many more nuts or fruits in a cup if they are already chopped, ground, or slivered.

pies, and candy. Their many shapes and flavor variations make them great for decorating, too. When exposed to heat during baking or toasting, they release their oils, thus intensifying their wonderful flavors—but they also burn easily, so keep on eye on them. Nuts go rancid quickly; store them in the freezer to prevent spoiling.

The way that nuts and seeds are prepared also affects their flavor and texture. Whether they're left whole, sliced, chopped, or ground makes a big difference, since each technique exposes a different amount of surface area. The smaller the pieces, the more pervasive the flavor they contribute. Nuts ground into a paste offer a creamy texture. Adding a little sugar helps make the process easier, encourages the nuts to absorb the oils, and provides a sweeter taste. Nut butters contain nuts that have been roasted and ground into a smooth texture and include peanut butter, almond butter, and cashew butter.

## Coconut

Coconut comes in many forms: fresh, dried, sweetened, unsweetened, shredded, flaked, and desiccated. Fresh coconut can be shredded with a peeler or food processor for a natural flavor. Unsweetened coconut allows you to control the amount of sugar in the recipe. Sweetened coconut is soaked in corn syrup, making it sweeter and moister than unsweetened coconut. The flaked and shredded varieties can be used interchangeably (I like to use large coconut flakes as a topping or for texture). Desiccated coconut is dried and very finely ground and usually comes unsweetened. Toasting coconut dramatically changes the flavor by bringing out the natural oils. Toasted coconut is more common when you want a crispy texture such as in baked goods, but when making candy you typically look for the chewiness of untoasted coconut.

# ESSENTIAL TECHNIQUES

Confectionary, especially working with chocolate, tends to be a skill that culinary crafters take on as a challenge later in their careers. Baking with chocolate does not require as many special skills as working with chocolate on a stove. This section focuses on the most basic techniques you'll need to master melting and tempering and then shaping that chocolate into a finished product.

## Melting Chocolate

Melting requires heating chocolate to change it from a solid to a liquid. Since chocolate is a fragile ingredient, the process must be done with great care. Melting is the first step in tempering, a process that changes the structure of the chocolate through heating and cooling, allowing it to set quickly and giving it a shiny, crisp finish. Pretempered chocolate and candy melts (chocolate discs with wax added to hold their shape) can be purchased at cake and candy supply stores, crafts stores, and some supermarkets, where they are packaged and labeled as dipping or molding chocolates. The quality of molding chocolate ranges widely, and most of the time it is not the highest-quality chocolate, though there are some pretty good brands out there (I like Guittard). Even as a chocolate snob, I admit to using these sometimes when I'm in a rush. However, to achieve high-quality results in taste and texture, it is useful to learn how to temper your own chocolate.

### STEPS AND TIPS FOR MELTING CHOCOLATE

1. Dry all countertops, double boilers, bowls, knives, and everything with which you will be working. Avoid getting water or any liquid on the chocolate, as it will ruin the batch.

2. To ensure quick, uniform melting, use a chef's knife to chop the chocolate into evenly sized pieces smaller than 1 inch (preferably ½ inch).

3. Always melt the chopped pieces in a double boiler over low heat, or in a microwave (see the section about melting chocolate in the microwave on page 29), never over direct

---

### MELTING CHOCOLATE IN THE MICROWAVE

1. Chop chocolate into small, uniform pieces (about ½ inch).
2. Place pieces in a microwave-safe bowl that will remain cool or gets only slightly warm after several minutes in the microwave.
3. Start with a low setting (50 percent power) to avoid scorching.
4. Heat initially for 1 minute; then heat 20 seconds at a time, stirring in between.
5. You don't need to melt the chocolate all the way in the microwave—just heat it until it's almost completely melted, and stir to melt the rest.

heat in a saucepan. Do not cover the double boiler, as condensation will form and ruin the chocolate.

4. Be patient and melt the chocolate slowly. Stir the chocolate frequently with a wooden spoon or rubber spatula to equalize the temperature. Be careful not to whip too much air into the chocolate while stirring since you will need to remove all air bubbles later in the process.

5. Watch carefully. Semisweet, milk, and white chocolate melt at lower temperatures and are harder to melt properly than dark chocolate. Do not let dark chocolate exceed 120°F, semisweet chocolate 113°F, and milk or white chocolate 110°F.

6. Allow the chocolate to cool, bringing it to room temperature after melting and before adding to cake batters, cookie dough, and piecrusts. It also adds a thicker layer when used for dipping if cooled to room temperature. Chocolate can be reheated and melted again if it thickens too much.

## TROUBLESHOOTING

- If the chocolate becomes lumpy, it has "seized" (this occurs when liquid gets into the chocolate or when the chocolate gets too hot). Try adding 1–2 teaspoons vegetable oil or shortening to the chocolate to smooth it out. This fix doesn't always work, and if it does, chocolate used for dipping or coating will take longer to set.
- If the chocolate has been scorched or burned, it cannot be restored. Next time make sure it is melted slowly over indirect heat. If it is not too burned and tastes fine, slightly scorched or burned chocolate can be reused in recipes where appearance is not an issue.

- If the chocolate has cooled too much and becomes excessively thick, warm the bowl over a double boiler or add some warm chocolate to the batch. If necessary, repeat the tempering process.
- If bubbles appear in the finished piece, the chocolate was too agitated during mixing, the temperature of the melted chocolate was too low, or the chocolate cooled too quickly. Next time check the temperature to make sure it's correct and allow the chocolate to cool slowly.
- If you have extra melted chocolate, spread it into a thin layer on a piece of parchment paper and let it set for several hours. Remelt this chocolate to be used in cakes, cookies, or fudge, or reuse it for molding and coating.

# Tempering Chocolate

Tempering is a heating and cooling process that changes the crystal structure of chocolate, providing stability and giving it a smooth mouthfeel, with an attractive sheen and a crispy snap. Chocolate should be tempered before you use it for shaping and dipping. It sets much more quickly than untempered chocolate and, if tempered properly, will not show streaks when set. Tempered chocolate shrinks slightly upon hardening, making it easy to release your chocolates from the molds. Use a thermometer when learning to temper; once you know how the chocolate should look, a thermometer may not be necessary. Be sure to heat only to the target temperature provided in the method described here, as going over can cause scorching.

Tempering chocolate is not necessary for recipes in which you will use melted chocolate, such as fudge or cakes, although it is crucial to achieve a professional glossy finish in candy making and dipping. To complicate matters, different brands of chocolate melt at different temperatures. Thus, the temperatures in this book are close approximates, even though they seem so specific. Once you find a brand you like, keep track of the heating and cooling temperatures and adjust the recipe accordingly.

There are three ways to temper chocolate: the easy stove-top method, which many home chocolatiers use, and the seed and tabling methods, which are professional techniques. Try them all to see which one provides consistent results for you. Always temper more chocolate than you think you'll need to ensure that you don't run out in the middle of a recipe.

**EASY METHOD**

1. Chop the chocolate into uniform ½-inch pieces and place in the top of a double boiler. Be very careful to keep any water or moisture away from the chocolate or it will not temper properly.

2. Melt the chocolate over low heat while stirring constantly with a rubber spatula. Measuring the temperature with a candy thermometer, bring dark chocolate to 115°F, semisweet and milk chocolate to 112°F, and white chocolate

to 110°F. Remove from the heat and let cool to 82–85°F, 80–83°F, and 78–81°F, for dark, semisweet and milk, and white chocolate, respectively.

3. Heat the chocolate over low heat again, until dark chocolate has reached 89–91°F and semisweet, milk, or white chocolate have reached 87–89°F (this will be quick). The chocolate should be tempered. To test it, spread a thin layer on a plate or dip a knife into it, and allow it to cool for 7–8 minutes. Properly tempered chocolate should be hard, not sticky, and shiny, not streaked, and it should not look wet. Once tempered, it can be used for piping, pouring, and dipping.

### SEED METHOD

1. Chop the chocolate into uniformly sized pieces and divide them into two batches, one with two-thirds the volume and the other with one-third. Weigh the batches on a kitchen scale to double-check the proportions.

2. Melt the larger amount of chocolate in the top pan of a double boiler over simmering water to about 115°F for dark chocolate, 112°F for semisweet and milk chocolate, and 110°F for white chocolate. Remove from the heat and add the remaining chopped chocolate. Stir vigorously until the chocolate has melted. Let sit for 1–2 minutes to cool.

3. Check the chocolate's temperature. If it's below 86°F for dark chocolate or 84°F for semisweet, milk, or white chocolate, put it back on the heat until the thermometer reads between 86°F–90°F for dark chocolate and 84°F–87°F for semisweet, milk, and white chocolate.

### TABLING METHOD

1. Melt all the chocolate in a double boiler, until a thermometer reads 115°F for dark chocolate, 112°F for semisweet or milk chocolate, and 110°F for white chocolate.

2. Pour two-thirds of the melted chocolate onto a marble slab at room temperature and spread it into a thin layer (about $\frac{1}{16}$ inch) using a metal offset spatula. Scrape it back into a pile and then spread it into a thin layer again, repeating until you achieve a thick but sludgy consistency.

3. Return it to the warm chocolate in the double boiler. Stir until a thermometer reads between 86°F–90°F for dark chocolate and 84°F–87°F for semisweet, milk, and white chocolate.

## Shaping and Finishing

Chocolate can be colored and shaped into many different forms, from cups to curls. These can stand on their own as finished pieces or are fantastic for decorating and finishing cakes, cupcakes, cookies—you name it. When handling chocolate, use disposable gloves, and if your hands are warm, hold the chocolate with a paper towel to avoid fingerprints and melting.

### COLORING CHOCOLATE

Starting with white chocolate, use an oil- or cocoa butter–based colorant, not food coloring (which is water based and will ruin your chocolate). Add to the chocolate according to the manufacturer's directions. Keep in mind that white is your base color, so pastels are easier to achieve than dark colors like black. Luster dust, an edible sparkly powder, can be dusted on the inside of a mold (Chocolate Liqueur-Filled Gems, page 188) or painted on after the chocolate has set (Solid Chocolate Wedding Cakes, page 121). Add a few drops of vodka to the luster dust to achieve the level of transparency you desire then brush on with a pastry brush and let dry.

### CHOCOLATE CUPS

Line muffin tins with foil liners. Pour the chocolate into the liners, about $\frac{1}{8}$ inch thick on the bottom and the sides, and let them set for 20 minutes. Pipe in the filling, leaving about $\frac{1}{4}$ inch on the top. Seal the molds with the remaining melted chocolate. Let sit for 20 minutes. Chill in the refrigerator for 20 minutes before unmolding.

## CURLS

Decorative curls of chocolate are used to finish baked goods. They can be made from a store-bought block of solid chocolate, or you can create your own block using multiple chocolates to create striped curls (Rich Chocolate Cupcakes with White Chocolate Buttercream, page 108). Bring a block of chocolate to room temperature. Use a vegetable peeler to apply pressure to the block and scrape the peeler over the chocolate along the longest edge, trying to make a continuous curl. If the curl breaks almost immediately, the chocolate is too cold. To make a striped block, melt two different types of chocolate and pour them to a ⅜–½-inch thickness side by side on a piece of parchment paper. Peel with a vegetable peeler as described above.

Long curls (Chocolate Layer Cake with Ganache, page 102) are made using a rolling pin or acetate as a form. Roll a piece of acetate into a tube, or use a rolling pin covered with parchment paper, and tape together the seam. Secure the form to a baking sheet using nontoxic tape. Brush tempered chocolate over the form in one long strip, following the curve along the shape and size you desire. After the chocolate has set, carefully remove it from the form.

## CUTTING AND SHAPING CHOCOLATE

Depending on the thickness and texture of mix-ins, chocolate can either be cut all the way though with a chef's or utility knife, or scored and snapped. Straight lines are much easier to cut than curved lines, so when my final results need curved lines, I mold the chocolate into the shape rather than try to cut it (pouring melted chocolate into cookie cutters a good way to do this). To cut chocolate, use a sharp knife to score the chocolate in a straight line about halfway through, then either make smaller cuts until you have made it all the way through or break the chocolate along the line with your hands.

## USING CHOCOLATE FOR DIPPING

Set out a cooling rack with a rimmed baking sheet underneath to catch drippings. Temper the chocolate and let it cool. To dip just part of an

## BLOOM

Although "bloom" sounds so pretty, it's really quite ugly when it refers to chocolate. Bloom refers to the streaks in chocolate that occur when chocolate is improperly melted, tempered, or stored. Even though the chocolate looks unattractive, the taste is still pretty accurate. Bloom will disappear if the chocolate is remelted and tempered properly. You should take precautions to avoid the two types of bloom.

- Fat bloom, characterized by gray streaks on the chocolate, occurs when the cocoa butter has risen to the surface due to hot temperatures caused by improper tempering or storage. Follow the prescribed tempering and storage techniques to avoid fat bloom.
- Sugar bloom looks like a whitish film covering the chocolate, the result of sugar crystals forming on the surface due to moisture. Avoid this by never refrigerating chocolate unless necessary, always drying all equipment and surfaces when working with chocolate, and never covering pots when melting or tempering chocolate.

item, hold it on one end and dip it into the chocolate, leaving about an inch uncovered. To dip a whole item, use a fork to submerge the entire piece into the chocolate. You might need to do this six or seven times to ensure a thick, even coating. After removing your dipped item from the chocolate, shake it over the pot several times to remove excess chocolate; then place it on a cooling rack or parchment paper. Return the excess chocolate from the baking sheet to the pot and remelt if needed. Let the pieces harden at room temperature.

### DRIZZLING AND PIPING

Melted chocolate can be drizzled (Cake Pop Truffles, page 123) or piped (Hamantaschen, page 204) as decoration or to create contrasting flavors. Although each brand of chocolate differs in texture, melted chocolate is generally thinner than icings and frostings, so the hole used for piping or drizzling should be small.

For thin lines, use a piping bag without a tip. Snip the very end of the piping bag with scissors to create a small hole, then add the melted chocolate to the bag. Fold the top to seal. Hold the bag about 4 inches above your target and squeeze, allowing the chocolate to flow out. You can also create thin lines by drizzling the chocolate directly from a spoon about 6 inches above your target. To pipe larger lines, fit a piping bag with a small round tip. Add the chocolate and seal the bag. Squeeze the bag and pipe directly onto the finished cake, candy, or cookie, or pipe decorations onto parchment paper or acetate and allow them to harden. Once they're set, transfer to the final piece.

Since frostings and whipped cream are thicker than chocolate, you will need a larger tip when piping them. Use a large star tip to create a grooved piping effect (Chocolate Carrot Cupcakes, page 198), a medium star tip for borders (Caramel Mocha Ice Cream Cake, page 105), or a round tip to make smooth shapes (Chocolate Cherry Coconut Tapioca Pudding, page 95). If using chocolate or icing, design details such as flowers can be piped directly onto finished pieces (Chocolate-Coated Almond-Flavored Easter Eggs, page 197) or onto a piece of parchment paper or acetate and, when hardened, transferred to the finished piece (Rich Chocolate Cupcakes with White

Chocolate Buttercream, page 108). To create flowers, place a petal tip on your piping bag. Pipe sets of about five flat petals in a circle so they overlap, and then pipe different colored dots in the center. Let dry and transfer to the final piece.

**FEATHERING**

Feathering can be done with two contrasting colors of chocolate (Chocolate Marble Cheesecakes, page 159). Melt the two chocolates in separate double boilers. When both chocolates are melted, pour one chocolate over the cakes. Add the remaining chocolate to a piping bag with a small round tip and, while the poured chocolate is still wet, drizzle the second chocolate over the poured chocolate. With a toothpick or small pastry brush, drag the piped chocolate into the poured chocolate to create a feathered pattern.

**CHOCOLATE FLOWERS AND LEAVES**

Chocolate flowers and leaves add a touch of nature to cakes, tarts, cookies, and candy. They can be made a few different ways. The easiest method is to pour melted chocolate into flower- or leaf-shaped molds, let them set, and then remove. These will form thick pieces (Pumpkin Tart, page 224). For thinner flowers and leaves (Chocolate Layer Cake with Ganache, page 102), paint a thin layer of chocolate in the mold using a medium pastry brush and let the chocolate set. Paint additional layers on top for thicker flowers and leaves, if necessary, allowing the chocolate to set again, and then remove from the mold. Leaves can also be made using real natural leaves that have a waxy coating. Choose nontoxic, chemical-free leaves, and wash and dry them first. Paint the chocolate on the leaves with a pastry brush; then refrigerate to set. Repeat for thicker flowers and leaves, if necessary. Carefully peel the leaf off the chocolate when hardened.

**GANACHE COATING FOR CAKES**

First cover the top and sides of the cake with a crumb coat—a thin layer of icing that covers loose crumbs and prepares a smooth surface for the ganache. Remove any large lumps or crumbs and clean the spatula. Let the topping harden for about 20 minutes in the refrigerator. Place the cake on a wire rack with a baking sheet under it. Heat your ganache and let it cool to room temperature before pouring it over the top of the cake. Let it set and then pour on another coat if necessary.

## MOLDING CHOCOLATE

Once chocolate is tempered, it's easy to mold. For solid chocolate pieces, simply pour directly into the mold with a ladle, filling the cavity to the top. Tap the mold on the countertop to allow air bubbles to rise to the surface (which will be the bottom of the finished chocolate piece). Place the mold on the countertop while the chocolate sets completely. Remove the chocolate from the mold and clean off any excess chocolate on the bottom of each piece with a sharp paring knife. Filled chocolates' centers are made by creating a hard outer shell, then filling and sealing it. Use a ladle to fill the mold halfway with tempered chocolate. Shake the mold around so every surface is coated. Pour excess chocolate back into the bowl. Set the mold on a countertop and let the chocolate set for about 5 minutes. Once it has begun to harden, use a knife to scrape off any excess chocolate on the top of the mold. Using a piping bag, add the filling to the chocolate shell, stopping 1/8–1/4 inch from the top of the mold. Allow solid fillings to set. Next, ladle or pipe tempered chocolate up to the top of the mold to create the bottom of the filled chocolate piece. Scrape off the excess with a knife. Allow the chocolate to set completely on the countertop, or place in the refrigerator for 15 minutes and then let the chocolate return to room temperature. Invert the mold over a piece of parchment paper and tap to release.

To include decorative lines in your molded candy, add chocolate to a piping bag cut with a small tip. Drizzle chocolate in lines in the mold, and let set. Add melted chocolate to the mold to create a shell or solid piece, and allow to harden.

## CHOCOLATE AS COATING

Set out a cooling rack with a rimmed baking sheet underneath. Temper the chocolate in a double boiler and dip the bottoms of the pieces you will be coating. Let set. Invert the item on the cooling rack so the chocolate is on the bottom. With a ladle or heatproof measuring cup, pour the melted chocolate over the treats, allowing the excess to drip onto the baking sheet. Add a second layer if desired. Let set at room temperature.

## SHAVED CHOCOLATE

Chill the chocolate in the refrigerator for 30 minutes. Set out a piece of waxed paper. Using the large grid side of a box grater for medium pieces (Mocha Cappuccino Mousse, page 96), or the small side for tiny shavings (Chocolate Marble Cheesecakes, page 159), grate the cold chocolate over the waxed paper. For large amounts of grated chocolate, use the grater disc on your food processor and feed the chocolate through the tube while the machine is running.

## TRANSFERS

Patterned transfers are edible sheets of colored sugar available in thousands of different designs, from classic to modern, used for decorating chocolate. They are available at candy supply stores, and if you're going to be using a lot of them, you can even have your own custom design made into a transfer. Cut to size and add them to the mold before pouring in the chocolate. When you unmold the chocolate, the transfer will have adhered to the top. Melted, tempered chocolate can also be spread over the transfer sheet and allowed to harden. Once the chocolate is dry, the sheet can be cut into various shapes or made into bark.

## PAIRING SUGGESTIONS

Consider assembling a chocolate board, much like you would a cheese board, at your next party. Set chocolates out on a platter with some of these other foods items to provide tasty flavor combinations.

- Candied foods (ginger, lemon peel, orange peel)
- Dried fruits (cherries, mangos, raisins)
- Fresh fruits (apricots, apples, cranberries, figs, pears)
- Gummy candies
- Jams and fruit spreads
- Marshmallows
- Nuts (macadamia, toasted almonds)
- Orange and lemon peel
- Salty snack foods
- Sweet baguette

# SERVING, GIFTING, AND TRANSPORTING

Eating chocolate is an experience that is meant to engage all the senses. Appreciate the sight of a beautifully formed baked good or the attractive gloss on a piece of candy. Inhale the rich aroma of the chocolate, the sweet smell of fruit, toasted nuts, and coconut. Listen to the satisfying snap of well-tempered chocolate when it breaks. Feel the crisp bite and smooth texture of a good piece of chocolate. Finally, savor the taste of the chocolate and its complementary add-ins. It simply cannot be matched.

Throughout the book you will find many opportunities for pairing chocolate with various drinks, including wine (page 190). Try a tasting party, a fun event during which you pair chocolate with beer, liqueur, coffee, or tea.

## Serving

When looking at the images throughout the book, take special note of the display. In addition to showing you the finished recipes, all the photos were designed to offer presentation suggestions. The main goal is to be minimal and let the treat shine. Single platters, multiple plates, pedestals, and boxes can all make edible objects look precious and appetizing. Choose either colors that complement the treat or neutral colors. Avoid patterns and overly bright, harsh colors. Give items space on the plates, and use multiple plates if necessary. Arrange objects in a graphic layout, or scatter them organically.

I also provide suggestions for serving your chocolate creations at parties. The Milk and Cookies Party photo (page 111) shows how to hold a milk and cookies party; the Easter candy image (page 192) offers ideas on how to display candy on pedestals and plates and in glasses, while the Filled Molded Chocolates (page 189) were photographed as if arranged for holding a wine and chocolate tasting.

## Gifting

Many of the recipes in this book make ideal gifts when they're dressed up and prettily packaged. These recipes are all relatively stable and are strong enough to easily package and transport. Package the goodies in boxes, plates, foil, cellophane bags, tins, bottles, glass jars, or airtight containers, and add customized labels. Use waxed paper between layers when needed for particularly sticky or oily treats. Some popular gift suggestions are listed here:

COOKIES AND BARS
Brownies
Chocolate chip
    cookies
Easter cookies
Fortune cookies
French macarons
Gingerbread men
Granola bars
Hamantaschen
Moon cakes
Rugelach

CANDY
Caramel popcorn
Chocolate lollipops
Dried and candied
    fruits
Fudge
Halloween bark
Hard pretzels
Marshmallows
Salted caramels
Trail mix
Truffles

SAUCES AND SPREADS
Barbecue sauce
Chocolate butter
Chocolate spread
Hot fudge
Mole sauce

CAKES AND BREADS
Bundt cake
Cake pops
Challah
Cupcakes
Gingerbread
Loaf cakes
Mochi
Panforte
Soft pretzels

RECIPES PACKAGED AS KITS FOR
THE RECIPIENT TO MAKE
Cake-decorating kit
Chocolate caramel
    apple kit
Chocolate-dipped
    pretzels or potato
    chips kit
Cookie-decorating kit
Dried and candied
    fruits kit
Hot cocoa mix
Kid's lollipop-making kit
Molded chocolate
    candy-making kit
Pancake or waffle mix

PIES AND TARTS
Date tartlets
Heart-shaped pies

# Transporting and Mailing Chocolate

When transporting chocolate, keep it in a cooler or thermal container with ice packs (use towels to separate the chocolate from the ice packs to avoid moisture contamination). Place the chocolate on the floor of the car, either by an air conditioner vent in hot weather or away from the hot air vents in cold weather. Always keep it out of direct sunlight. Avoid bringing chocolate to outdoor events. Although I love to give chocolate as gifts, I generally only do hand deliveries for my local friends, as mailing it is rather risky. Try to avoid shipping chocolate, or at least save it for the colder months. In warm weather, the chocolate will sit in hot trucks, warehouses, or airplanes during transport, so you cannot guarantee its quality upon delivery. Mailing a do-it-yourself hot cocoa or cake kit with powdered ingredients makes the most sense because the recipient will add the perishable ingredients. Canned spreads (page 139) or sauces (page 242) shipped in vacuum-sealed packages or break-resistant containers are another option.

If you absolutely must mail chocolate, choose items that are easy to mail, such as firm cookies (White and Milk Chocolate Icebox Spirals, page 115), bars (Brownies, page 67), cakes (Chocolate-Cherry Almond Panforte de Sienna, page 232, and Chocolate Gingerbread Cake, page 230), and Candy Bars (page 48). Lay them between pieces of cardboard, wrap them in bubble wrap to protect them, and place the chocolate in a box that is at least 2 inches smaller than the packing box. Fill in the space between the two boxes with an insulator (popcorn or earth-friendly foam peanuts both serve as good cushions and insulators). If you're very concerned about protecting the chocolate, pack the box with frozen gel packs, dry ice, or another cold source, making sure to wrap it in plastic so the condensation doesn't soak through the cardboard box. Ship overnight at the beginning of the week so your package won't sit around over the weekend—the less time in transit, the better. Shipping the chocolate via two- or three-day delivery may be okay and is definitely cheaper than overnight service, but check the cost difference and decide if it's worth it. Tell the recipient to be home expecting the package, or mail it to a workplace; otherwise, the chocolate may go back to the warehouse for another day or be left out on a doorstep in the heat.

# Chapter 2

# Everyday Chocolate

## CANDY

A little bite of candy every day might be just enough to satisfy your sweet tooth. Although candy making seems mysterious, it's really quite easy once you have the chocolate. Here are a few simple recipes and techniques that can be savored as your daily pleasure.

### Hand-Dipped Salted Caramels

*Makes about 50 pieces*

The days have passed when salt was just a seasoning for bland meals. Salt stimulates our taste for sweetness, and modern pastry chefs and confectioners worldwide have learned to use the distinctive flavors of salts from different regions to enhance flavors in all types of sweets, including chocolate. These milk-chocolate-covered caramels utilize common coarse sea salt (sal del mar), black Hawaiian sea salt (hiwa kai), and pink Himalayan salt (see "Types of Salt," page 44). When topping your caramels, add just a little salt at a time until they're flavored to your taste.

½ cup water

2 cups granulated sugar

1 teaspoon vanilla extract

1 cup light corn syrup

1 can (14 ounces) sweetened condensed milk, warmed

12 tablespoons (1½ sticks) unsalted butter, softened and cut into chunks

6 ounces dark chocolate (at least 65% cacao), chopped

16 ounces dark chocolate (at least 65% cacao), melted and tempered (page 29)

½–1 teaspoon sea salt, ground

1. Line a 7 x 7-inch square baking pan with parchment paper, allowing 1 inch of the paper to hang over the edges on two sides. Butter the parchment.

2. Combine the water, sugar, vanilla, and corn syrup in a medium saucepan over medium heat and stir constantly until boiling. Continue cooking until the mixture reaches 245–250°F. It should be firm but not hard. Remove from the

heat and stir in the condensed milk and softened butter. The temperature should go down slightly. Return to the heat and continue to cook until the temperature reads 244°F and the caramel is golden brown. Remove from the heat and stir in the chopped chocolate.

3. Spread the mixture into the prepared pan. Let sit at room temperature for 3 hours to cool completely. Once it's firm, lift the caramel slab from the baking pan and place it on a cutting board. Cut into 1-inch squares.

4. Line a baking sheet with parchment paper. Place the melted chocolate in a bowl and allow it to cool for about 10 minutes, until it starts to thicken. Using a dipping fork or large dinner fork, submerge a caramel square in the chocolate. Repeat a few times to coat completely, then tap against the edge of the bowl to remove excess chocolate. Transfer to the baking sheet. Repeat with the remaining caramels. Let dry for about 5 minutes, sprinkle on the sea salt, and allow them to dry completely.

**Variations**

CHOCOLATE ALMOND SALTED CARAMELS: Add ⅓ cup ground almonds to the caramel in step 2. Top with almond pieces.

CHOCOLATE-COATED GINGER SALTED CARAMELS: Omit the chopped chocolate from the caramel, and add 1½ teaspoons ground ginger at the same time as the vanilla. Top with crystallized ginger.

CHOCOLATE-COATED VANILLA SALTED CARAMELS: Omit the chopped chocolate from the caramel.

*Clockwise from top left: Almond Rochers Nut Clusters, Turtles, Candy Bars, Peanut Rochers Nut Clusters*

5 cups toasted pecans

7 ounces sweetened condensed milk

½ cup whole milk

1 cup granulated sugar

6 tablespoons unsalted butter

1 teaspoon vanilla extract

¼ teaspoon salt

8 ounces milk chocolate (at least 30% cacao), melted and tempered (page 29)

# Turtles

*Makes forty 2 ½–3-inch pieces*

Originally named because they look like little turtles, these treats have pecans for the head and legs and a caramel and chocolate mound in the center to mimic the shell. These days this classic chocolate treat can be formed into any cluster shape. The main goal is to pack in as many pecans as you can.

1. Line two baking sheets with parchment paper. Form 40 clusters or turtle shapes of 6 pecan halves (4 legs sticking out and 2 in the center—one for the body and one for the head) 1½ inches apart on the parchment.

2. To make the caramel, combine the condensed milk, whole milk, sugar, butter, and vanilla in a medium-size heavy-bottomed saucepan. Bring to a boil over medium heat, stirring constantly. Continue cooking until the caramel is firm at 245°F. Remove from the heat and stir in the salt. Set aside and continue measuring the temperature until it reaches 140–150°F.

3. Spoon 1½–2 tablespoons of hot caramel in the center of each pecan cluster to "glue" the pecans together, covering the center pecans but leaving the ends of the "legs" exposed. Let cool completely for about 30 minutes.

4. Spoon the chocolate over the caramel and pecans to cover most of the caramel. Allow the clusters to fully set at room temperature for 1 hour or in the refrigerator for 30 minutes. Place in an airtight container with waxed paper between the layers and store in a dry, cool place or the refrigerator for up to 1 week. Return to room temperature to soften the caramel before eating.

## Rochers Nut Clusters

*Makes forty 2-inch clusters*

These rock-shaped nut clusters (*rochers* is French for "rocks") can be made with any type of nut or dried or candied fruit you like. Here I have made two types in one batch. I dipped the toasted almond clusters in amaretto liqueur for extra flavor and left the peanut ones plain. To identify the nuts inside, top each candy with a whole nut after you have poured the chocolate.

2 cups whole almonds, freshly toasted (page 27)

½ cup amaretto liqueur

2 cups toasted whole peanuts

16 ounces dark chocolate (at least 65% cacao), melted and tempered (page 29)

20 whole almonds for topping (optional)

20 whole peanuts for topping (optional)

1. Line two baking sheets with parchment paper. While they're still warm from toasting, soak the almonds in the amaretto in a small bowl, tossing occasionally. After 1 hour, strain out the amaretto. Dry the bowl and return the almonds to it.

2. Place the peanuts in a second small bowl. Pour half the melted chocolate into the bowl with the almonds and the other half into the bowl with the peanuts. Mix quickly to coat the nuts evenly.

3. Spoon clusters onto the baking sheet 1½–2 inches apart, then spoon the remaining melted chocolate over the clusters. Top each piece with whole nuts. Allow the clusters to fully set at room temperature for 1 hour or in the refrigerator for 30 minutes. Place in an airtight container with waxed paper between the layers and store in a dry, cool place or the refrigerator for up to 1 month.

### Variation

FRUIT AND NUT CLUSTERS: Prepare the recipe as one batch and use 2 cups dried fruits and 2 cups nuts.

## Candy Bars

*Makes one 2-pound bar*

1½ pounds chocolate (any kind), chopped

½ cup whole nuts (almonds, hazelnuts, peanuts, macadamia nuts, pistachios) or nut and dried fruit mixture (raisins, dried cranberries, dried cherries, dried apricots)

Shaping a chocolate nut or dried fruit mixture in candy bar molds gives you a clean, professional finish. Break the bar into chunks to serve. This recipe yield fits nicely in a 2-pound mold, although you can adjust proportions to fit your mold. The candy bar combinations shown on page 45 are white chocolate hazelnut, milk chocolate almond, and dark chocolate with peanuts, walnuts, and raisins.

1. Melt the chocolate in the top of a double boiler set over simmering water. Pour half into the mold and tilt the mold around to evenly coat the surface. Add the nuts and pour in the remaining chocolate. Tap the mold on the countertop to allow air bubbles to rise to the top. Let set for 2 hours. Unmold the chocolate.

## Chocolate Fudge

*Makes thirty-six 1½-inch squares*

4 cups granulated sugar

½ cup light corn syrup

½ cup heavy cream

1 cup whole milk

6 ounces unsweetened solid baking chocolate (100% cacao), chopped

1 teaspoon vanilla extract

American-style chocolate fudge was popularized by recipes developed at women's colleges in the Northeast (most notably Vassar, Wellesley, and Smith) in the late 1800s, probably as part of the home economics curriculum, and used for fund-raisers. This soft fudge recipe does not use butter but relies on the fat in the cream and milk. It's made in just three steps—cook, cool, and beat until thick and creamy. When making fudge, keep in mind that the higher the temperature, the harder the fudge, since sugar dissolves and liquid evaporates more rapidly at high temperatures. So if you prefer harder fudge, cook the mixture until it reaches 238–240°F instead of the 236°F specified here. Beating, too, requires a keen eye. When the mixture slightly lightens, thickens, and begins to lose its shine, it is ready. To vary the flavors of your fudge, add chopped nuts, sweetened flaked coconut, chopped dried fruit, a little peppermint extract, or a touch of dried red chili flakes.

1. Butter a 9 x 9-inch baking pan. Set out a 9 x 13-inch baking pan.

*Chocolate Walnut Fudge, Coconut Fudge, Chocolate Fudge*

2. Combine the sugar, corn syrup, cream, milk, and chocolate in a heavy saucepan. Cook over medium heat, stirring constantly, until the chocolate is melted and the temperature has reached the soft ball stage (235–240°F). Remove from the heat and stir in the vanilla.

3. Pour the mixture into the 9 x 13-inch pan, spreading it into a thin layer. Let it cool to room temperature, about 20 minutes. Do not disturb the fudge as it cools.

4. Scrape up the mixture with a metal spatula and transfer it to a bowl. Mix with an electric mixer on medium speed for about 3 minutes, or until the fudge thickens, lightens slightly, and begins to lose its sheen.

5. Spread the mixture in the buttered 9-inch square baking pan and smooth the surface with an offset spatula or a knife. Cover with plastic wrap and set aside at room temperature for 1 hour, allowing the fudge to crystallize.

6. Cut into 1½-inch pieces and serve. Cover leftovers tightly with plastic wrap and store at room temperature for 1 week or in the refrigerator for up to 3 weeks.

**Variations**

CHOCOLATE WALNUT FUDGE: Mix 1½ cups chopped walnuts into the fudge in step 4.

COCONUT FUDGE: Mix 1 cup sweetened coconut flakes into the fudge in step 4. After cutting but before serving, cover the cubes with coconut.

CRANBERRY FUDGE: Mix 1 cup chopped dried cranberries into the fudge in step 4.

Outer ring from top: Dark Chocolate Almond, Dark Chocolate with White Chocolate Coating, Dark Chocolate Cocoa Powder, White Chocolate Mint, Dark Chocolate Cherry, Dark Chocolate Almond, Dark Chocolate with White Chocolate Coating, Milk Chocolate Hazelnut; inner ring clockwise from top: Raspberry Cream, Chai Tea, Milk Chocolate Espresso; outer container: Candy Dish

PEPPERMINT FUDGE: Reduce the vanilla to ½ teaspoon and add ½ teaspoon pure peppermint extract along with the vanilla.

CHOCOLATE CHILI FUDGE: Add ½ teaspoon dried red chili flakes (or more to taste) along with the vanilla.

## Ganache Truffles in Candy Dish
*Makes about fifty 1–1¼-inch truffles*

The ultimate candy experience, these dark, milk, and white chocolate ganache-filled truffles are creamy, smooth, and moist, with a dense chocolate outer shell. I've included instructions for several flavors made by using an assortment of ganache fillings and various toppings.

### Basic Ganache

1. Place the chopped chocolate in a heatproof bowl. Place the heavy cream and corn syrup in a saucepan over medium heat, stirring occasionally, until the cream comes to a boil and a candy thermometer reads 95°F. Remove from the heat, add the butter, and stir until melted.

2. Pour the hot mixture over the chocolate and let sit for 2–3 minutes to melt the chocolate. Stir until blended.

3. Either use the melon baller method (page 52), transfer the centers to a baking dish, and refrigerate, or let the ganache sit for 1 hour and then transfer it to a piping bag to follow the hand method.

### Dark Chocolate Truffle Flavors

DARK CHOCOLATE COCOA POWDER: Scatter ¾ cup natural unsweetened cocoa powder on a flat dish. Dip the fillings in dark chocolate (at least 65% cacao); then roll them in cocoa powder while still wet to cover completely. Remove from the cocoa. When the chocolate has completely set, roll each truffle in cocoa again if necessary.

DARK CHOCOLATE ALMOND: Add ⅔ cup ground almonds and 2 tablespoons amaretto liqueur to the filling. After dipping the filling in dark chocolate (at least 65% cacao) and while the truffles are still wet, sprinkle them with ¼ cup ground almonds and cocoa powder.

---

### Outer Coating

*16 ounces dark chocolate (at least 65% cacao), milk chocolate (at least 30% cacao), or white chocolate, melted and tempered (page 29) or compound coating, melted.*

---

### Dark Chocolate Ganache

*12 ounces dark chocolate (at least 65% cacao), chopped*

*1 cup heavy cream*

*1½ tablespoons light corn syrup*

*2 tablespoons unsalted butter*

### Milk Chocolate Ganache

*12 ounces milk chocolate (at least 30% cacao), chopped*

*1 cup heavy cream*

*3 tablespoons butter*

### White Chocolate Ganache

*12 ounces white chocolate, chopped*

*⅔ cup heavy cream*

*½ cup (1 stick) unsalted butter*

## FORMING THE GANACHE CENTERS

Unlike the recipes for the ganache used to cover cakes, those for ganache truffle centers call for less cream, making the mixture more dense and easier to shape. The ganache must be firm in order to be formed into a ball, which is made either by scooping the ganache out of the bowl with a melon baller or by filling a piping bag, squeezing out a dollop, and then shaping it into a 1–1¼-inch ball with your hands. If using the hand method, allow the ganache to sit for 1 hour before transferring it to the piping bag. After they are formed, the ganache centers need to be left out on the counter for 2 hours to dry out, and then allowed to harden in the refrigerator for 1–2 hours; alternatively, you can set them out overnight to dry and harden. When finishing the truffles with the outer coating, focus on one truffle at a time so that the dipped chocolate stays sticky enough to hold the topping. Dip the truffles twice if you want a thicker shell.

DARK CHOCOLATE CENTER WITH WHITE CHOCOLATE COATING: Dip the dark chocolate ganache into a white chocolate outer coating and let set. To finish, add 1 ounce melted dark chocolate (at least 65% cacao) to a piping bag with a small cut tip and 1 ounce melted milk chocolate to another piping bag with a small cut tip. Drizzle the chocolates in lines over the truffles.

DARK CHOCOLATE CHERRY: Add ½ cup finely chopped dried cherries to the dark chocolate ganache. Dip the filling in dark chocolate (at least 65% cacao), and top with grated pink chocolate.

### Milk Chocolate Truffle Flavors

MILK CHOCOLATE ESPRESSO: Add ¼ cup finely ground French roast coffee to the milk chocolate ganache. Dip the filling in the milk chocolate outer coating, and top with small shavings of milk and dark chocolate while still wet.

MILK CHOCOLATE HAZELNUT: Scatter 2 cups ground hazelnuts on a flat dish. Add ⅔ cup ground hazelnuts to the milk chocolate ganache. Dip the filling in the milk chocolate outer coating; then roll in hazelnuts while still wet.

### White Chocolate Truffle Flavors

RASPBERRY CREAM: Puree 1½ cups fresh raspberries and strain through a sieve to remove the seeds. Add to the white chocolate ganache. Dip the filling in dark chocolate (at least 65% cacao) and let set. Add 2 ounces melted pink chocolate to a piping bag with a small cut tip. Drizzle the chocolate in lines over the truffles.

WHITE CHOCOLATE MINT: Steep a sprig of mint (bearing about 10 leaves) in the cream for the white chocolate ganache during heating. Add 3–4 drops natural mint extract after the ganache is mixed. Dip the filling in milk chocolate and let set. Add 2 ounces melted green chocolate to a piping bag with a small cut tip. Drizzle chocolate lines over the truffles.

CHAI TEA: Steep 3 tablespoons strong black loose tea leaves in the cream of the white chocolate ganache during heating. Remove from the heat and let the tea steep for another 5 minutes before straining. Add ½ teaspoon each ground ginger and ground cinnamon, ¼ teaspoon each ground allspice, ground cardamom, and ground cloves, and ⅛ teaspoon black pepper before adding the butter. Let sit and stir. Dip the filling in white chocolate and top with brown crystal sugar while still wet.

WHITE CHOCOLATE GREEN TEA: Add 2 teaspoons matcha powder to the white chocolate ganache. Dip the filling in white chocolate and sprinkle each truffle with a pinch of matcha powder while still wet.

## Candy Dish

*Makes one 5½-inch dish*

Most candy dish molds on the market contain the pattern of the classic crystal candy dish. Since it is what's inside the dish that I want to shine, I poured the chocolate over the smooth, convex back of the mold, not the concave inside. Make the chocolate extra thick (at least ¼ inch) so it doesn't break. For a simpler method, pour the chocolate in the mold.

*6 ounces dark chocolate (at least 65% cocoa), melted and tempered (page 29)*

1. Pour half the chocolate on the outside of the mold. Let it set, then pour the remaining chocolate on top until the chocolate is at least ¼-inch thick. Place the mold on a baking sheet, clean up the edges, and let set.

2. Once the chocolate is set, remove the dish from the mold. Clean up the edges of the dish with a sharp paring knife to create a clean rim. Place the truffles inside the dish.

# CAKES AND MUFFINS

Make every day a celebration with flavors and textures that work together to make supremely satisfying cakes and muffins. For a casual breakfast, enjoy thick pound cakes with your coffee, or top them with fruit for an after-dinner dessert. For an afternoon snack, indulge in a slice of intensely chocolaty, fluffy multilayer cake with creamy frosting. If you want your own little personalized treat, choose individual muffins. Whatever you create, they'll all taste great with a tall glass of milk.

## Devil's Food Cake with Semisweet Chocolate Frosting

*Makes one 9-inch six-layer cake*

There's more than one recipe for this classic chocolate layer cake—the only requirement is that it be moist, rich, and topped with swoops of chocolate frosting. It's intended for everyday snacking, no special skills or fancy tools are required, and a simple dinner plate and butter knife will work just fine for presentation. However, there are a few tools that will make assembling and frosting this cake a snap—see "Specialized Cake-Making Equipment" on page 14 for a list. Bake this cake in round 9-inch pans that are 2 inches deep to ensure an extra-tall cake.

1. To make the cake, preheat the oven to 375°F. Butter and flour three 9-inch round pans.

2. Combine the flour, cocoa powder, baking soda, baking powder, and salt in a medium mixing bowl.

3. Beat the butter and sugar in a large mixing bowl with an electric mixer on medium speed until fluffy. Add the eggs one at a time, beating well after each addition. Stir in the melted chocolate.

4. Gradually add the flour mixture, alternating with the buttermilk, on low speed until blended. Add the whole milk and vanilla.

5. Pour the batter into the pans and bake for 30–35 minutes, or until a knife inserted in the center comes out clean. Cool in the pans for 5 minutes. Transfer to a rack to cool completely.

## Cake

*Makes one 9-inch round cake*

3½ cups all-purpose flour

¼ cup natural unsweetened cocoa powder

1 teaspoon baking soda

2 teaspoons baking powder

¼ teaspoon salt

¾ pound (3 sticks) unsalted butter, at room temperature

3 cups firmly packed light brown sugar

5 large eggs

5 ounces bittersweet chocolate (at least 70% cacao), melted

1 cup buttermilk

1½ cups whole milk

1½ tablespoons vanilla extract

## Semisweet Chocolate Frosting

*Makes about 6 cups*

24 ounces semisweet chocolate (at least 50% cacao), chopped into ½-inch pieces

¾ cup water

¾ cup milk

1½ cups (3 sticks) unsalted butter, at room temperature

3–4 cups sifted confectioners' sugar

## TIPS ON PREPARING LAYER CAKES

To cut a single cake into layers, place the baked cake on a lazy Susan or a cutting board covered with waxed paper. To create two layers, use a ruler to find the midpoint of the cake and mark it with a toothpick. Rotate the cake, marking it at the same height five more times around the perimeter, spacing the toothpicks evenly. Cut the cake horizontally along the toothpick line with a long serrated knife, using a sawing motion while rotating the cake; then remove the toothpicks. To create three or more layers, use the same measuring, marking, and cutting technique at the appropriate heights. When all the layers have been cut, choose the order of assembly, making the most even layers the top and bottom of the cake while the others serve as the middle layers.

To level a domed cake, remove it from the pan, set it on a plate, and place that plate in a larger baking pan. The sides of the pan should come up to the topmost straight edge of the cake, just below where the slope of the dome begins. Lay a long serrated knife flat against the top of the pan, with the blade facing the cake. Slowly cut the cake dome off, making sure to keep your knife level as you gently saw back and forth. Eat or save the domed top for later.

To construct a multilayer cake, simply stack the layers on top of one another, frosting after each one. To frost, you should first cover the top and sides of the cake with a crumb coat—a thin layer of frosting that covers loose crumbs and prepares a smooth surface for the rest of the frosting. Remove any large lumps or crumbs and then clean the spatula. Leave the cake on the counter to let the frosting set or in the refrigerator to let it harden for about 20 minutes. Mound additional frosting in the center of the top layer and spread it evenly to cover the entire stack of layers.

6. To make the frosting, combine the chocolate, water, and milk in a double boiler over medium-high heat. Stir constantly, until the chocolate is melted. Remove from the heat and let cool for 10 minutes. Add the butter, stirring until the mixture is smooth. Gradually beat in the confectioners' sugar until the frosting reaches a spreadable consistency.

7. Cut each of the three layers in half lengthwise to make six layers. Place one cooled layer on a serving plate and top with one-eighth of the frosting. Place a second layer on top and spread with another eighth of the frosting. Continue to add layers and frosting until all six are stacked. Top with the remaining layer; then spread the remaining frosting on the sides and top of the cake with a large icing spatula.

## Muffin Batter

2½ cups all-purpose flour

2 teaspoons baking powder

½ teaspoon baking soda

¼ teaspoon salt

½ cup (1 stick) unsalted butter, at
  room temperature

⅔ cup granulated sugar

2 large eggs

2 teaspoons vanilla extract

1½ cups mashed ripe banana
  (3–4 whole bananas)

½ cup buttermilk

2 cups semisweet miniature chocolate chips (at least 50% cacao)

¼ cup crystal sugar

## Chocolate Cream Cheese Filling

1 package (8 ounces) cream
  cheese, at room temperature

⅓ cup granulated sugar

3 tablespoons all-purpose flour

1 teaspoon vanilla extract

½ cup semisweet chocolate chips
  (at least 50% cacao), melted
  and cooled

## Topping

2 bananas sliced into ¼-inch
  rounds

## Chocolate Chip Banana Muffins

*Makes 10 jumbo muffins, 20 regular muffins, or 32 mini muffins*

There are a few tricks to baking muffins like these with big crunchy tops. The recipe contains a large amount of baking powder and a bit of baking soda to ensure a high rise. Fill the batter three-quarters of the way to the top of each muffin cup, sprinkle with crystal sugar, and bake. Eat the muffins unadorned, or include the cream cheese filling and fresh fruit topping—either way, they're guaranteed to start your day off right.

1. Preheat the oven to 350°F. Line two jumbo (3½-inch) muffin tins with large paper liners, two medium (2¾-inch) muffin tins with regular paper liners, or three mini (2-inch) muffin tins with small paper liners.

2. To make the muffins, combine the flour, baking powder, baking soda, and salt in a medium bowl and set aside.

3. Beat the butter and sugar with an electric mixer until light and fluffy. Add the eggs and vanilla and mix until blended. Beat in the banana and buttermilk.

4. Gradually add the flour mixture until just blended. Do not overbeat. Fold in the chocolate chips. Fill the liners three-quarters of the way full and sprinkle with crystal sugar. Bake for 25–30 minutes, or until a knife inserted in the center comes out clean. Set the pan on a rack to cool.

5. To make the filling, combine the cream cheese, sugar, flour, and vanilla in a bowl and blend until smooth. Beat in the melted chocolate.

6. To construct the muffins, cut the tops off the muffins and spread each bottom with 1–2 tablespoons filling. Place 3–4 banana slices on top and add another 1–2 tablespoons filling. Place the muffin top over the filling.

### Muffin Batter

1¾ cups all-purpose flour

⅔ cup Dutch-process cocoa
  powder

1 teaspoon baking powder

1 teaspoon baking soda

¾ teaspoon salt

½ cup (1 stick) unsalted butter, at
  room temperature

1¼ cups firmly packed light
  brown sugar

2 large eggs

1 cup whole milk

2 teaspoons vanilla extract

1 cup semisweet chocolate chips
  (at least 50% cacao)

1 cup toffee pieces

3 tablespoons crystal sugar

### Cream Cheese Filling

1 package (8 ounces) cream
  cheese, at room temperature

¼ cup granulated sugar

3 tablespoons all-purpose flour

1 teaspoon vanilla extract

1 cup whole blueberries

# Chocolate Blueberry Toffee Muffins

*Makes 10 jumbo muffins, 20 medium muffins, or 24 mini muffins*

One of the best chocolate-fruit flavor combinations out there is chocolate and blueberries. The toffee pieces and brown sugar in this recipe create a buttery caramel and molasses flavor, while the cream cheese filling adds a pleasant tang.

1. Preheat the oven to 400°F. Line two jumbo (3½-inch) muffin tins with large paper liners or one regular (2¾-inch) muffin tin with medium paper liners.

2. To make the muffins, combine the flour, cocoa powder, baking powder, baking soda, and salt in a medium bowl. Set aside.

3. Beat the butter and sugar together until fluffy. Add the eggs, milk, and vanilla and beat until blended.

4. Gradually add the flour mixture until just blended. Fold in the chocolate chips and toffee pieces. Fill the liners three-quarters full and sprinkle with crystal sugar. Bake for 25–30 minutes, or until a knife inserted in the center comes out clean. Set the pan on a rack to cool.

5. To make the filling, combine the cream cheese, sugar, flour, and vanilla in a bowl, and blend until smooth.

6. Cut the tops off the muffins and spread each bottom with 1–2 tablespoons filling. Arrange a row of blueberries around the perimeter of the muffin and spoon on another 1–2 tablespoons filling. Place the muffin top over the filling.

### Variations

CHOCOLATE BLUEBERRY MUFFINS: Omit the toffee pieces. Add 1½ cups fresh or frozen blueberries to the batter after adding the flour.

CHOCOLATE TOFFEE RASPBERRY MUFFINS: Replace blueberries with raspberries.

*Clockwise from left: Chocolate Chip Banana Muffin, Chocolate Toffee Raspberry Muffin, Chocolate Blueberry Toffee Muffin*

## Orange Chocolate Marble Pound Cake

*Makes one 4½ x 8½-inch loaf (8 servings, 2 slices per serving)*

Start your day right with small slices of this casual cake paired with a few slices of fresh fruit and a large cup of coffee. Loaf cakes are baked in a relatively tall, rectangular pan. I bake about six loaves at a time, each with a different chocolate accompaniment, and then freeze them to enjoy for the rest of the month. Here are a few of my favorites.

2 cups all-purpose flour

1 teaspoon baking powder

½ teaspoon salt

½ pound (2 sticks) unsalted butter, at room temperature

1⅔ cups granulated sugar

5 large eggs

2 tablespoons freshly squeezed orange juice

½ teaspoon grated orange zest

½ cup whole milk

3 ounces semisweet chocolate (at least 50% cacao), melted

1. Preheat the oven to 350°F. Butter and flour a 4½ x 8½-inch loaf pan.

2. Combine the flour, baking powder, and salt in a mixing bowl.

3. Using an electric mixer on medium speed, beat the butter and sugar in a large mixing bowl until creamy. Add the eggs one at a time, beating well after each addition. Beat in the orange juice and zest.

4. Gradually add the flour mixture, alternating with the milk, on low speed until blended.

5. Divide the batter in half and add the chocolate to one batch.

6. Pour the batter into the pan one on top of the other and swirl together with a knife. Bake for 55–70 minutes, or until a knife inserted in the center comes out clean. Cool in the pan for 10 minutes. Transfer to a rack to cool completely.

### Variations

MOCHA CHIP POUND CAKE: Replace the orange juice and zest with 1½ teaspoons vanilla. Replace the whole milk with ¼ cup double-strength brewed espresso. Add 2 ounces melted dark chocolate and 1 ounce mini semisweet chocolate chips to the batter.

MARBLE POUND CAKE: Replace the orange juice and zest with 1½ teaspoons vanilla.

*Front: Orange Chocolate Marble Pound Cake; back: Mocha Chip Pound Cake*

## Chocolate Pound Cake

2 cups all-purpose flour

1 teaspoon baking powder

½ teaspoon salt

½ pound (2 sticks) unsalted
  butter, at room temperature

1⅔ cups granulated sugar

4 large eggs

1½ teaspoons vanilla extract

¼ cup whole milk

3 ounces dark chocolate (at least
  65% cacao), melted and cooled

## Strawberry Rhubarb Topping

½ cup water

½ cup light agave nectar

1 pound rhubarb, sliced

1½ pounds strawberries, hulled
  and quartered

## Chocolate Pound Cake with Strawberry Rhubarb Topping

*Makes one 4½ x 8½-inch loaf (8 servings, 2 slices per serving)*

For the short time that both strawberries and rhubarb are in season, serve a slice of this rich chocolate pound cake topped with whipped cream or add the agave nectar–sweetened topping to your favorite chocolate recipes, such as Chocolate Marble Cheesecakes (page 61) or Semisweet Chocolate Ice Cream (page 91). Don't cook the strawberries—they are way too good fresh.

1. Preheat the oven to 350°F. Butter and flour a 4½ x 8½-inch loaf pan.

2. To make the cake, combine the flour, baking powder, and salt in a mixing bowl.

3. Using an electric mixer on medium speed, beat the butter and sugar in a large mixing bowl until creamy. Add the eggs one at a time, beating well after each addition. Beat in the vanilla.

4. Gradually add the flour mixture, alternating with the milk, on low speed until blended. Mix in the chocolate.

5. Pour the batter into the pan and bake for 55–70 minutes, or until a knife inserted in the center comes out clean. Cool in the pan for 10 minutes. Transfer to a rack to cool completely.

6. To prepare the strawberry rhubarb topping, place the water, agave nectar, and rhubarb in a saucepan. Simmer over low heat for 10 minutes, until the rhubarb is softened. Remove from the heat and let cool for 10 minutes. Stir in the strawberries.

7. Cut the pound cake into ½-inch slices and top each with whipped cream. Spoon the topping over the whipped cream.

# COOKIES AND BARS

Classic and comforting, these cookies and bars are the fastest home-made baked treats to make, and they work great as an on-the-go breakfast or after-school snack. So for some not-so-fussy cookies, get started baking with the recipes here. (For additional cookies, see the selection offered in the Milk and Cookies Party, page 110.)

## Florentines

*Makes 24 chocolate almond Florentines, 18 chocolate-dipped Florentines, 10 Florentine chocolate sandwiches, 10 Florentine ice cream sandwiches, or 18 cream-filled Florentines*

Florentines are ultrathin, crunchy, caramelly nut cookies from Italy that are traditionally filled, dipped, or topped with chocolate. Here I show you how to prepare them in many different shapes and sizes, from rolled or cream-filled cookies to chocolate ice cream sandwiches. Vary the nuts and chocolate in each batch and the possibilities are endless.

1. Preheat the oven to 350°F. Butter two cookie sheets. Set out a double boiler for melting chocolate.

2. Bring the butter, cream, and sugar to a boil in a saucepan over medium heat. Remove from the heat and let cool for 3–5 minutes.

3. Add the hazelnuts and almonds and stir to combine. Stir in the flour and salt. Follow one of the methods below to finish.

CHOCOLATE-DIPPED FLORENTINES: Drop 1¼-tablespoon portions of dough 4 inches apart on the cookie sheets. Bake for 10–12 minutes, until the cookies are thin and an even golden brown. Remove from the oven and cool for 5 minutes. Transfer to a rack to cool completely. Melt and temper 6 ounces dark chocolate (at least 65% cacao) in the top of a double boiler set over simmering water and dip each cookie halfway in the melted chocolate. Set on a rack to dry.

CHOCOLATE ALMOND FLORENTINES: Drop 1-teaspoon portions of dough 3 inches apart on the cookie sheets. Flatten with a wet fork to make 1½–2-inch rounds. Bake for 8–10 minutes, until the cookies are thin

### Cookies

6 tablespoons unsalted butter

½ cup plus 2 tablespoons heavy cream

1 cup superfine sugar

¾ cup hazelnuts, chopped

⅓ cup almonds, chopped

½ cup all-purpose flour

¼ teaspoon salt

*Clockwise from top: Chocolate Almond Florentines, Chocolate Buttercream Florentines, Florentine Ice Cream Sandwiches, Florentine Chocolate Sandwiches, Chocolate-Dipped Florentines*

and an even golden brown. Remove from the oven and cool for 5 minutes. Transfer to a rack to cool completely. Melt and temper 4 ounces dark chocolate (at least 65% cacao) in the top of a double boiler set over simmering water. Spoon ½ teaspoon melted chocolate on the top of each cookie. Add 3–5 whole almonds to the top. Set on a cooling rack to dry.

FLORENTINE CHOCOLATE SANDWICHES: Drop 1¼-tablespoon portions of dough (to make 3¼–3½-inch rounds) 4 inches apart on the cookie sheets. Bake for 10–12 minutes, until the cookies are thin and an even golden brown. Remove from the oven and cool for 5 minutes. Transfer to a rack to cool completely. Melt 6 ounces milk chocolate (at least 30% cacao) in the top of a double boiler set over simmering water. Spread 1 tablespoon melted chocolate on top of each cookie. Press two cookies together to create a sandwich.

FLORENTINE ICE CREAM SANDWICHES: Prepare the Florentine chocolate sandwiches as instructed above, but add a large scoop of chocolate ice cream (page 91) between the cookies before pressing them together to create a sandwich. Serve immediately, or wrap in plastic wrap and freeze until ready to eat.

CHOCOLATE BUTTERCREAM FLORENTINES: Drop 1½-tablespoon portions of dough (to make 4-inch rounds) 4 inches apart on the baking sheets. Bake for 10–12 minutes, until the cookies are thin and an even golden brown. Remove from the oven and wrap around a ¾-inch wooden rod, overlapping the edges of the cookie to form a tube. Let cool for 10 minutes to set. Slide off the rod and transfer to a rack to cool completely. Add chocolate buttercream frosting (page 243) to a pastry bag with a round tip and fill each cookie roll with frosting. Melt and temper 6 ounces semisweet chocolate (at least 50% cacao) in the top of a double boiler set over simmering water. Dip the end of each Florentine into the chocolate, and then dip the chocolate-tipped end of each cookie in chocolate sprinkles while still wet. Let dry on a rack for 1 hour.

**Variation**

MILK CHOCOLATE MACADAMIA FLORENTINES: Replace the almonds and hazelnuts with 1¼ cups ground macadamia nuts. Replace the dark chocolate with milk chocolate (at least 30% cacao).

*Opposite, front: Brownies; back: Salted Chocolate Brownies*

## Brownies

*Makes 12 brownies*

A chocolate recipe collection is not complete without a very good basic brownie recipe. These rich and chewy delights tempt your taste buds to finish every last morsel.

1 cup all-purpose flour

1 teaspoon baking powder

⅛ teaspoon salt

12 ounces semisweet chocolate (at least 50% cacao), chopped

½ pound (2 sticks) unsalted butter

1⅓ cups granulated sugar

4 large eggs

1½ teaspoons vanilla extract

1½ cups chopped walnuts

1. Preheat the oven to 350°F. Butter and flour a 9 x 13-inch baking pan.

2. Combine the flour, baking powder, and salt in a bowl and set aside.

3. Melt the chocolate and butter in a small saucepan over low heat. Add the sugar and stir to mix. Transfer the mixture to a bowl and let cool. Beat in the eggs one at a time, then stir in the vanilla. Gradually add the flour mixture and stir until blended.

4. Spread the batter into the baking pan and smooth out the top with a palette knife. Top with the walnuts. Bake for 30–35 minutes, until a knife inserted in the center comes out clean. Place the pan on a rack to cool. Cut into 3-inch squares or 3 x 4-inch rectangles to serve.

### Variation

SALTED CHOCOLATE BROWNIES: These taste great with or without walnuts. Increase the salt in the recipe to ½ teaspoon. Use bittersweet chocolate (at least 70% cacao) instead of semisweet chocolate. After spreading the brownie batter into the pan, sprinkle with 2 teaspoons coarse sea salt.

## Cereal Pops

4 tablespoons unsalted butter

3 cups miniature marshmallows

1 teaspoon vanilla extract

4 cups puffed rice cereal (plain or chocolate)

½ cup semisweet chips (at least 50% cacao) or milk chocolate chips (at least 30% cacao)

## Coating

12 ounces dark chocolate (at least 65% cacao) or milk chocolate (at least 30% cacao), melted and tempered (page 29)

1 ounce white chocolate shavings

# Chocolate Rice Cereal Pops

*Makes 12 pops*

Inspired by my favorite breakfast cereal bar, these crisp and chewy pops are a perfect on-the-go treat. Use plain rice cereal, or choose chocolate rice cereal for extra chocolate taste.

1. Line a 9 x 9-inch baking pan with parchment paper, leaving 2 inches hanging over two of the sides to use as handles. Set out a cooling rack over a rimmed baking sheet.

2. Melt the butter in a large saucepan over low heat. Add the marshmallows and stir until completely melted. Remove from the heat and stir in the vanilla. Add the rice cereal, and then stir in the chocolate chips until the rice cereal and chocolate chips are well coated. Press into the prepared pan and cool.

3. When ready, lift the parchment paper from the pan and place on a cutting board. Cut into 2 x 3-inch rectangles. Press a pop stick into a short side of each bar.

4. Dip a pop into the chocolate and shake it over the pan several times to remove excess chocolate. Place the pop on the cooling rack. Sprinkle with white chocolate shavings. Repeat with the remaining pops. Return the excess chocolate on the baking sheet to the pot and remelt if needed. Let the pops harden on the countertop for 1 hour. Place in an airtight container with waxed paper between the layers and store for up to 2 weeks at room temperature.

## Oatmeal Raisin Chocolate Chip Cookies

*Makes 24 large cookies*

⅔ cup all-purpose flour

3 tablespoons Dutch-process
  cocoa powder

1 teaspoon ground cinnamon

½ teaspoon salt

½ teaspoon baking soda

12 tablespoons (1½ sticks) unsalted butter, at room temperature

½ cup granulated sugar

½ cup light brown sugar

1 large egg

3 tablespoons apple juice

1 teaspoon vanilla extract

3 cups rolled oats (not instant)

¾ cup raisins

¾ cup chopped walnuts

1 cup semisweet chocolate chips
  (at least 50% cacao)

Oatmeal raisin cookies and semisweet chocolate chips produce what I call "flavor harmony." The ingredients blend together to create a one-of-a-kind taste. Feel free to swap out the raisins and walnuts for the dried fruits and nuts of your choice.

1. Preheat the oven to 350°F. Butter two cookie sheets.

2. Combine the flour, cocoa powder, cinnamon, salt, and baking soda in a medium bowl and set aside.

3. Cream the butter and sugars until fluffy. Add the egg and beat well. Mix in the apple juice and vanilla.

4. Gradually add the flour mixture until well blended. Stir in the oats, raisins, nuts, and chocolate chips.

5. Drop 2-tablespoon portions of dough 2½ inches apart on the cookie sheets. Bake for 10–12 minutes, until edges are golden. Remove from the oven and let cool for 2 minutes. Transfer to a rack to cool completely.

### Variations

OATMEAL CRANBERRY MOLASSES COOKIES: Replace the apple juice with unsulfured molasses and the raisins with dried cranberries.

OATMEAL CHOCOLATE MACADAMIA NUT COOKIES: Replace the raisins with chopped dried pineapple and the walnuts with chopped macadamia nuts.

OATMEAL APRICOT COOKIES: Replace the walnuts with almonds and the raisins with chopped dried apricots.

# MAKING COOKIES

Here are some hints that will help you make the best cookies possible.

## Baking Preparation

- Arrange the racks close together in the center of the oven. Leave enough room to pull out the sheets and rotate their positions while baking if necessary.
- Place a thermometer inside the oven.
- Preheat the oven 10–15 minutes before baking. Double-check the oven thermometer to ensure the correct baking temperature and adjust if necessary.
- Grease the sheets or pans or cover them with parchment paper or a silicone mat. Flour is not necessary unless a recipe recommends it (often a recipe doesn't need it if the cookies contain a lot of butter).
- Dust a work surface with flour if necessary, but don't add too much.

## Preparing Dough

- Measure accurately.
- Mix the dry ingredients and set aside.
- Cream the butter and sugar next. To do this properly, use a low mixer speed to begin and increase if needed. The mixture may look curdled, but when the flour is added it will become uniform. If mixing by hand, use a wooden spoon and beat about 150 strokes per minute, until blended smoothly together.
- Gradually add the flour mixture to the wet ingredients, and do not overmix. The more you work it, the tougher the dough, and consequently the final product, will be.
- Add any mix-ins (chips, nuts, berries) next.
- If the dough is soft or the recipe requires it, wrap the mixture tightly in plastic wrap and chill for 20–30 minutes. Chilling dough ensures that the butter doesn't melt too fast while baking, so the cookies don't spread.
- Form the dough, and follow the method for whatever type of cookie you're making. The cookies should all be the same size and shape to ensure even baking, or place similarly sized cookies on the same sheets and adjust baking times accordingly. Make sure spacing on sheets is appropriate for the style of cookie (for example, drop cookies need more space than those made with cookie cutters).

## Baking Cookies

- Since cookies bake quickly, keep an eye on them so they don't overbake. Check cookies often and rotate cookie sheets in the oven if necessary to ensure even cooking. Do not allow too much heat escape when opening and closing the oven while baking.
- Check cookies a few minutes before the shortest listed baking time. When they're done, the edges should be slightly golden, a bit darker than the center. Lift edges with a spatula to look underneath to make sure cookies are not doughy.
- Most cookies are best when removed from the oven slightly before they are completely done and then left to finish cooking on the hot baking sheet, which keeps them chewy. However, some recipes require cookies to be left in the oven with the temperature off until the cookies have cooked through.

## Cooling Cookies

- The general rule is to remove the cookies quickly from the baking sheets to prevent them from browning on the bottom and sticking to the sheet. Allow the cookie sheets to cool, and then wash and regrease them to prevent spreading before putting on the next batch.
- Cool individual cookies on a cooling rack and bar cookies in the pan on a cooling rack, or if the recipe is prepared with parchment paper, remove from the pan and cool on a rack. Bar cookies are easiest to cut when cold or frozen.
- Most cookies can be eaten 10 minutes after they are removed from the oven. Cool completely if decorating.

## Chocolate Lemon Bars

*Makes 12 lemon bars*

½ pound (2 sticks) unsalted
  butter, at room temperature

⅔ cup confectioners' sugar

2 cups flour

½ teaspoon ground ginger

1 teaspoon grated lemon zest

3 ounces semisweet chocolate (at
  least 50% cacao), melted and
  cooled

4 large eggs

2 cups granulated sugar

⅓ cup freshly squeezed lemon juice

¼ cup all-purpose flour

½ teaspoon baking powder

This recipe is a real delight. The lemony tart flavor of the custard mixed with the chocolate and ginger of the crust gives the bars a bit of bite. These bars are quick and easy to make, so prepare them when you're short on time but want to make a treat.

1. Preheat the oven to 350°F. Butter and flour a 9 x 13-inch baking pan.

2. To make the crust, beat the butter and confectioners' sugar until fluffy. Stir in the flour, ginger, and lemon zest, then stir in the melted chocolate. Press into the bottom of the prepared pan and bake for 15–20 minutes, until firm. While the crust is baking, prepare the lemon layer.

3. To make the custard, combine the eggs, granulated sugar, and lemon juice in a medium bowl and beat with an electric mixer until blended. Add the flour and baking powder. Remove the chocolate layer from the oven, pour the filling over the baked crust, and place back in the oven for 20–25 minutes. Remove from the oven and cool for 20 minutes.

4. Dust with confectioners' sugar and cut into 3-inch squares or 3 x 4-inch rectangles. Serve at room temperature.

## Chocolate Macaroons

*Makes twenty-four 2-inch macaroons*

3 large egg whites

½ teaspoon cream of tartar

½ cup granulated sugar

3 tablespoons natural unsweetened
  cocoa powder, sifted

⅛ teaspoon salt

2 teaspoons vanilla extract

1½ cups shredded unsweetened
  coconut

The refreshing lightness of these macaroons makes them a perfect snack or end to a meal. Try them with Chocolate Spice Sorbet (page 85).

1. Preheat the oven to 325°F and line two cookie sheets with parchment paper.

2. Beat the egg whites until foamy. Add the cream of tartar and continue to beat until soft peaks form. Gradually add the sugar 1 tablespoon at a time and continue to beat until all the sugar is absorbed and the peaks are shiny and stiff.

Gently stir in the cocoa powder, salt, vanilla, and coconut, being careful not to deflate the eggs.

3. Add half the mixture to a piping bag with a large star tip and pipe onto the baking sheets into 2-inch-wide, 1-inch-tall mounds. Bake for 15–20 minutes, or until the cookies look a bit dry. Keep an eye on them, being careful not to overbake. Cool on the baking sheet for 5 minutes. Transfer to a rack to cool.

**Variation**

CHOCOLATE-DIPPED MACAROONS: Melt and temper (page 29) 4 ounces dark chocolate (at least 65% cacao). Remove from the heat and add 1½ tablespoons butter to the chocolate. Stir until melted. Dip the macaroons halfway into the chocolate. Place on waxed paper or a cooling rack for 1–2 hours to set.

## Chocolate Madeleines

*Makes 20 madeleines*

Madeleines are spongy, cake-like cookies baked in a traditional shell-shaped pan, although if you don't have a madeleine mold you can use mini muffin pans. Serve with Chocolate Hot Toddies (page 166) for a comforting snack.

*¾ cup plus 2 tablespoons sifted cake flour*
*¼ cup natural unsweetened cocoa powder*
*½ cup (1 stick) unsalted butter, melted and cooled*
*¾ cup granulated sugar*
*2 large eggs*
*Zest of 1 lemon*
*½ teaspoon vanilla extract*

1. Preheat the oven to 375°F. Butter two madeleine molds and line a baking sheet with waxed paper.

2. Combine the flour and cocoa powder in a small bowl and set aside.

3. Using an electric mixer on medium speed, beat the butter and sugar together until light and fluffy. Add the eggs one at a time, beating well after each addition. Add the lemon zest and vanilla and beat for 2–3 minutes.

4. Gradually add the flour mixture and beat on low speed for about 2 minutes, until the batter thickens. Pour rounded teaspoonfuls of the batter into the prepared molds. Do not spread.

5. Bake for 12–15 minutes, or until the cakes are just beginning to pull away from the sides of the molds. Remove from the pans and transfer to racks to cool slightly.

## STORING COOKIES

There's nothing like freshly baked cookies straight from the oven, when the chocolate is still melted and the dough still warm. To prevent myself from eating a whole batch in one sitting, I usually make a double batch of dough. I then freeze half of one batch and refrigerate the other half, from which I prepare fresh-baked cookies later that week. I bake one entire batch and freeze some of the baked cookies, which I can thaw out at a later date.

- Cool cookies before storing.
- Cream-filled cookies have a short shelf life and should be refrigerated, although refrigeration dries out cookies in a few days.
- Store crisp and soft cookies in separate containers; otherwise, the crisp ones will soften.
- Bar cookies and shortbread can be cut and stored in containers or stored in the pan they were baked in. If you know you will be storing them, bake them in a pan that has a lid.
- Crisp cookies can be recrisped by returning them to a baking sheet and heating them at 300°F for 3–4 minutes.
- Separate sticky, moist, or decorated cookies with waxed paper.
- If you need to store cookies for a few days before gifting, choose airtight containers and transfer to a gift container if necessary.
- Freeze cookies, icing, and filling separately. Assemble when ready to eat.
- When freezing baked cookies, keep them in freezer-safe, airtight containers to prevent sogginess. Line containers with paper towels to absorb moisture. When you're ready to eat the cookies, take them out of the freezer, remove the cookies from the containers, and place them on fresh paper towels on a baking sheet for 1–2 hours to thaw at room temperature. Place any uneaten cookies back into airtight containers.
- Most prepared cookie dough can be stored in the refrigerator for up to 2 weeks. If the dough contains eggs, milk, or cream, I usually play it safe and use it within 5 days.
- Frozen dough should stay good for 3–4 months, although mine is usually gone within 2 months because why freeze it for that long when I can eat it? Defrost the dough for 30 minutes before dropping or rolling it. Icebox cookies can be sliced within 5 minutes of removing the dough from the freezer.
- To moisten dry cookies, add a piece of fruit to the container. An apple, pear, orange, lemon, or lime slice works. Let stand for a day or two and then remove the fruit. The cookies will pick up the flavor of the fruit, so choose complementary flavors. If you don't want added flavor, try using a piece of bread.

# PIES, TARTS, AND PASTRIES

It is always nice to have homemade treats around the kitchen, and no other foods say "home" more than the irresistible pies, tarts, and pastries found in this chapter. The greatest advantage to making a crust from scratch is that it gives you the opportunity to vary the taste and texture. For example, besides the more traditional pastry or graham cracker crusts, have you ever seen chocolate puff pastry piecrusts, chocolate butter crusts, or oatmeal crusts in the store? In addition to these recipes, you will also find fillings that deliciously complement or contrast the flavor of chocolate.

## Banana Chocolate Cream Pie

*Makes one 9-inch pie*

If you love cream pies, then this is the recipe for you. Combining banana cream pie and chocolate cream pie in a chocolate butter crust creates a pie that is a new American classic. I made the border of this pie from appliqué crust leaves. After rolling out the dough, assemble the border along the crust's edge and freeze it for about an hour before baking. This allows the leaves and the veins to hold their shape better when heated. The appliqué requires a lot of dough, so if you choose to make a fluted edge instead, you will have extra dough. In that case, prepare some extra filling to make an additional, smaller pie.

1. Butter and flour a 9-inch pie pan. On a floured work surface, roll out the large pastry disc to ⅛ inch thick and 13 inches round and place over the pie pan, allowing the excess to hang over the rim. Crimp the edges to build up a tall border around the rim.

2. On a floured work surface, roll out the small pastry disc to ⅛ inch thickness. Cut out about thirty-two ¾-inch leaves for the rim decoration. Draw veins in the leaves using a bamboo skewer. Brush the edge of the crust with egg white, and then press the leaves around the rim. Brush the tops of the leaves and entire crust with egg white. Cover in with plastic wrap and place in the freezer for at least 1 hour.

## Crust

Chocolate Butter Crust (page 241)

1 egg white, beaten

## Chocolate Pie Filling

¼ cup cornstarch

⅛ teaspoon salt

½ cup granulated sugar

4 large egg yolks

2½ cups whole milk

2 tablespoons unsalted butter

4 ounces semisweet chocolate (at least 50% cacao), melted

1 teaspoon vanilla extract

3 ripe medium bananas

2¼ teaspoons freshly squeezed lemon juice

## Topping

3½–4 cups Chocolate Whipped Cream (page 244)

3 ripe medium bananas, sliced, or ¾ cup dried banana chips

2¼ teaspoons freshly squeezed lemon juice

2 ounces large chocolate shavings

## HOW TO MAKE AN ALUMINUM FOIL PIE SHIELD

A pie shield covers the edges of a piecrust to prevent it from browning too much. To make a shield for a 9-inch pie, fold a 12-inch square of aluminum foil into quarters. Use scissors to cut out a semicircle from the center, leaving a 3-inch ring around the edges. Unfold the ring and place over the pie's rim during baking, just before the crust reaches a nice golden color. Continue to bake for 5–10 minutes, or until the center is done.

## PIE WEIGHTS

Metal, ceramic, or clay pie weights are used to bake pie and tart pastries without a filling. Lining a crust with parchment paper and weighting it helps the crust retain its shape and keeps it from shrinking or puffing. Dry beans and rice can also be used as weights. Fill the shell with weights until they reach $\frac{1}{4}$ inch from the top; this will prevent the sides of the crust from slipping down into the pan.

3. To make the filling, combine the cornstarch, salt, and sugar in a small bowl; set aside. Beat the egg yolks and milk in a medium saucepan over low heat. Gradually add the cornstarch mixture, stirring continuously, until the mixture comes to a boil. Reduce the heat and continue stirring for about 5 minutes, until the mixture thickens. Remove from the heat and stir in the butter and melted chocolate until the butter is melted and the ingredients are combined. Add the vanilla. Place plastic wrap over the filling, making sure it touches so that a skin does not form on the surface, and refrigerate for 45–60 minutes.

4. Preheat the oven to 350°F. Line the piecrust with parchment paper and fill it with pie weights. Bake the crust for 20 minutes. Remove the paper and weights and bake for an additional 10–15 minutes, until the crust is cooked in the center (it will appear dry). Cool on a rack.

5. Slice the bananas into $\frac{1}{4}$-inch rounds on a diagonal and gently toss with the lemon juice. Add the sliced bananas to the shell in overlapping circles. Spread the chocolate filling over the bananas, pressing down to remove any air gaps.

6. Using a spatula, spread half the whipped cream over the filling to create a smooth mound. Add the remaining whipped cream to a pastry bag set with a star tip and pipe around the edges of the filling. Chill for 1–2 hours. When ready to serve, slice the bananas for the topping into $\frac{1}{4}$-inch-thick rounds on a diagonal and gently toss with the lemon juice. Top the pie with the banana slices or dried banana chips and chocolate shavings.

## Crust

Sweet Chocolate Tart Crust (page 241)

## Chocolate Ganache Filling

2¾ cups heavy cream

1½ teaspoons grated clementine zest

24 ounces dark chocolate (at least 65% cacao), chopped and melted

¼ cup light corn syrup

3 clementine slices

# Chocolate Clementine Tart

*Makes one 12 x 6-inch tart*

Savor the wonderful taste of sumptuous chocolate mingling with fresh citrus. Juicy, sweet, and less acidic than oranges, clementines enhance the flavor of a rich chocolate tart perfectly.

1. Preheat the oven to 375°F. Butter and flour a 12 x 6-inch tart pan.

2. On a floured surface, roll out the crust to a ⅛-inch-thick rectangle roughly 14 x 8 inches. Drape the dough in the pan, pressing it into the bottom corners. Push the rim against the top edges of the pan. Prick the bottom with a fork. Place a piece of parchment paper large enough to cover the sides onto the crust and fill with pie weights.

3. Bake the crust for 15–20 minutes. Remove the weights and bake for an additional 10–15 minutes, until the rim appears slightly dry or cooked. Let cool for 20 minutes, remove the rim from the pan (leaving the metal base on the bottom), and transfer to a rack to cool completely.

4. To make the filling, heat the cream in a small saucepan over low heat until bubbles appear, but it's not yet boiling. Remove from the heat and add the clementine zest.

5. Mix in a medium bowl with the dark chocolate and corn syrup until smooth.

6. Using a large metal spatula, transfer the shell from the metal tart pan base to a serving plate. Pour the filling into the tart shell, and smooth the top with an offset palette knife if necessary. Cover with plastic wrap, and chill for 2 hours. Top with clementine slices when ready to serve.

## Crust

*Sweet Chocolate Tart Crust (page 241)*

## Filling

*1 cup hazelnuts, chopped*

*1 cup chopped dates*

*2 tablespoons apple juice*

*3 large eggs*

*1 cup clover honey*

*½ cup granulated sugar*

*½ teaspoon salt*

*¼ cup unsalted butter, melted*

*2 ounces dark chocolate (at least 65% cacao), melted and cooled*

*2 teaspoons vanilla extract*

*18 whole hazelnuts for topping*

# Chocolate Hazelnut Date Tarts

*Makes eighteen 2½-inch mini tarts*

If you like the chocolate and hazelnut combination commonly found in spreads like Nutella (see page 139 for a homemade recipe), you'll love these tarts. They have all that goodness, as well as the gooeyness of pecan pie and fruitiness of dates. I like to eat these bite-size treats on the go—or have one every time I pass through the kitchen.

1. Butter and flour eighteen 2½-inch tart pans. Preheat the oven to 350°F.

2. On a floured work surface, roll out the chilled dough into a circle about ⅙ inch thick and 15 inches in diameter. Place the tart pans upside down on the dough and score it by pressing the entire rim of each pan lightly into the dough. Using a knife, cut the dough into circles slightly larger than the diameter of the pans. You can also use cookie cutters that are larger than the tart pans; use cutters with fluted edges to make decorative borders.

3. Drape the dough over the tart pans, allowing the excess to hang over the rim. Press the dough into the bottom and up the sides, so the dough rises slightly above the rims of the pans. Decoratively crimp the edges.

4. Add the hazelnuts, dates, and apple juice to a food processor and pulse until the mixture resembles a thick paste. Set aside.

5. Combine the eggs, honey, and sugar in a medium mixing bowl. Beat with an electric mixer on medium speed until combined. Add the salt, butter, chocolate, and vanilla, and blend well. Add the nut-date mixture.

6. Spoon the filling into the crusts. Press a whole hazelnut on top of each tart. Bake for 18–20 minutes, or until the crust is deep brown and the filling has puffed. Cool in the pans on a rack for 30 minutes. Remove from the pans and serve warm.

*Chocolate Hazelnut Date Tarts*

**Variation**

CHOCOLATE FRUIT TARTS: Prepare the shells without the filling and let cool. Fill with Chocolate Whipped Cream (page 244) and top with fresh berries and Chocolate Leaves (page 162).

## Chocolate Croissants

*Makes 6 croissants*

Say good morning with these cream cheese- and chocolate-filled croissants. You can make homemade puff pastry with the plain butter recipe shown here; use one 14-ounce package of all-butter frozen puff pastry, thawed; or, for a real chocolate overload, use the Chocolate Puff Pastry (page 82).

1. To make the pastry, mix the flours and salt in a large bowl. Toss the butter in the flour mixture until coated, breaking it up a bit with your fingertips.

**Puff Pastry**

3 cups all-purpose flour

1 cup cake flour

½ teaspoon salt

1 pound (4 sticks) cold unsalted butter, cut into tablespoon-size slices

1⅓ cups ice water

Chocolate Croissants

## Cream Cheese Filling

*Makes about 1½ cups*

*1 package (8 ounces) cream cheese, at room temperature*

*¼ cup sugar*

*3 tablespoons all-purpose flour*

*1 large egg yolk*

*1 teaspoon freshly squeezed lemon juice*

*1 teaspoon vanilla extract*

## Chocolate Filling

*Makes about 1½ cups*

*2½ tablespoons unsalted butter*

*8 ounces semisweet chocolate (at least 50% cacao), chopped, or about 1⅓ cups semisweet chocolate chips (at least 50% cacao)*

*2 tablespoons light corn syrup*

*1 teaspoon vanilla extract*

*3 large egg whites, beaten*

2. Form a well in the center of the dough. Gradually add the water and mix until the flour is slightly moistened.

3. Turn out the dough on a floured surface and knead 8–10 times. Form into a ball. Flatten the dough into a rectangle.

4. Roll the dough out into a 15-inch square. Fold horizontally into thirds, forming a 15 x 5-inch rectangle. Rotate the dough a quarter turn, and then fold horizontally into thirds again to form a 5-inch square. Cover with plastic wrap and chill for 30 minutes.

5. Repeat the rolling and folding process twice more, chilling for 30 minutes each time.

6. To make the cream cheese filling, combine the cream cheese, sugar, flour, egg yolk, lemon juice, and vanilla in a bowl, and blend until smooth.

7. To make the chocolate filling, melt the butter in a double boiler over medium-high heat. Add the chocolate and corn syrup and cook, stirring constantly, until the chocolate is melted. Remove from the heat, stir in the vanilla, and let cool.

8. Preheat the oven to 400°F. Line two baking sheets with parchment paper.

9. On a floured surface, roll out the pastry into a ⅛-inch-thick, 16 x 15-inch rectangle. Using a pastry wheel or pizza cutter, cut the dough into six 8 x 5-inch rectangles.

10. Spoon the cream cheese and chocolate fillings into the center of each pastry, leaving a 1-inch border on the longest (8-inch) edges. Brush egg white along the clean edges and fold the pastry over to create a rectangle. Press and pinch the edges with your fingertips to seal tightly. Use a knife to score the top with lines to create air vents.

11. Place the croissants on the baking sheets. Brush the tops with egg white and chill for 20 minutes.

12. Bake for 15 minutes. Reduce the heat to 350°F and rotate the baking sheets. Bake for an additional 10–15 minutes, or

until golden brown. Cool on the baking sheets for 5 minutes. Transfer to a rack to cool for an additional 15 minutes. Serve warm or at room temperature.

**Variation**

CHOCOLATE PUFF PASTRY CROISSANTS: Prepare using Chocolate Puff Pastry (below).

## Chocolate Raspberry Turnovers

*Makes nine 5-inch pastries*

Fall in love with these fruity chocolate turnovers. One of the main advantages to homemade puff pastry is that it can be any flavor you like. Here it's chocolate. Prepare the fresh raspberry filling or, if you are short on time, use a 14-ounce package of all-butter frozen puff pastry and high-quality raspberry preserves. Since you won't get the chocolate pastry kick, you may want to add a bit more chopped chocolate to the filling.

1. To make the dough, sift the flours and cocoa powder together in a large bowl. Add the sugar and salt. Toss the butter in the flour mixture until coated. Mix by breaking up the butter a little with your fingers.

2. Form a well in the center, add the water, and mix until the flour is slightly moistened.

3. Gather the dough and knead 8–10 times by pressing it on a floured work surface until blended. Gather the dough into a ball and then flatten it into a rectangle.

4. On a floured work surface, roll the dough into a 15 x 15-inch square. Fold horizontally into thirds, forming a 15 x 5-inch rectangle. Rotate the dough a quarter turn; then fold horizontally into thirds again to form a 5 x 5-inch square. Cover the dough with plastic wrap and chill for 30 minutes.

5. Repeat the rolling and folding process twice more. Chill for 30 minutes each time.

### Chocolate Puff Pastry

2¾ cups all-purpose flour

1 cup cake flour

⅓ cup natural unsweetened cocoa powder

¼ cup superfine sugar

1 teaspoon salt

1 pound (4 sticks) cold butter, cut into tablespoon-size slices

1⅓ cups ice water

2 large egg whites

¼ cup crystal sugar

### Fresh Raspberry Filling

½ cup apple juice

¼ cup cornstarch

½ cup firmly packed light brown sugar

¼ teaspoon salt

1 tablespoon freshly squeezed lemon juice

2 tablespoons instant tapioca

3 cups raspberries

4 ounces semisweet chocolate (at least 50% cacao), chopped into ½-inch pieces

Kneading develops the gluten in dough, providing the strength it needs to hold air pockets and rise adequately. If the gluten is not stretched and worked properly, the bread is not able to hold air, and it becomes dense and tough.

To knead, simply push the dough down with the palm of your hands, fold it, turn it ninety degrees, and repeat. It takes 8-10 minutes, depending on the recipe, and can be a real workout. Most people don't knead long enough. You'll know you're done when the dough is smooth and almost satiny. When you poke your finger into it, the indentation should remain.

6. To make the filling mix the juice, cornstarch, sugar, and salt in a medium saucepan over medium heat. Stir until thick. Remove from the heat and stir in the lemon juice and tapioca. Allow to cool for 10 minutes. Fold in the raspberries.

7. On a floured work surface, roll out the dough into a ⅛-inch-thick, 15 x 15-inch square. Using a pastry or pizza cutter, cut the dough into nine 5 x 5-inch squares.

8. Place ⅓ cup filling in the center of each pastry, leaving a ½-inch border around the edges. Divide the chopped chocolate evenly among them. Brush egg white along the clean edges, then fold in half to make a triangle. Pinch the pastry edges with your fingertips to seal tightly.

9. Line two baking sheets with parchment paper and place the turnovers on them. Brush the tops with egg white and sprinkle with crystal sugar. Chill for 20 minutes. Preheat the oven to 400°F.

10. Bake for 15 minutes, reduce the heat to 350°F, and rotate the baking sheets. Bake for an additional 10–15 minutes, or until golden brown. Let sit for 5 minutes. Transfer the turnovers to a rack for 15 minutes to cool. Serve warm or at room temperature.

**Variations**

BANANA CHOCOLATE TURNOVERS: Omit the Fresh Raspberry Filling. Prepare the Hot Fudge (page 242). Slice 3 medium bananas into ¼-inch-thick slices cut diagonally. Add 2–3 tablespoons fudge to each pastry. Distribute the bananas among the pastries, seal, and bake.

CHOCOLATE CHERRY TURNOVERS: Omit the Fresh Raspberry Filling. Fill the turnovers with Hot Fudge (page 242) and add 5–6 fresh, pitted cherry halves to each one. Seal and bake.

# ICE CREAM AND FROZEN DELIGHTS

Anytime and anywhere, melt-in-your-mouth icy-cold chocolate feels good on the taste buds and on the soul. Whether eaten by itself from a small bowl, dressed up with waffles or cookies, or drunk through a straw in a float, it is always sure to please.

## Chocolate Spice Sorbet

*Makes 2½ cups*

The recipe for this light and refreshing sorbet calls for infusing the sugar syrup with cinnamon, cardamom, and vanilla, or you can try infusing it with other flavors such as mint, ginger, lavender, raspberry, or orange. Serve with Chocolate Macaroons (page 71).

3 cups water

½ cinnamon stick

1 vanilla bean

1¼ cups granulated sugar

¾ cup natural unsweetened cocoa powder

⅛ teaspoon salt

6 ounces bittersweet chocolate (at least 70% cacao), finely chopped

¼ teaspoon ground cardamom

1. Combine the water, cinnamon stick, vanilla bean, and sugar in a large saucepan. Cook over medium-high heat for 20 minutes, until the mixture has reduced to about 2¼ cups. Remove from the heat and let cool. Remove the cinnamon stick and vanilla bean.

2. Return the pan to the stove top and add the cocoa powder and salt. Slowly bring to a boil over medium heat, whisking occasionally. Once it starts boiling, whisk constantly for an additional 30 seconds.

3. Remove from the heat and stir in the bittersweet chocolate and cardamom. Stir until the chocolate has melted. Cover and chill in the refrigerator for 30 minutes, until thick but still pourable.

4. Freeze the sorbet in an ice cream maker according to the manufacturer's instructions. Scoop onto plates immediately before serving.

## Milk Chocolate Fudge Pops

*Makes six 6-ounce pops*

Made with either whole or almond milk, these pops are light and refreshing. The stripes are not just pretty, but also offer contrasting tastes. For a quicker pop, just add the melted chocolate along with the cocoa powder. Enjoy as an afternoon pick-me-up.

3 cups whole milk or almond milk

⅓ cup unsalted butter or almond butter

½ cup natural unsweetened cocoa powder

1 teaspoon vanilla extract

⅓ cup agave nectar

4 ounces milk chocolate (at least 30% cacao), melted and cooled

1. Combine the milk and butter in a small saucepan over low heat and stir until the butter is melted. Turn off the heat.

2. Place the cocoa powder in a small bowl. Add ¼ cup of the milk mixture to the powder and stir to create a smooth paste. Return the paste mixture to the milk mixture and stir until blended. Stir in the vanilla and agave nectar.

3. Transfer half the cocoa mixture to a bowl. Add the melted milk chocolate to one of the bowls. Fill each pop mold one-quarter to one-third full with one of the mixtures. Freeze for at least 30 minutes, until firm.

4. Remove from the freezer. Fill the molds with the second mixture until two-thirds full, and place the pop stick in the mold. Freeze for at least 2 hours, until firm. Fill the mold to ¼ inch from the top with the first mixture, straighten the sticks if necessary, and freeze for 3–4 hours, until firm.

5. Remove from the freezer. Let stand at room temperature for 5 minutes before removing the pops from the molds.

1 cup granulated sugar

¼ cup Dutch-process cocoa powder

½ cup cornstarch

¼ teaspoon salt

3 cups milk

3 tablespoons unsalted butter

1 teaspoon vanilla extract

¾ cup semisweet chocolate chips

¾ cup miniature marshmallows

¾ cup chopped peanuts

*Opposite: Rocky Road Pudding Pops, Milk Chocolate Fudge Pops, Chocolate Malt Pops, Balboa Bars*

## Rocky Road Pudding Pops

*Makes twelve 4-ounce pops*

Lay-flat, horizontal silicone molds were used to make these rocky road and malt pudding pops. I love these molds because the pops are very easy to remove, making them great to use for soft, creamy ingredients with a high fat content, such as pudding and ice cream. Since the surfaces of the pops are exposed in the mold, you can fill the mold with mix-in ingredients to enhance the visual appeal. If you don't have a horizontal mold, I recommend making these pops in disposable paper or plastic cups. After adding all the ingredients to the cup, wrap the top with a piece of foil and make a small slit in the middle with a utility knife. Stick the wooden stick through the slit to hold it upright while the pop is freezing. When ready, remove the cup to serve.

1. To make the pudding, stir together the sugar, cocoa powder, cornstarch, and salt in a large saucepan. On the stove over medium heat, add the milk and bring to a boil, stirring constantly. Remove from the heat as soon as the mixture thickens.

2. Stir in the butter and vanilla and cool to room temperature. Stir in ½ cup of the chocolate chips, ¼ cup of the marshmallows and ¼ cup of the peanuts.

3. Scatter about half the remaining chocolate chips, peanuts, and marshmallows into the molds. Spoon the chocolate pudding into the molds; then add the remaining chocolate chips, nuts, and marshmallows to the pop. Insert sticks and place in the freezer for 4–6 hours.

**Variation**

CHOCOLATE MALT POPS: Add 1 tablespoon malt powder to the pudding along with the cocoa powder. Replace the marshmallows and peanuts with 1½ cups chopped malt balls.

## Balboa Bars

*Makes 12 pops*

Balboa bars are decadent rectangular ice cream pops with a thin shell of chocolate coating and playful toppings. They originated on Balboa Island, a small island off Newport Beach in Southern California (island residents also claim to have invented chocolate-dipped frozen bananas). Coat the outer chocolate with nuts, coconut, chocolate bits, dried bananas, toffee, or sprinkles. Experiment with different chocolates, including white, dark, and bittersweet. This recipe uses store-bought ice cream packaged in a rectangular container. If you make the ice cream yourself, mold it into a rectangular or square baking pan, as it will be easier to cut into the traditional bar shape. Soften the ice cream for five minutes and then cut with a large, warm chef's knife.

*4 cups high-quality chocolate ice cream (page 91), packaged in a rectangular container*

*2 cups white chocolate, milk chocolate (at least 30% cacao), or bittersweet chocolate (at least 70% cacao), melted and tempered (page 29)*

*1 cup sprinkles, slivered almonds, dried banana chips, unsweetened coconut flakes, and/or chopped chocolate*

1. Line a baking sheet with parchment paper. Using a warm knife, cut the ice cream into pieces that are 2¼ inches wide, 3 inches tall, and 1 inch thick. Place on the baking sheet and insert the sticks in the center of the bars. Cover with plastic wrap and place in the freezer for 2 hours to harden.

2. When the pops are frozen, heat the chocolate in the top of a double boiler set over simmering water and then cool to room temperature. Quickly dip a pop into the coating until

covered. Allow the excess to drip onto a plate. Sprinkle the toppings of your choice over the coating. Press lightly with a knife to adhere. Return the pop to the baking sheet in the freezer. Repeat this process one at a time with the remaining pops. When all the pops are ready, serve immediately or lay on a baking sheet lined with parchment paper, cover with plastic wrap, and freeze until ready to serve.

### Chocolate Ice

*4 cups water*

*⅔ cup granulated sugar*

*1 cup natural unsweetened cocoa powder*

### Fruit Syrup

*1 cup granulated sugar*

*1 cup water*

*1 cup peeled and pureed fresh pineapple, peach, or kiwifruit*

### Plain Ice

*24–30 large ice cubes (enough to make 4 cups crushed ice)*

### Garnish

*8 slices fresh peach, pineapple, or kiwifruit*

## Fruity Chocolate Snow Cones

*Makes eight 8-ounce snow cones*

Peach and chocolate, pineapple and chocolate, kiwi and chocolate—all are refreshing flavor combinations perfect for a hot summer day. You can crush the ice using a snow cone machine, a blender, or an 8 x 8-inch baking dish as directed below. Instead of serving the ice in paper cones, you can scoop it into small juice glasses or sherbet dishes.

1. To make the chocolate ice, combine the water, sugar, and cocoa powder in a large saucepan. Cook over medium heat until the mixture starts to bubble. Continue to cook for 1–2

minutes, until the mixture thickens slightly. Pour the mixture into an 8 x 8-inch ceramic baking dish and let cool for 30 minutes. Cover with plastic wrap and freeze for 45 minutes. When ice crystals have formed around the edges, stir the mixture thoroughly with a fork. Freeze for another 3 hours, stirring every 45 minutes, until the mixture is completely frozen and has achieved a shaved texture. Alternatively, pour the hot mixture into two ice cube trays, allow to cool to room temperature, and then freeze for 4 hours. Crush the cubes a few at a time in a blender or in a snow cone maker according to the manufacturer's instructions. Transfer to an 8 x 8-inch ceramic baking dish and freeze for 20–30 minutes to harden.

2. To make the fruit syrup, combine the sugar and water in a medium saucepan over medium heat and stir until the sugar has dissolved. Add the pureed fruit and cook for an additional 5–7 minutes, until thickened. Remove from the heat and let cool in the pan for 1 hour. Strain the syrup through a fine-mesh sieve into a tall pitcher, cover, and refrigerate for 1 hour until cold.

3. To make the plain ice, crush the ice cubes a few at a time in a snow cone machine or blender until you have 4 cups crushed ice. Transfer to an 8 x 8-inch ceramic baking dish and freeze for 20–30 minutes to harden.

4. To serve, scoop about ½ cup of the chocolate ice and ½ cup of the plain ice into each of the paper cones. You can place the plain and chocolate ice side by side, in concentric circles, or one on top of the other. Pour about ¼ cup fruit syrup over the ice. Freeze until ready to serve, and garnish with fresh fruit.

## Semisweet Chocolate Ice Cream

*Makes 4½ cups*

*6 large egg yolks*

*1 cup granulated sugar*

*⅛ teaspoon salt*

*2 cups heavy cream*

*1½ cups whole milk*

*3 ounces semisweet chocolate (at least 50% cacao), chopped*

*1 tablespoon vanilla extract*

## Brownie Waffle Sundae

*Makes 6–8 sundaes, depending on the size of the waffle iron*

When preparing homemade ice cream, forget waffle cones and go for homemade brownie waffles instead. Top the ice cream with chocolate sauce and nuts to make a dreamy snack, dessert, or, yes, even breakfast.

1. To make the ice cream, combine the egg yolks, sugar, and salt in a medium mixing bowl. Beat with an electric mixer on medium speed until the mixture forms ribbons when the beaters are lifted. Set aside.

2. Combine the cream, milk, and chocolate in a medium saucepan and heat over medium heat until just below the boiling point. Slowly whisk in the egg mixture and cook, stirring constantly, about 5 minutes, or until the mixture coats the back of a wooden spoon. Make sure the chocolate is melted completely.

## Brownie Waffles

*Makes 8 waffles*

¾ cup (1½ sticks) butter, melted

1½ cups granulated sugar

4 large eggs

2 teaspoons vanilla extract

½ cup unsweetened cocoa

2 cups all-purpose flour

¾ cup chopped walnuts

### Toppings

¾ cup Chocolate Sauce (page 242)

⅓ cup chopped walnuts

3. Return the mixture to the mixing bowl and stir in the vanilla. Place the bowl inside a larger bowl filled halfway with ice water and let cool, stirring occasionally. Cover and chill for 1 hour.

4. Transfer to an ice cream maker and freeze according to the manufacturer's instructions.

5. To make the waffles, heat a waffle iron. Spray with nonstick cooking spray. Place a covered baking dish on the middle rack of the oven and preheat the oven to 225°F.

6. Mix the butter, sugar, eggs, vanilla, and cocoa in a large bowl. Add the flour and nuts and mix until just combined. Spoon about ⅔ cup batter into the waffle iron and cook until crisp. Remove and place in the covered baking dish to keep warm while you cook the rest. Repeat with the remaining batter.

7. To serve, place each waffle on an individual serving plate. Spoon the chocolate ice cream on top. Drizzle with chocolate sauce and sprinkle with nuts.

5 cups cold carbonated water

1½ cups Chocolate Sauce (page 242)

2 cups Semisweet Chocolate Ice Cream (page 91)

1½ cups Chocolate Whipped Cream (page 244)

## Chocolate Soda Ice Cream Floats

*Makes four 1¾-cup floats*

The trick to making good chocolate soda is to use homemade chocolate sauce. What makes it even tastier? Turning it into a float made with homemade ice cream and whipped cream.

1. Add the carbonated water to a large pitcher. Slowly add 1 cup of the chocolate sauce and stir until mixed.

2. Pour the soda you just made into four ice cream float glasses and scoop ½ cup ice cream into each glass. Top with the remaining chocolate sauce and whipped cream.

### Variation

CREAMY CHOCOLATE ICE CREAM SODA: Add the chocolate sauce to 1 cup whole milk. Reduce the carbonated water to 4 cups.

# PUDDINGS AND CREAMY TREATS

When the urge for creamy chocolate strikes, what's the best solution? Bring on the chocolate pudding! Or maybe a chocolate mousse or fresh fruit and yogurt parfait. Inspired by my favorite selection of pudding recipes and some of the all-time best flavor combinations, such as chocolate and coffee or chocolate and cherry, the tastes and textures you will find in this section are whipped into smooth, refreshing goodness that is easy to tackle and ready to enjoy for any occasion.

## Chocolate Pear Raisin Bread Pudding

*Makes one 9 x 11-inch bread pudding (about 8 servings)*

Bread pudding made with day-old Chocolate Chip Challah (page 208) and Chocolate Rolls (page 150) fits right in to today's "zero waste" trend, and I cannot think of a better way to give these recipes a second life. If you don't want to make the bread from scratch, just use store-bought challah or sourdough bread and add an additional 2 ounces of dark chocolate.

I prefer to make my bread pudding without a water bath to get a really nice golden color on top. If you prefer to use the traditional method and bake the pudding more evenly, set the baking dish in a water bath that comes about halfway up the sides. It will take an additional 15 minutes or so to cook. Serve plain or with white or dark Chocolate Sauce (page 242).

2 tablespoons unsalted butter

2 large Bartlett or other firm, juicy pears, peeled, cored, and chopped

2 tablespoons granulated sugar

6 large eggs

½ cup firmly packed light brown sugar

1½ cups whole milk

1½ cups heavy cream

2 tablespoons maple syrup

1 teaspoon vanilla extract

⅛ teaspoon salt

8 slices day-old bread, cut into 1-inch cubes

¾ cup golden raisins, soaked in 3 tablespoons hot water or bourbon

6 ounces dark chocolate (at least 65% cacao), chopped into 1-inch pieces

1. Preheat the oven to 375°F. Butter a 9 x 13-inch baking dish.

2. Melt the butter in a medium sauté pan over low heat. Add the pears and granulated sugar and stir occasionally for about 5 minutes, until the pears are slightly softened and glazed. Remove from the heat and set aside.

3. Whisk the eggs and brown sugar in a large bowl until blended. Add the milk, cream, maple syrup, vanilla, and salt. Add the bread to the mixture and let soak for 15 minutes. Stir in the pears. Drain the raisins and add to the mixture. Add 4 ounces of the chocolate and stir.

4. Put the pudding in the baking dish and add the remaining 2 ounces of chocolate, pressing the pieces into the top of the batter.

5. Bake on the center rack for 50–60 minutes, or until the top is golden brown and a knife inserted in the center comes out clean. Transfer to a rack and serve warm.

## Chocolate Cherry Coconut Tapioca Pudding

*Makes ten 8-ounce servings*

When cherries are in season and at their sweetest, I buy as many as I can and add them to several of my chocolate recipes. The addition of coconut milk in this rich chocolate tapioca pudding gives it a tropical flair.

1⅓ cups small pearl tapioca
5 cups whole milk
2 cans (15 ounces each) coconut milk
½ cup unsweetened coconut flakes
½ teaspoon salt
4 ounces dark chocolate (at least 65% cacao), melted
2 large eggs
1½ cups cherries, pitted and chopped
1 cup Chocolate Whipped Cream (page 244)
10 whole cherries

1. Combine the tapioca and milk in a large saucepan. Cover and refrigerate for 8 hours.

2. Place the saucepan on the stove top and add the coconut milk, coconut, and salt. Heat over medium heat to a simmer until the pearls are clear and smooth, 15–20 minutes. Stir in the dark chocolate and remove from the heat.

3. In a small bowl, beat the eggs until frothy. Add 1½ cups of the hot pudding to the eggs and mix until combined. Add the egg mixture back into the pudding and mix until blended. Let sit for 15 minutes to cool. Stir in the chopped cherries.

4. Spoon the pudding into cups, cover with foil, and refrigerate for 3 hours. Top with chocolate whipped cream and whole cherries when ready to serve.

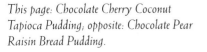

*This page: Chocolate Cherry Coconut Tapioca Pudding; opposite: Chocolate Pear Raisin Bread Pudding.*

## Mousse

*Makes about 6 cups*

1 teaspoon instant coffee granules

1 cup double-strength brewed
   espresso

2 cups whole milk

1½ tablespoons cornstarch

⅛ teaspoon salt

1 can (14 ounces) sweetened
   condensed milk

2 large eggs

1 teaspoon vanilla extract

3 ounces dark chocolate (at least
   65% cacao), melted

3 ounces milk chocolate (at least
   30% cacao), melted

12 White Chocolate Cookies
   (page 114) or soft chocolate
   wafer cookies

## Meringue

*Makes about 2 cups*

2 large egg whites

Pinch of salt

⅛ teaspoon cream of tartar

½ teaspoon vanilla extract

3 tablespoons superfine sugar

## Topping

3 ounces dark chocolate (at least
   65% cacao), half chopped into
   ½-inch pieces and half grated

¼ cup espresso beans

¼ cup chocolate-covered espresso
   beans

# Mocha Cappuccino Mousse

*Makes eight 8-ounce servings*

Ooh la la! This creamy mousse pudding, layered with both chocolate and coffee flavors, has a hidden surprise cookie that separates the layers. Make it yourself using the White Chocolate Cookie recipe (page 114) or use store-bought wafer cookies. Keep in mind that the diameter of your cookies should be smaller than the diameter of your serving container. Top with toasted meringue or, for a simpler choice, use Chocolate Whipped Cream (page 244).

1. Dissolve the instant coffee granules in the double-strength espresso and set aside to cool.

2. To make the mousse, combine the milk, cornstarch, and salt in a medium saucepan over medium heat and stir until the cornstarch is dissolved. Add the condensed milk and cook until the mixture thickens. Turn off the heat.

3. Beat the eggs in a small bowl and whisk in ¼ cup of the hot mixture. Add the egg mixture to the saucepan and whisk to combine. Place over medium heat and continue whisking until the mixture thickens and bubbles begin to form. Remove from the heat and add the vanilla.

4. Divide the mixture into three bowls. Add ⅔ cup of the espresso to one, the dark chocolate to another, and the milk chocolate to the third. Cover the bowls and refrigerate for 30 minutes to thicken until firm enough to form layers.

5. Spoon the dark chocolate mousse into six 8-ounce dessert glasses and top each with a cookie. Brush the cookie with half the remaining espresso to soak the layer. Add the milk chocolate mousse, top with another cookie, and brush the cookie with the remaining espresso to soak the layer. Top with the espresso mousse. Cover and refrigerate for 3 hours to set.

6. To make the meringue, combine the egg whites, salt, cream of tartar, and vanilla in a large mixing bowl. Beat with an electric mixer on medium speed until soft peaks form. Beat

in the sugar a little at a time, until the egg whites are stiff but not dry. Do not overbeat.

7. Spread the meringue on the top of each cup. Toast the meringue one cup at a time. Hold a kitchen torch 4 inches from the meringue and rotate the cup until all the meringue is toasted. Refrigerate for 1 hour to chill. Garnish with chopped chocolate, grated chocolate, espresso beans, and chocolate-covered espresso beans.

## Chocolate Cranberry Oat Granola

4½ tablespoons honey

4 tablespoons olive oil

4½ tablespoons firmly packed light brown sugar

2 teaspoons vanilla

½ teaspoon salt

1 teaspoon ground cinnamon

¼ teaspoon ground cloves

¼ teaspoon ground allspice

3 cups oatmeal

½ cup dried cranberries

½ cup yogurt-covered raisins

½ cup chocolate-covered raisins

½ cup white chocolate chips

½ cup semisweet chocolate chips (at least 50% cacao)

### Parfait

3 cups plain or vanilla low-fat yogurt

3 tablespoons natural unsweetened cocoa powder

¼ cup clover honey

3 cups total chopped fresh kiwis, peaches, and mangoes

3 cups berries (whole raspberries and blueberries, chopped strawberries)

## Chocolate Yogurt and Fruit Parfaits with Granola Topping

*Makes six 2½-cup parfaits*

Enjoy a taste of the good-for-you life with this fruit, yogurt, and granola parfait that includes a hint of chocolate. Prepare as a full breakfast or lunch—main course and dessert included! Really indulge by adding granola between the layers in addition to the topping. If you make the full batch of granola, you will have some extra, which tastes great as your morning cereal with, of course, chocolate milk.

1. Preheat the oven to 325°F. Butter a large baking sheet. Heat the honey, olive oil, sugar, and vanilla in a small heavy-bottomed saucepan over low heat until the sugar is dissolved. Remove from the heat and stir in the salt, cinnamon, cloves, and allspice.

2. Place the oatmeal in a medium bowl and coat with the honey mixture. Spread out the mixture on the prepared baking sheet. Bake for 10 minutes, stir, bake for 10 more minutes, stir, and bake again for 7–10 more minutes, until crisp. Let cool on the baking sheet.

3. In a large bowl, combine the oat mixture, dried cranberries, yogurt-covered raisins, chocolate-covered raisins, white chocolate chips, and semisweet chocolate chips. Set aside.

4. To make the parfait, stir together the yogurt, cocoa powder, and honey in medium bowl.

5. Fill the parfait cups a quarter full with about 1 cup of the fresh fruit; divide half the yogurt among the cups. Add about 1 cup more fresh fruit and top with the remaining yogurt. Add the remaining 1 cup fruit. When the cups are close to full, top with the granola.

**Chapter**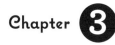

# Chocolate for Special Occasions

## BIRTHDAYS

If you bake only a few times a year, it is most likely for a loved one's birthday. Homemade chocolate cake, cupcakes, or cookies define "Happy Birthday," and each recipe here sets the mood for the occasion. A retro-style classic Bundt cake makes a statement of old-fashioned warm feelings. Celebrate stylishly with a chocolate cake adorned with chocolate toppings. Chocolate cupcakes at a milk and cookies party appeal to kids and adults alike.

### Chocolate Chocolate Chip Birthday Bundt Cake

*Makes one 8-inch cake*

I believe that a birthday is not a celebration without a cake. And for a chocolate lover, a cake is not a cake without chocolate. This easy-to-make chocolate lover's cake uses three types of chocolate to celebrate the special day.

1. Preheat the oven to 350°F. Butter and flour a 4½-inch-tall, 8-inch-wide Bundt pan. Place a rimmed baking sheet under a cooling rack.

2. Place the cocoa in a small bowl. Pour in the hot milk and whisk until all lumps are dissolved. Mix in the bittersweet

### Cake

⅓ cup Dutch-process cocoa powder

1⅓ cups hot (almost boiling) milk

4 ounces bittersweet chocolate (at least 70% cacao), coarsely chopped

1⅓ cups all-purpose flour

1 teaspoon baking soda

⅛ teaspoon salt

½ pound (2 sticks) unsalted butter, at room temperature

1 cup granulated sugar

3 large eggs

1 teaspoon vanilla extract

⅔ cup plain low-fat yogurt, at room temperature

1 cup milk chocolate chips (at least 30% cacao)

chocolate, whisking until the chocolate is melted and the mixture is smooth. Set aside to cool.

3. Combine the flour, baking soda, and salt in a mixing bowl.

4. Beat the butter and sugar in a large mixing bowl with an electric mixer on medium speed until fluffy. Add the eggs one at a time, beating well after each addition. Beat in the vanilla.

5. Mix in half the flour mixture on low speed until blended. Blend in the yogurt. Add the remaining flour mixture and combine. Add the chocolate mixture on low speed until just blended. Do not overmix. Stir in the chocolate chips.

6. Pour the batter into the pan and bake for 45–55 minutes, or until a tester inserted in the center comes out clean. Cool in the pan for 20 minutes. Invert onto a rack to cool completely.

7. Pour the hot fudge over the cooled cake, allowing it to drip over the sides and down the center of the ring without covering the cake completely. Top with chopped pecans.

## Chocolate Layer Cake with Ganache

*Makes one 9-inch oval or round cake*

For an exceptionally elegant birthday celebration, this cake is a decorator's delight. Four layers of moist chocolate cake are covered in fluffy buttercream frosting and then coated with a smooth chocolate ganache. Decorate as elaborately as you like, using chocolate flowers, leaves, and curls and white chocolate piping. To create textured sides, run a decorating comb around the first chocolate buttercream layer.

1. Preheat the oven to 350°F. Butter and flour two 9-inch oval pans.

2. To make the cake, place the chocolates in two separate small bowls and pour ¼ cup of the boiling water over each. Allow to melt for 5 minutes and stir to blend.

## Chocolate Ganache

12½ ounces chopped dark chocolate (at least 65% cacao)

1½ cups heavy cream

3 tablespoons butter, cut into small
cubes

## Decorations

2 ounces white chocolate, melted

3 ounces semisweet chocolate (at
least 50% cacao), melted and
tempered (page 29)

3. Combine the sugar and eggs in a heatproof bowl and beat until blended. Transfer to a double boiler over medium heat or place the bowl over hot water and beat for 6–8 minutes, until the mixture thickens and has doubled in volume. Remove from the heat and beat in the vanilla.

4. Using a rubber spatula, gently fold in the flour until blended. Divide the mixture in two and add the semisweet chocolate to one batch and the milk chocolate to the other. Pour the batters into the prepared pans (semisweet chocolate in one, milk chocolate in the other), and bake for 30–35 minutes, or until a knife inserted in the center comes out clean. Set the pans on a rack for 7–10 minutes to cool. Remove the cakes from the pans and allow to cool completely.

5. If the cake tops have rounded, once the cakes have cooled, cut the rounded tops off with a long serrated knife. Cut each cake in half to create four layers (page 56).

6. Put aside 1½ cups of the buttercream for the final piped border. Place one layer of the cake on a cake board or other movable surface and frost the top with buttercream. Add the next layer and frost. Repeat with the rest of the layers. Cover the top and sides of the cake with a crumb coat—a thin layer of buttercream—using a large offset spatula, to prepare a smooth surface for the glaze on top. Drag a decorating comb around the sides of the cake to create a grooved surface. Remove any large lumps or crumbs. Let the frosted cake set for about 20 minutes in the refrigerator.

7. To make the chocolate ganache, place the chocolate in a heatproof bowl. Bring the cream to a boil over low heat and pour over the chocolate. Stir gently to blend. Add the butter and stir until blended. Allow the mixture to cool to room temperature. Place the cake on a wire rack with a rimmed baking sheet under it. Pour the chocolate mixture over the top of the cake. Let it set, and pour another coat over the cake if necessary. Let set for 2 hours on the countertop or 1 hour in the refrigerator.

8. To make the decorations, use the melted chocolate to mold flowers, leaves, and a large chocolate spiral (pages 36–37), setting aside about 1 ounce of the white chocolate. Let set. Add the remaining white chocolate to a piping bag with a small round tip.

9. Transfer the cake to a serving plate. Pipe the pattern on the top of the cake with the white chocolate. Prepare a pastry bag set with a large star tip. With the reserved buttercream, pipe a center in each flower and a scalloped border around the bottom of the cake. Attach the flowers and leaves to the cake, using buttercream to adhere if necessary.

### Variations

CHOCOLATE RASPBERRY CAKE: Omit the buttercream. Heat 2½ cups raspberry preserves in a medium saucepan over medium heat with 3 tablespoons water. Stir until thickened. Spread between the layers and on the outside of the cake for the crumb coat.

BLACK FOREST CAKE: Add 2 tablespoons Kirsch to the buttercream. Soak the cake layers in ⅓ cup Kirsch by brushing it on with a pastry brush. Distribute 2 cups halved, pitted black cherries between the layers along with the buttercream. Top with ¾ cup whole black cherries.

### Brownie Crust

2 ounces semisweet chocolate (at least 50% cacao), chopped in ½-inch pieces

¼ cup unsalted butter

1 teaspoon vanilla extract

¼ cup all-purpose flour

½ teaspoon baking powder

¼ cup granulated sugar

¼ cup firmly packed dark brown sugar

1 large egg

### Caramel Mocha Ice Cream Cake

*Makes one 4½ x 8½-inch cake*

When I was growing up, my birthday was always celebrated with a store-bought ice cream cake. Recently I learned how to make even better ones at home. There are a few tricks to making a great ice cream cake: Bake the cake in the same pan you will assemble it in, or bake it in a similarly sized pan. Freeze the baked cake before adding it to the ice cream cake. To assemble, soften the ice cream, but do not let it melt. Line the bottom of the pan with a sheet of parchment paper that hangs 3 inches over the long sides of the pan to make the cake easy to remove when frozen. Make sure the cake is completely hard before removing it from the pan. Note that cake will need to go in the freezer before serving, so make sure you use a freezer-safe serving plate.

*Caramel Mocha Ice Cream Cake*

## Ice Cream Layers

3 cups high-quality chocolate ice
cream

½ cup semisweet chocolate chunks
(at least 50% cacao)

3 ounces caramel sauce

2 cups high-quality coffee ice
cream, softened

2 cups Coffee Buttercream (page
243)

1 cup Whipped Cream (page 244)

1½ cups Semisweet Chocolate
Frosting (page 55)

## Toppings

Chocolate chunks, grated chocolate, crushed caramel candy,
chocolate-covered espresso beans

1. Preheat the oven to 350°F. Butter and flour a 4½ x 8½-inch loaf pan.

2. To make the crust, melt the chocolate and butter in a double boiler over medium heat, stirring until melted. Remove from the heat and stir in the vanilla. Set aside to cool.

3. Combine the flour and baking powder in a mixing bowl and set aside.

4. Using an electric mixer on medium speed, beat both sugars and the egg in a large mixing bowl until creamy.

5. Gradually add the flour mixture, alternating with the chocolate mixture, with the mixer on low speed, until well mixed.

6. Pour the batter into the pan and bake for 15–20 minutes, or until a tester inserted in the middle comes out clean. Cool for 15 minutes in the pan. Transfer to a rack to cool completely. Once the crust has cooled, cover and place in the freezer for 1 hour. Wash and dry the pan.

7. To make the ice cream layers, line the bottom and sides of the same loaf pan with waxed paper, leaving a 2-inch overhang on all sides.

8. Place the chocolate ice cream in a bowl and let it soften, but do not let it melt. Mix in the chocolate chunks. Make a rectangular well of ice cream in the pan by spreading it about ¾ inch thick on the bottom and ½ inch thick on the sides. Spread the caramel over the ice cream, covering the top completely.

9. Measure the thickness of the brownie crust, which should be ¼–½ inch. Spread the coffee ice cream over the caramel sauce, leaving enough room at the top of the loaf pan for the brownie crust. Press the brownie crust on top. Cover with foil and freeze for 5–6 hours, or until firm.

10. Remove the cake from the freezer and let sit for 5 minutes. Unmold the cake by lifting it by the waxed paper and inverting it onto a freezer-safe serving plate.

11. Use a large icing spatula to frost the cake with coffee buttercream. Press grooves into the frosting with a cake comb, or use the tines of a fork or edge of a serrated knife. Add the chocolate frosting to a piping bag with a medium star tip and pipe around the edges. Add chocolate-covered espresso beans to the corners of the cake. Add the whipped cream to a piping bag with a large star tip and pipe rosettes on top. Sprinkle with crushed caramel candy and grated chocolate. Top with chocolate chunks. Place in the freezer for at least 1 hour before serving. Cut with a sharp knife and serve with whipped cream.

## Rich Chocolate Cupcakes with White Chocolate Buttercream

*Makes 24 medium 2¾-inch cupcakes*

Cupcakes are a birthday favorite for kids and adults alike. Glowing with luster dust and decorated with just a few simple toppings, these cupcakes are ready to shine.

1. Preheat the oven to 325°F. Line cupcake pans with liners.

2. To make the cupcakes, place the butter and chocolate in a large bowl. Pour the boiling water over them and let stand until melted. Stir to combine. Stir in the vanilla, sugar, and sour cream and mix until fully integrated.

3. In a separate medium bowl, combine the flour, baking soda, and baking powder. Gradually add the flour mixture to the chocolate mixture using an electric mixer on medium speed, until the batter is smooth.

4. In another medium bowl, beat the egg whites with a clean electric mixer until stiff. Gently fold the egg whites into the batter using a rubber spatula.

5. Fill the cupcake liners three-quarters full. Bake for 20–25 minutes, or until a toothpick inserted in the center of a cupcake comes out clean. Set the pan on a rack to cool.

### Cupcakes

½ cup (1 stick) unsalted butter

3 ounces (½ cup) unsweetened chocolate, coarsely chopped

1 cup boiling water

1 teaspoon vanilla extract

2 cups granulated sugar

½ cup sour cream

2 cups all-purpose flour

1 teaspoon baking soda

1 teaspoon baking powder

2 large egg whites

### White Chocolate Buttercream

¼ cup hot whole milk

4 ounces white chocolate, melted and cooled

6 tablespoons (¾ stick) unsalted butter, at room temperature

2¼ cups confectioners' sugar

1 teaspoon vanilla extract

2 drops each purple, pink, and green food coloring

### Toppings

1 teaspoon luster dust

¼ cup total colored sugar, chocolate shavings, candy pieces, and candy flowers

Foreground: Rich Chocolate Cupcakes with White Chocolate Buttercream; background: Red Velvet Cupcake

## Cake

3 cups all-purpose flour

⅔ cup natural unsweetened cocoa powder

2 ½ teaspoons baking powder

1 teaspoon baking soda

1 teaspoon salt

¾ cup (1 ½ sticks) unsalted butter, at room temperature

2 cups granulated sugar

3 large eggs

2 teaspoons vanilla extract

1 ½ cups buttermilk

⅔ cup canola oil

1 tablespoon vinegar

8 drops (or more) red food coloring

3 ounces dark chocolate (at least 65% cacao), melted and cooled

6. To make the buttercream, combine the milk and white chocolate in a small bowl, stirring until smooth. Set aside to cool.

7. In a medium bowl, beat the butter and gradually add the confectioners' sugar until blended. Add the white chocolate mixture and vanilla and beat for 1–2 minutes, until fluffy.

8. Divide the frosting into three equal batches. Stir 2 drops of a different food coloring into each batch. Sprinkle each cupcake with luster dust. Add the frosting to a piping bag set with a large star tip and pipe on top of each cupcake. Sprinkle on the colored sugars and top with assorted chocolate and candy pieces and flowers.

## Red Velvet Cupcakes

*Makes 24 medium 2 ¾-inch cupcakes*

Visit a cupcake bakery and you are bound to see a red velvet cupcake proudly displayed. A favorite of the American South, this red chocolate cake uses buttermilk, vinegar, and cream cheese frosting to create its famous tang.

1. Line two medium muffin pans with paper liners. Preheat the oven to 350°F.

2. To make the cake, combine the flour, cocoa powder, baking powder, baking soda, and salt in a medium bowl, and set aside.

3. In a separate medium bowl, use a mixer to cream the butter and sugar. Beat in the eggs and vanilla until well blended.

4. In another small mixing bowl, stir together the buttermilk, oil, and vinegar, and tint the mixture with the red food coloring. Gradually beat the flour mixture into the butter mixture, alternating with the buttermilk mixture, until well combined. Stir in the melted chocolate.

Chocolate for Special Occasions • 109

5. Fill the cupcake liners three-quarters full. Bake for 20–25 minutes, until a knife inserted in the center comes out clean. Let cool in the pans.

6. To make the frosting, beat the cream cheese and butter with an electric mixer until smooth. Slowly add the confectioners' sugar, and continue beating until all the lumps are gone and the frosting is thick and smooth. Add the vanilla and mix until fully blended. Sprinkle each cupcake with luster dust. Add the frosting to a piping bag set with a large star tip and pipe onto the top of each cupcake. Sprinkle on the red crystal sugar.

# Milk and Cookies Party

Kids and adults alike will enjoy this fabulous selection of chocolate cookies at a playful birthday party.

*1¾ cups all-purpose flour*

*⅓ cup granulated sugar*

*½ cup natural unsweetened cocoa powder*

*1 teaspoon baking soda*

*¼ teaspoon salt*

*3 large eggs*

*1 teaspoon vanilla extract*

*1 cup semisweet chocolate chips (at least 50% cacao)*

*6 ounces milk chocolate (at least 30% cacao), chopped*

## Triple Chocolate Biscotti

*Makes 24 cookies*

These low-fat chocolate biscotti contain no butter and are drizzled with chocolate.

1. Preheat the oven to 300°F. Butter two cookie sheets.

2. Combine the flour, sugar, cocoa powder, baking soda, and salt in a medium bowl, and set aside.

3. In a medium mixing bowl, beat the eggs and vanilla. Stir in the chocolate chips. Add the flour mixture and mix until blended.

4. Divide the dough in half and shape into two logs that are ¾ inch thick, 1½ inches wide, and 6 inches long. Place on the cookie sheets at least 2 inches apart.

5. Bake for 50 minutes, remove from the oven, and let cool for 5 minutes.

6. Using a serrated knife, slice ½-inch-thick cookies. Lay the cookies flat on the baking sheet and bake for 10 minutes.

*Opposite: Butter Cookie Bears, White Chocolate Macadamia Cookies, Triple Chocolate Biscotti, Chocolate Chip Brownie Cookies, Walnut Brownie Cookies, Chocolate Chip Cookies, Chocolate Candy Icebox Cookies, White and Milk Chocolate Icebox Spirals*

Flip and then bake for 10 more minutes. Transfer to a rack to cool completely.

7. Melt the milk chocolate in the top of a double boiler set over simmering water. Dip the bottom of each cookie into the chocolate. Set on a rack with the chocolate side facing up to dry. Once all the cookies are dry, place them with their tops facing up and drizzle melted chocolate on top.

## Butter Cookie Bears

*Makes fifteen 4½-inch cookies*

A bite with just a few chocolate chips can be enough to satisfy a craving. These butter cutout cookies add a playful touch to a cookie buffet.

*½ pound (2 sticks) butter, at room temperature*
*1 cup superfine sugar*
*1 large egg yolk*
*1 large egg*
*½ teaspoon salt*
*2 teaspoons vanilla*
*3½ cups all-purpose flour*
*½ cup semisweet chocolate chips (at least 50% cacao)*
*¼ cup Vanilla Icing (page 243)*

1. Preheat the oven to 350°F. Line two cookie sheets with parchment paper.

2. Beat the butter and sugar until light and fluffy. Add the egg yolk and mix until blended. Add the whole egg, salt, and vanilla and combine.

3. Gradually add the flour while beating with a mixer at low speed until combined. Flatten the dough into two disks and chill for 2 hours before rolling.

4. Roll out the dough on a floured work surface. Cut out the bears using a cookie cutter.

5. Transfer to cookie sheets and bake for 12–14 minutes, until the cookies are firm and light brown. Cool on the cookie sheets for 30 minutes. Attach the chocolate chips to the bears with icing. Let dry for 1 hour.

### Variation

CHOCOLATE BUTTER COOKIE BEARS: Reduce the flour to 3 cups. Add 3 tablespoons butter and ¼ cup sugar to the butter-sugar mixture and add ¾ cup natural unsweetened cocoa powder with the flour.

## Chocolate Chip Brownie Cookies

*Makes 18 large cookies*

These cookies are rich and chewy just like brownies. Prepare them using just chocolate chips, or you can add walnuts or any of your favorite brownie mix-ins.

½ cup flour

¼ teaspoon baking powder

¼ cup unsalted butter

12 ounces semisweet chocolate (at least 50% cacao), chopped

¾ cup firmly packed light brown sugar

1 teaspoon vanilla extract

2 large eggs

1¼ cups semisweet chocolate chips

1. Preheat the oven to 350°F. Line two baking sheets with parchment paper.

2. Combine the flour and baking powder in a small bowl; set aside.

3. Heat the butter and chocolate in the top of a double boiler set over simmering water, stirring constantly until melted.

4. Remove from the heat, stir in the sugar and vanilla, and let cool for 5 minutes. Blend in the eggs. Gradually add the flour mixture. Stir in the chocolate chips. Cover the bowl and refrigerate for 20 minutes.

5. Drop the cookies 2 tablespoons at a time onto the cookie sheets, spacing them 2½ inches apart. Bake for 12–16 minutes, until the cookies are set around the edges and soft in the center. Transfer to racks to cool.

**Variation**

WALNUT BROWNIE COOKIES: Add 1 cup walnuts with the chocolate chips.

## Chocolate Chip Cookies

*Makes 18 large cookies*

These melt-in-your-mouth drop chocolate chip cookies are easy to make and are best enjoyed warm with a tall glass of milk.

2¼ cups all-purpose flour

1 teaspoon baking powder

½ teaspoon salt

½ pound (2 sticks) unsalted butter, at room temperature

¾ cup firmly packed dark brown sugar

¾ cup granulated sugar

2 large eggs

1 teaspoon vanilla extract

1 cup semisweet chocolate chips (at least 50% cacao)

1. Preheat the oven to 375°F. Butter two cookie sheets.

2. Combine the flour, baking powder, and salt in a medium bowl and set aside.

3. Cream the butter and sugars together until light and fluffy. Add the eggs and vanilla and beat until combined.

4. Gradually add the flour mixture until blended. Stir in the chocolate chips.

5. Drop the dough 2 inches apart in portions of 1½ heaping tablespoons on the prepared cookie sheets. Bake for 10–12 minutes, until lightly browned. Remove from the oven and transfer to a rack to cool.

### Variations

CHOCOLATE CHIP RAISIN COOKIES: Add 1 cup raisins with the chocolate chips.

CHOCOLATE CHIP WALNUT COOKIES: Add 1 cup walnuts with the chocolate chips.

## White Chocolate Cookies

*Makes 18 large cookies*

Featuring melted white chocolate in the dough and white chocolate chunk mix-ins, these cookies will transport you to white chocolate heaven.

1. Preheat the oven to 350°F. Butter two cookie sheets.

2. Combine the flour, baking soda, and salt and set aside.

3. Cream the butter and sugar until fluffy. Beat in the eggs and vanilla until blended. Stir in the melted white chocolate and chopped white chocolate.

4. Drop 1½-tablespoon dollops of dough 2 inches apart on the cookie sheets. Bake for 10–12 minutes, until golden around the edges. Remove from the oven and let sit for 5 minutes. Transfer to a rack to cool.

### Variation

WHITE CHOCOLATE MACADAMIA: Add 1 cup macadamia nuts with the chopped white chocolate.

2¼ cups all-purpose flour
¾ teaspoon baking soda
½ teaspoon salt
14 tablespoons (1¾ sticks) unsalted butter, at room temperature
2 cups firmly packed light brown sugar
3 large eggs
1½ teaspoons vanilla
4½ ounces white chocolate, melted and cooled to room temperature
¾ cup chopped white chocolate

1¾ cups all-purpose flour

1 teaspoon baking powder

½ teaspoon baking soda

¼ teaspoon salt

¾ cup (1½ sticks) unsalted butter, at room temperature

½ cup firmly packed light brown sugar

½ cup granulated sugar

1 large egg

1 teaspoon vanilla extract

2 ounces milk chocolate (at least 30% cacao), melted and cooled

2 ounces white chocolate, melted and cooled

2 large egg whites, beaten

¼ cup crystal sugar

## White and Milk Chocolate Icebox Spirals

*Makes 36 cookies*

Icebox cookies are made from dough that is rolled into a log, refrigerated or frozen, and then sliced into cookie rounds. This recipe is made with both white and milk chocolate. The two batches of dough are layered on top of each other and then rolled together to form a spiral pattern.

1. Preheat the oven to 350°F. Line two cookie sheets with parchment paper.

2. Combine the flour, baking powder, baking soda, and salt in a medium bowl and set aside.

3. In the bowl of an electric mixer, beat the butter and sugars on medium speed until fluffy. Add the egg and vanilla and beat well. On low speed, gradually add the flour mixture until well blended.

4. Divide the dough in two and put each half in a mixing bowl. Stir the milk chocolate into one batch and the white chocolate into the other batch. Flatten each batch into a disk, cover in plastic wrap, and chill for 45 minutes.

5. On a floured work surface, roll out each batch of dough into a rectangle that is 7½ inches long, 9½ inches wide, and ³⁄₁₆ inch thick. Brush half the egg white on one batch of dough, covering the entire top surface. Cover with the other rolled-out rectangle and press down lightly. Starting with the long side, roll the stack of dough away from you, forming a 9½-inch log about 2 inches in diameter. Cover in plastic wrap and freeze for 2 hours.

6. Unwrap the log and let soften for 5 minutes. Brush the surface on all sides with the remaining egg white and then roll the log in crystal sugar. Slice into ¼-inch slices and place the cookies 1½ inches apart on the cookie sheets. Sprinkle a little more crystal sugar around the edges of each cookie. Bake for 8–10 minutes, or until the white parts of the

cookies are lightly golden. Cool on the baking sheet for 5 minutes. Transfer to a rack to cool completely.

**Variation**

CHOCOLATE CANDY ICEBOX COOKIES: Omit the milk chocolate, increase the quantity of white chocolate to 3 ounces, and keep the dough in one batch. Add 1 cup assorted chocolate candies, such as M&M'S, chopped peanut butter cups, or chopped malt balls, to the dough when you add the white chocolate. After the cookies are cut and ready to bake, press an additional ¼ cup candies into the tops of the cookies.

## Chocolate-Covered Pretzels
*Makes 24 pretzels*

Pretzels are a classic party food; people love them for their crunchy saltiness. Dipping them in chocolate gives them a sweet-and-salty flavor twist. You can use any shape pretzel—sturdy rods will have more of a carbo-loaded crunch, whereas twists have more surface area, meaning more chocolate after they're dipped. In addition to being great party snacks, chocolate-covered pretzels make tasty gifts. To add another dimension of flavor, top the pretzels with colored sprinkles or small candies while the chocolate is still wet. For a stronger flavor contrast, the same technique can be used to make chocolate-covered potato chips. Be sure to use ridged potato chips, as they are sturdier than flat chips. Since potato chips are thin and fragile, they tend to be trickier than pretzels, so I prefer not to decorate chips.

1. Set out a cooling rack with a rimmed baking sheet underneath it to catch drippings.

2. Hold each pretzel rod by one end and dip it in the melted and tempered milk chocolate, leaving an inch of the pretzel uncovered. To dip pretzel twists, use a fork to press the whole piece into the chocolate. Remove from the chocolate with the fork, shake over the pot several times to remove excess chocolate, and place on the cooling rack. Return the excess chocolate on the baking sheet to the pot and remelt if needed.

24 6–7-inch-long pretzel rods or 3-inch pretzel twists

16 ounces milk chocolate (at least 30% cacao), melted and tempered (page 29)

6 ounces dark chocolate (at least 65% cacao), melted and tempered (page 29)

*Opposite, clockwise from top: Chocolate-Covered Pretzel Rods, Chocolate-Covered Pretzel Twists, Chocolate-Dipped Ginger Caramel Corn, Chocolate-Covered Potato Chips*

3. Let the pretzels harden for 20 minutes to set the chocolate; then dip the uncoated ends of the rods and let dry for 20 minutes.

4. Drizzle the melted dark chocolate over the pretzels in a decorative pattern. Let set for 1 hour. Peel the pretzels off the cooling rack and serve. To store, place the pretzels in an airtight container with waxed paper between the layers. Store at room temperature for up to 2 weeks.

**Variations**

WHITE CHOCOLATE PEPPERMINT PRETZELS: Replace the milk chocolate with white chocolate. Top the dipped pretzels with crushed red and white peppermint candies.

CHOCOLATE-COVERED POTATO CHIPS: Replace the pretzels with 36–40 unbroken, firm, ridged potato chips.

## Chocolate-Dipped Ginger Caramel Corn

*Makes 4 quarts*

Milk chocolate adds creaminess and ginger infuses a spicy bite into the buttery flavor of the brown sugar in this decadent caramel corn. The baking soda in the caramel aids with browning and aerates the caramel, making it more delicate than usual. For an interesting texture contrast, make a batch coating some of the kernels in both caramel and chocolate, and leave some without the chocolate.

*4 quarts freshly popped popcorn, unpopped kernels removed*
*½ teaspoon ground ginger*
*½ teaspoon salt*
*½ cup light corn syrup*
*½ cup (1 stick) unsalted butter*
*1½ cups firmly packed light brown sugar*
*½ teaspoon baking soda*
*1 teaspoon vanilla extract*
*1½ teaspoons vegetable shortening*
*6 ounces milk chocolate (at least 30% cacao), melted and tempered (page 29)*

1. Preheat the oven to 250°F. Line a baking sheet with parchment paper.

2. Mix the popcorn, ginger, and salt in a large heatproof bowl and set aside.

3. Combine the corn syrup, butter, and sugar in a heavy saucepan. Stir over medium heat until the sugar dissolves. Stir in the baking soda. Bring the syrup to a boil. Lower the heat and simmer for 5 minutes, until the syrup thickens, stirring occasionally. Remove from the heat and stir in the

vanilla. Pour the caramel over the popcorn, stirring until all the popcorn is coated.

4. Spread the popcorn on a baking sheet and bake for 15 minutes. Remove from the oven and stir. Bake and stir every 15 minutes two more times, for a total of 45 minutes. Separate the individual kernels while still warm. Let cool.

5. Set up a cooling rack with a rimmed baking sheet underneath. Add the shortening to the melted and tempered milk chocolate and stir until the shortening is just melted.

6. Using a fork, dip a few popcorn kernels at a time into the chocolate. Remove and shake the popcorn over the pot several times to remove excess chocolate. Place the chocolate-dipped popcorn on the cooling rack. Repeat with half the remaining popcorn, leaving some kernels uncoated. Return the excess chocolate on the baking sheet to the pot and remelt if needed. Store in an airtight container for up to 3 weeks.

**Variation**

CARAMEL PEANUT POPCORN: Add 1 cup unsalted peanuts to the bowl of popcorn before caramelizing.

# WEDDINGS

Share the fun of chocolate with friends at the biggest party of a life-time, whether it's in a hip take-home favor or a small bite of something different at the reception. Food is an important part of the wedding, and the flavors can set the look or mood on this special day. Highlight the bride's and groom's favorite treats or prepare an assortment and allow everyone to choose their favorites.

## Solid Chocolate Wedding Cakes

*Makes ten 1½-ounce pieces*

*16 ounces dark chocolate (at least 65% cacao), milk chocolate (at least 30% cacao), or white chocolate, melted and tempered (page 29)*
*1 teaspoon luster dust*
*A few drops of vodka*

Surprise each guest with his or her own individual wedding cake as a thank-you at the end of the event. Solid chocolates (compared to filled) are a good choice when making a large quantity. Wedding cake molds are easy to find at candy supply stores. If the mold does not label the volume for each candy, melt and temper a bit of chocolate and make one candy. Weigh the piece once it has hardened, multiply by the number of pieces you need, and this will give you the weight of chocolate you need to melt and temper. If you have time on your hands, prepare candy cakes filled with ganache (page 51) or dulce de leche (page 217) or peanut butter filling (page 134), or add a whole nut in the center. Play up the event colors by painting the details formed from the mold (such as ribbons and dots) with a glittery luster dust.

1. Using a ladle, pour the chocolate to the top of the mold. Tap the mold on the countertop to allow air bubbles to rise to the surface. Place the mold on a countertop and let the chocolate set for about 5 minutes. Once it has begun to set, use a knife to scrape off any excess chocolate that is on the top of the mold (not in the cavities). Allow the chocolate to set completely, 30–60 minutes depending on the size of the mold. Unmold the chocolate and clean off excess chocolate with a sharp paring knife. Set the chocolates upright on a plate.

2. Dissolve the luster dust in a few drops of vodka to thin to the level of transparency you desire. Brush on the details of the molded chocolates with a small brush.

**Variation**

NUT CENTER WEDDING CAKES: To make candy with a nut center, first coat the mold with an outer shell (page 37). Let the outer shell set and then add a whole nut in the center. Fill the rest of the mold with chocolate and let set.

## Chocolate Liqueur with Chocolate Shot Cups

*Makes 24 cups*

Looking for something a little different to give out as wedding favors? Prepare homemade chocolate liqueur accompanied by chocolate shot cups. You can purchase the liqueur and the cups or make everything yourself. Leave the cups with no labels on them, as shown in the photo, or prepare a label with the happy couple's names and the date of the occasion. Mold the cups in 1½-inch plastic candy cup molds, available at candy supply stores, or use foil liners set in a mini muffin pan.

### Chocolate Cups

1. Fill the cups a quarter of the way with chocolate. Use a pastry brush to paint the chocolate all the way up the sides of the cup, completely coating the surface and making it as thick as you can. Let set for 15 minutes to harden.

2. Add a second layer of chocolate, brushing it onto the sides until they are ⅛–¼ inch thick. Let set for 1 hour; then place in the refrigerator for 30 minutes. Peel off the papers or press out of the plastic molds to serve.

---

### Chocolate Cups

16 ounces dark chocolate (at least 65% cacao), milk chocolate (at least 30% cacao), or white chocolate, melted and tempered (page 29)

### Chocolate Liqueur

*Makes 36 ounces (twelve 3-ounce servings)*

2 cups water

¼ cup natural unsweetened cocoa powder

¾ cup granulated sugar

½ cup sweetened condensed milk

1 teaspoon vanilla extract

1 cup vodka

---

## Chocolate Liqueur

1. Bring the water to a boil in a medium saucepan over medium heat. Add the cocoa powder and dissolve. Reduce to a simmer. Add the sugar, stirring until dissolved.

2. Add the sweetened condensed milk. Remove from the heat and add the vanilla, stirring to combine. Set aside to cool. Strain through a fine mesh sieve.

3. Add the vodka and stir well. Using a funnel, transfer to the bottles and seal.

### Cakes

1¼ cups all-purpose flour

⅓ cup Dutch-process cocoa powder

½ teaspoon baking powder

¼ teaspoon salt

¾ cup (1½ sticks) unsalted butter, at room temperature

¾ cup granulated sugar

3 large eggs

1 teaspoon vanilla extract

### Coating

8 ounces dark chocolate (at least 65% cacao), melted and tempered (page 29)

8 ounces white chocolate, melted and tempered (page 29)

1 cup Semisweet Chocolate Frosting (page 55)

## Cake Pop Truffles

*Makes 24 cake pops*

Most wedding cakes are beautiful and extravagant, so if you're looking to add a bit of playfulness to the dessert table, cake pops are fun to design, fun to make, and fun to eat. These pops, filled with chocolate cake, are designed to look like truffles, but feel free to follow the technique here and prepare them using the bride and groom's favorite cake recipe. To coat the cakes with both white and dark chocolate

you will need two double boilers; to simplify the process use just one type of chocolate or melt the decorating chocolate in the microwave. To apply the decorative lines around the pop, stick the pops standing upright into a piece of Styrofoam after they are dipped.

1. Preheat the oven to 350°F. Butter and flour two 24-count cake pop pans.

2. Combine the flour, cocoa powder, baking powder, and salt in a large mixing bowl.

3. With an electric mixer on medium speed, beat the butter and sugar in a large mixing bowl until fluffy. Add the eggs one at a time, beating well after each addition. Beat in the vanilla.

4. Gradually add the flour mixture on low speed until blended.

5. Pour the batter into the molds and bake for 12–15 minutes, or until a tester inserted in the center comes out clean. Cool in the pans.

6. Unmold the cakes, spread the flat side of each cake with the frosting, and press two cakes together, flat sides touching, to form balls. Press lollipop sticks three-quarters of the way into each ball, making sure it passes through the seam.

7. Line a baking sheet with waxed paper or ready a piece of Styrofoam. Reserve a quarter of each batch of melted chocolate. Hold a cake pop by the stick and dip it in either of the melted chocolates, covering it completely and twisting to let any excess chocolate fall back into the double boiler. Stand it upright in a piece of Styrofoam or set it down upside down on the baking sheet to dry.

8. When the coating is dry, remelt the reserved 2 ounces decorating chocolate and transfer to a piping bag with a small cut tip. For pops standing in Styrofoam, pipe lines over the base layer of chocolate on all sides of the cakes. For pops that are sitting on the baking sheet, pipe lines over the areas not touching the surface of the baking sheet.

## Dark Chocolate Soft Pretzels

*Makes eight 4½-inch pretzels*

Celebrate tying the knot with soft chocolate pretzel twists. Based on recipes used by classic New York street vendors, these pretzels have a chocolaty, salty flavor combination that is sure to please.

1½ cups warm water

¼ cup plus 3 tablespoons granulated sugar

2¼ teaspoons active dry yeast

4¼ cups all-purpose flour

⅓ cup Dutch-process cocoa powder

2 teaspoons kosher salt

5 tablespoons unsalted butter, melted

Vegetable oil

⅔ cup baking soda

1 large egg yolk beaten with 1 tablespoon water

Pretzel salt or sea salt

½ cup nuts, sprinkles, nonpareils, or white chocolate chips

1. Combine the water, 3 tablespoons of the sugar, and the yeast in a small bowl. Let sit for 5 minutes, or until the mixture begins to foam.

2. Combine the flour, cocoa powder, salt, remaining sugar, and butter in a large bowl. Mix with an electric mixer on low speed until well blended. Transfer to a floured work surface.

3. Knead until the dough is smooth, 8–10 minutes. Grease a large bowl with vegetable oil and place the dough in the bowl. Cover the bowl with either plastic wrap or a clean dish towel and set in a warm place for 50–60 minutes, or until the dough has doubled in size.

4. Preheat the oven to 450°F. Line two baking sheets with parchment paper and lightly brush with vegetable oil. Fill a large pot with water (10–12 cups) and stir in the baking soda. Cover and bring to a rolling boil over high heat.

5. Turn the dough out onto a lightly oiled work surface and divide into 8 pieces. Roll out each piece of dough into a 24-inch rope. Make a U shape with the rope and, holding the ends of the rope, cross them over each other to form the shape of a pretzel. Press the dough to secure the shape, then place on the baking sheets.

6. Add the pretzels one at a time to the boiling water for 30–40 seconds, 15–20 seconds on each side. Remove the pretzels from the water using a slotted spoon. Return to the baking sheet, brush the top of each pretzel with the egg-water glaze, and sprinkle with the salt, nuts, sprinkles, or candies. Bake for 12–14 minutes, until dry and dark. Transfer to a rack to cool for 10 minutes before serving.

# BABY CELEBRATIONS

When real cigars went out of fashion, chocolate cigars came into being. They are easy enough to prepare in a cigar-shaped mold if you like, but here you will find a different take on celebrating the arrival of a baby—miniature, playful, and cute chocolate treats. Celebrate a new baby with bite-size, feel-good chocolate treats. You won't be able to stop at just one.

## Chocolate French Macarons

*Makes 24 sandwich cookies*

I have been to more French-themed baby showers in the past few years than I can count on one hand. I don't know what started this trend, but as long as French macarons are served, it is fine with me. They are both childlike and sophisticated—a perfect choice to celebrate a sweet new baby. Paint them with patterns or the baby's name or initials using luster dust. Use prepared almond flour or almond meal, or grind your own from whole almonds.

### Cookies

1 cup almond meal

3 tablespoons natural unsweetened cocoa powder

2 cups confectioners' sugar

3 large egg whites

¼ teaspoon salt

Pinch of cream of tartar

3 tablespoons granulated sugar

### Decoration

1½ teaspoons luster dust

1 tablespoon vodka

### Filling

½ cup heavy cream

2 tablespoons natural unsweetened cocoa powder

½ cup (1 stick) unsalted butter

5 ounces bittersweet chocolate (at least 70% cacao), chopped in ½-inch pieces

1. Line two baking sheets with parchment paper.

2. To make the macarons, pulse the almond meal, cocoa powder and confectioners' sugar in a food processor until finely blended. Sift and set aside.

3. In a large bowl, use an electric mixer to beat the egg whites with the salt just until the whites form soft peaks. Add the cream of tartar and granulated sugar and beat again just until the whites form stiff peaks. Sprinkle the almond mixture over the egg whites and gently fold in with a rubber spatula until just combined.

4. Transfer the batter to a pastry bag fitted with a large round tip. Pipe out mounds that are 1¾ inches in diameter spaced 2 inches apart on the prepared baking sheets. Tap the sheet against the work surface to create the flat macaron base. Let sit on the countertop for 30 minutes to dry.

5. Preheat the oven to 350°F. Bake one sheet at a time for 6–8 minutes, until the tops appear dry and are soft to the touch.

Transfer the cookies on the parchment paper to a rack and let cool for 5 minutes. Peel the paper off the macarons and transfer to wire racks to cool completely.

6. To decorate, combine the luster dust and vodka in a small bowl. Using a small brush, paint patterns on the tops of the cookies and let dry.

7. To make the filling, warm the cream in a double boiler over medium heat. Remove from the heat right before it comes to a boil. Add the cocoa powder and butter and stir until the butter is melted and the mixture is smooth. Stir in the chocolate until melted. Transfer to a bowl and let cool to room temperature. Cover and chill for about 30 minutes, until thickened but still spreadable.

8. Spoon the filling into a pastry bag fitted with large round tip. Pair macarons of similar size. Pipe about a tablespoon of filling onto the flat sides of half the cookies. Top with the remaining macarons, pressing together gently to form sandwiches. Store in the refrigerator for up to 2 days.

**Variations**

PISTACHIO CHOCOLATE MACARONS: Replace the cocoa powder with 3 additional tablespoons confectioners' sugar. Add 1–2 drops green food coloring and replace the almonds with 1 cup ground pistachio nuts. Add ¼ cup ground pistachios to the filling.

VANILLA MACARONS WITH CHOCOLATE FILLING: Replace the cocoa powder with 3 additional tablespoons confectioners' sugar. Add 1 teaspoon vanilla extract along with the egg.

ORANGE CHOCOLATE MACARONS: Replace the cocoa powder with 3 additional tablespoons confectioners' sugar. Add ¼ teaspoon grated orange zest and 1–2 drops orange food coloring along with the egg. Add ½ teaspoon grated orange zest to the filling when it is removed from the heat.

STRAWBERRY CHOCOLATE MACARONS: Replace the cocoa powder with 3 additional tablespoons confectioners' sugar. Add 1–2 drops strawberry flavoring and 1–2 drops red food coloring along with the egg. Add 1 tablespoon strained strawberry preserves to the filling when it is removed from the heat.

## Dough

1 tablespoon plus ½ teaspoon
   active dry yeast

½ cup warm water

1 cup granulated sugar

½ cup (1 stick) unsalted butter

⅔ cup milk

2 large eggs

4–6 cups all-purpose flour

½ cup Dutch-process cocoa
   powder

3 cups vegetable oil for frying

## Vanilla Icing

*Makes 1½ cups*

3 cups confectioners' sugar, plus
   more if necessary

3 tablespoons warm water

2 teaspoons vanilla extract

1–2 drops each red, blue, and
   brown food coloring

Nuts, sprinkles, unsweetened
   coconut flakes, and chopped
   dried fruits

## Raised Chocolate Doughnuts

*Makes about 18 doughnuts*

This soft and crispy raised doughnut is a real delight. If you're looking for the classic doughnut shape, use a doughnut cutter (page 131). Or break out the cookie cutters and cut the doughnuts into different shapes for the fun of it, always cutting a circle in the center so the dough cooks evenly. I also cook and frost the centers for bite-size treats. For tips on deep-frying, see page 131.

1. Combine the yeast, water, and 1 teaspoon of the sugar in a small bowl. Let sit for 10 minutes, or until foamy.

2. In a medium saucepan over low heat, mix the butter, milk, and remaining sugar until the butter is melted and the sugar is dissolved. Cool for 3 minutes.

3. Transfer to a large bowl and beat in the eggs with an electric mixer on medium speed. Beat in the yeast mixture. Add the cocoa powder and 4½ cups of flour; mix well on low speed. If the dough is sticky, continue to add flour, ½ cup at a time, stirring until smooth. Transfer to a floured work surface and knead until the dough is smooth and satiny, about 10 minutes. Place in a buttered bowl, cover loosely, and let sit for 75 minutes. Punch down the dough, cover, and let rise for an additional hour, or until doubled in volume.

4. Divide the dough into three batches. On a floured work surface, roll out the first batch of dough to ¼ inch thick. Prepare your cutting tool by dipping it in flour. Using doughnut cutters fitted with a 1-inch center, or using a 3–3½-inch cookie cutter on the outside and a 1-inch circle cutter on the inside, cut out circles, squares, or flowers. Add any leftover scraps to the following batch of dough. Roll and cut the other two batches of dough in the same way, making

Raised Chocolate Doughnuts

## DEEP-FRYING

- Frying dough or batter in oil or clarified butter makes cakes that are crisp on the outside and moist on the inside, since the oil holds in moisture and prevents the dough or batter from drying out.
- Always add enough oil to the pot to allow the batter or dough to move freely.
- Heat the fat gradually over low heat, monitoring the temperature with a deep-fat or candy thermometer, until it reaches the temperature specified in the recipe.
- Test the oil with a small piece of bread or a little batter to see if it browns quickly.
- Do not allow the oil to smoke, as that means it is too hot and the outside of the cake will cook more quickly than the inside.

## DOUGHNUT CUTTER

This metal tool is made of two concentric rings that are 1 inch high, available with plain or fluted edges. Convertible cutters allow you to take out the center ring to make round filled doughnuts (this dough recipe works for those as well). To use the cutter, first dip it in flour, and then press it into the dough.

about 18 doughnuts in total. Place on baking sheets and cover the doughnuts lightly with plastic wrap and let rise for 30 minutes.

5. Heat the oil over medium heat in a large, deep saucepan until it reaches 400°F. Test the oil temperature by frying one doughnut until lightly browned on both sides. It will take 60–90 seconds per side in the beginning, and a little less time in later batches. Smaller doughnuts will also fry more quickly than larger doughnuts. Cut open the first doughnut to see if the center is cooked. Adjust the frying time accordingly and make the doughnuts in batches. Add the first batch of room-temperature doughnuts to the oil, making sure the doughnuts are roughly equal in size so that they will cook evenly. Rotate or turn the doughnuts until browned on all sides. Lift them from the oil using a slotted spoon so the oil can drain back into the pot. Transfer the doughnuts to plates or a pan lined with paper towels. Remove any little pieces of dough floating in the oil. Bring the oil to the correct temperature again and fry the next batch. Cool for 10 minutes before icing.

6. To make the icing, put the sugar in a medium bowl and gradually beat in the water until the icing is smooth. Beat in the vanilla. If the icing is too thin (it should be a thick glaze), add more sugar. Divide the icing into three small bowls and color each with a different food coloring.

7. Dip the tops of the doughnuts into the icing, or pipe it on with a pastry bag, and top with coconut, nuts, dried fruits, and/or sprinkles. Let the icing set for 10 minutes before serving.

## Chocolate Pastry Cream

*Makes 2¼ cups*

½ cup granulated sugar

4 tablespoons all-purpose flour

2 cups whole milk

2 large egg yolks

1 tablespoon unsalted butter

3 ounces dark chocolate (at least
   65% cacao), melted

2 teaspoons vanilla extract

## Chocolate Choux Pastry

¾ cup water

5⅓ tablespoons (⅔ stick)
   unsalted butter

¾ cup all-purpose flour

4 tablespoons natural unsweetened
   cocoa powder

⅛ teaspoon salt

3 large eggs

## Garnish and Filling

30–40 fresh raspberries or blueberries (30 for éclairs, 40 for
   cream puffs)

⅓ cup melted white chocolate

## Bite-Size Cream Puffs and Éclairs

*Makes 20 cream puffs or 15 éclairs*

These chocolate choux-pastry cream puffs and éclairs are sized just right for a small, sweet bite. They are filled with chocolate pastry cream and a single blueberry or raspberry. Spraying them with water from a spray bottle before baking helps them puff up nicely. To assemble, place the fruit in the middle and pipe the cream around it. Top with another berry and secure with a toothpick. Serve immediately, or cover and store in the refrigerator until ready to serve.

1. To make the pastry cream, combine the sugar and flour in a heavy, heatproof mixing bowl and set aside.

2. In a heavy saucepan, heat the milk over low heat until bubbles begin to appear. Do not let the milk boil. Remove the skin that forms on the surface of the milk. Slowly pour the milk into the sugar mixture, whisking constantly. Pour the mixture into the top of a double boiler set over simmering water and cook for about 10 minutes, or until the mixture lightly coats the back of a spoon.

3. Add the egg yolks and cook, stirring constantly, for an additional 10 minutes, or until the mixture thickens and heavily coats the back of a spoon. Remove from the heat and add the butter, stirring until the butter is melted. Stir in the chocolate and vanilla.

4. Transfer to a bowl, cover with plastic wrap touching the surface, and chill for 2 hours.

5. To make the pastry, preheat the oven to 375°F. Line a baking sheet with parchment paper.

6. Combine the water and butter in a medium saucepan over medium heat and bring to a boil, stirring until the butter is melted. Remove from the heat and beat in the flour, cocoa powder, and salt.

7. Return the saucepan to low heat and cook, stirring constantly, until the mixture forms a ball and no longer

sticks to the sides of the pan. Remove from the heat and add the eggs one at a time, beating well after each addition. Continue to beat until the dough is smooth and satiny.

8. Transfer the dough to a pastry bag fitted with a large round tip. Pipe 1½-inch circles (for cream puffs) or 2-inch logs (for éclairs) onto the baking sheet about 1½ inches apart. Lightly spray with water from a spray bottle. Bake for 12–15 minutes, without opening the oven door, until the cream puffs are firm. Transfer the puffs to a rack to cool.

9. To assemble the pastries, cut the puffs in half and set the tops on one baking sheet and the bottoms on another baking sheet. Place a berry in the center of each bottom half.

10. Transfer the pastry cream to a pastry bag fitted with a small star-shaped tip. Pipe 1½–2 tablespoons cream around each berry. Place the top halves on top of the cream-filled bottoms.

11. Transfer the melted white chocolate to a pastry bag fitted with a small round tip and pipe a small amount in a decorative pattern on each top half. Allow the white chocolate to dry for about 15 minutes. Insert a toothpick into each of the remaining berries and spear one on top of each pastry.

## Peanut Butter Filling

24 ounces milk chocolate (at least 30% cacao) or dark chocolate (at least 65% cacao), melted and tempered (page 29)

1 cup creamy peanut butter

4 tablespoons (½ stick) unsalted butter

½ cup confectioners' sugar

4 cups White Chocolate Buttercream (page 108) or Chocolate Buttercream (page 243)

¼ cup total colored crystal sugar, nonpareils, sprinkles, nuts, grated chocolate, and/or chocolate chips, for garnish

## Peanut Butter Cupcake Truffles

*Makes forty-eight 1¼-inch truffles or twenty-four 2-inch truffles*

Peanut butter cups and cupcakes have two things in common. Most important, they are both delicious. Second, they both use paper or foil liners. These peanut butter cups are designed to look like cupcakes for a cute and tasty break from the norm. Prepare with any nut butter you choose, such as almond butter, cashew butter, Mocha Filling (opposite page), or Chocolate Hazelnut Spread (page 139). Once you get the technique down, the possibilities are endless. If you can find 1¼-inch mini muffin pans, you should use those, although larger ones will work, as well.

1. Line four mini muffin pans with foil liners. If the cavities of the pan are too big, that's okay. Pour the chocolate into the liners and pick up each liner one at a time, tilting it until there's a ⅛-inch-thick layer on the bottom and on the sides of each liner. Let set for 20 minutes.

2. Mix the peanut butter and butter in a double boiler over medium heat and stir until melted and blended. Transfer to a bowl and let cool for 2 minutes. Beat in the confectioners' sugar with an electric mixer for 2–3 minutes; then cool to room temperature. Add the mixture to a piping bag.

3. Pipe the peanut butter filling into the cups, leaving about ¼ inch of space on the top. Pour the remaining melted chocolate on the tops to seal. Let sit at room temperature for 20 minutes. Chill in the refrigerator for 20 minutes before unmolding.

4. Place the buttercream frosting in a piping bag set with a large star tip. Pipe buttercream on the tops of the candies and then sprinkle on the toppings.

### Mocha Filling

12 tablespoons (1½ sticks) butter, at room temperature

2½ cups confectioners' sugar

2 tablespoons coffee liqueur

⅛ teaspoon salt

1 tablespoon vanilla extract

2 tablespoons natural unsweetened cocoa powder

4 ounces semisweet chocolate (at least 50% cacao), melted and cooled

### Variation

MOCHA CUPCAKE TRUFFLES:

1. Follow directions in step 1 of previous recipe.

2. Cream the butter and sugar until smooth. Beat in the liqueur, salt, vanilla, and cocoa powder. Add more sugar if necessary to reach the desired piping consistency. Add the mixture to a piping bag.

3. Follow directions in steps 3 and 4 of previous recipe, using the mocha filling instead of the peanut butter filling.

# Chapter 4

# Party Chocolate

## Blueberry Cream Cheese

*1 package (8 ounces) cream cheese, at room temperature*

*1 cup fresh blueberries*

*1 teaspoon freshly squeezed lemon juice*

## Bagels

*2 cups cold water*

*2 tablespoons granulated sugar*

*½ teaspoon salt*

*1 tablespoon safflower oil*

*1 tablespoon diastatic malt powder or 1½ tablespoons diastatic malt syrup, honey, or firmly packed light brown sugar*

*7½ cups bread flour*

*5 teaspoons active dry yeast*

*¾ cup Dutch-process cocoa powder*

*1 tablespoon baking soda*

*2 tablespoons cornmeal*

## BRUNCHES

The impressive but understated chocolate treats in this chapter will tempt even late sleepers to come over for a weekend brunch. This section includes breakfast favorites and new lunch ideas with tons of chocolate goodies mixed in.

### Chocolate Bagels with Blueberry Cream Cheese

*Makes a baker's dozen*

Making bagels had always been a mystery to me. I thought they could be made correctly only in New York City, at a bagel shop with a brick oven. As a native New Yorker who grew up with the best superdense bagels in the world, it took me about twenty years of living in California to find bagels that are more than "rolls with holes." But after some experimenting, I found that I could make excellent bagels at home. I started with a basic dough and then topped the bagels with sesame seeds, coarse salt, poppy seeds, and "everything" flavors, which included onion flakes, caraway seeds, garlic, nuts, cheddar cheese, and jalapeños. Eventually I tried adding fresh blueberries, dried cranberries, chocolate, and peanut butter to the dough. This recipe makes delicious chocolate bagels.

1. To make the blueberry cream cheese, combine the cream cheese, ½ cup of the blueberries, and the lemon juice in the bowl of an electric mixer fitted with the paddle attachment

## MAKING BAGELS

- Adding malt (found in most health food stores) to the dough results in a dense texture, because malt does not fuel the yeast as extensively or as quickly as sugar does.
- If you don't have a stand mixer with which to knead the dough, knead it by hand.
- The dough rings in this recipe will be smaller than you expect, but they should expand during baking.
- Putting baking soda in the water is a classic technique used to make a crisper crust.
- If you don't have two baking stones or pizza stones, use two baking sheets lined with parchment paper or one baking stone and one baking sheet lined with parchment paper. Scatter the cornmeal on the parchment paper.

and mix on low speed until the berries are crushed and well incorporated. Fold in the remaining whole blueberries by hand and refrigerate for at least 30 minutes before serving. Clean the mixing bowl and paddle attachment.

2. To make the bagels, combine the water, sugar, salt, and oil in the bowl of an electric mixer fitted with the paddle attachment and blend on low speed. Replace the paddle attachment with the dough hook attachment.

3. In a large bowl, combine the malt, 6 cups of the flour, and the yeast. With the mixer set on low speed, gradually add the flour mixture to the water mixture until the dough holds together.

4. Add the remaining 1½ cups flour and cocoa powder and beat on low speed until smooth and a ball forms. Add a few drops of water if the mixture is not smooth and too dry, or a few teaspoons of flour if the mixture is too moist and sticky. Beat on medium speed for 5 more minutes.

5. Transfer to a bowl greased with a small amount of safflower oil, cover with a clean kitchen towel, and let rest for 10 minutes to rise slightly. Divide the dough into 13 pieces and keep covered while you form the rings.

6. Lightly grease two baking sheets with vegetable oil. Knead each piece of dough by folding it in half and punching out air pockets, and repeat 2–3 times. After you have kneaded all 13 pieces, start over with the first piece and repeat the kneading. Form each piece into a ball and let rest for 5 minutes. Then roll each ball into a log about 6 inches long, bring the ends together, and overlap them by 1 inch to create a circle. Roll the overlap between your hands until smooth. When all the rings are complete, place on a lightly greased baking sheet, cover with a clean towel, and let rest for 10 minutes to rise slightly.

7. Preheat the oven to 500°F. Fill a large pot with water and add the baking soda. Bring to a rapid boil. Drop a bagel into the boiling water; if it floats to the top within 10 seconds, the

dough has risen the correct amount. If the bagel takes longer than 10 seconds to float to the top, allow the remaining bagels to rise for an additional 5 minutes. When the bagels are ready, drop three bagels at a time into the water. After about 4 seconds, flip them over to the other side using a slotted spoon. Cook for 10 seconds total, or until the bagels rise to the top. Remove from the water with a slotted spoon and transfer to a rack set over a baking sheet to drain further. Repeat with the remaining bagels.

8. Dust two baking stones with the cornmeal. Place the bagels on the stones 2 inches apart and bake for 5 minutes. Reduce the heat to 450°F and bake for 5 more minutes, or until firm. Transfer to a rack to cool. Spread the chilled cream cheese on the bagels.

**Variation**

PEANUT BUTTER CHOCOLATE CHIP BAGELS: Omit the cocoa powder and increase the flour to 8 cups. Add 3 tablespoons creamy peanut butter and 1 cup semisweet chocolate chips (at least 50% cacao) when you add the remaining flour in step 4.

## Chocolate Hazelnut Spread

*Makes 3½ cups*

Quite addictive, chocolate nut spreads taste great on a plain piece of toast or with many of the baked goodies in this book. Use this on its own or with jam.

2 cups hazelnuts

2 tablespoons granulated sugar

8 ounces dark chocolate (at least 65% cacao), melted

¼ cup natural unsweetened cocoa powder

1 cup confectioners' sugar

2 teaspoons vanilla extract

A few drops of hazelnut oil or vegetable oil

1. Preheat the oven to 400°F. Place the hazelnuts on a rimmed baking sheet and toast for 8–10 minutes, until fragrant. Transfer them to a clean dishcloth and rub to remove the skins. Most should come off, although it's okay if a few skins stay on.

2. Combine the hazelnuts and sugar in a food processor, grind to a meal, and continue to process until smooth. Add the chocolate, cocoa powder, sugar, and vanilla and pulse until

smooth. Add the oil a few drops at a time and blend until the mixture reaches a spreadable consistency. Store in a glass jar or airtight container at room temperature for up to 3 weeks or in the refrigerator for up to 2 months.

**Variation**

CHOCOLATE ALMOND SPREAD: Replace the hazelnuts with toasted almonds (you don't need to remove the skins). Replace the hazelnut oil with coconut oil. Add 1 tablespoon honey when mixing.

## Almond Chocolate Chip Scones
*Makes 6 scones*

These sweet, tender, and hearty breakfast biscuits made with ground almonds and chocolate chips can be eaten plain or with a flavorful spread such as your favorite jam or jelly. If you are looking for a chocolate and almond overload, try the Chocolate Almond Spread (above).

¾ cup almonds

2 tablespoons granulated sugar

2½ cups all-purpose flour

2½ teaspoons baking powder

½ teaspoon baking soda

½ teaspoon salt

4 tablespoons (½ stick) unsalted butter, chilled and cut into chunks

⅔ cup buttermilk

1 large egg

1½ cups semisweet chocolate chips (at least 50% cacao)

3 ounces semisweet chocolate (at least 50% cacao), melted

1. Preheat the oven to 375°F. Butter and flour two baking sheets.

2. Grind the almonds and sugar together in a food processor. Add the flour, baking powder, baking soda, and salt and pulse to combine. Add the butter and pulse until the mixture is coarse and gritty and well blended. Add the buttermilk and egg, and process for 30 seconds. Transfer to a bowl and mix in the chocolate chips with a wooden spoon.

3. On a floured work surface, roll out the dough to ¼-inch thick. Use a cookie cutter or knife to cut the dough into 4-inch rounds. Transfer to the prepared baking sheets, spacing the rounds 3 inches apart. Bake for 18–22 minutes, until golden. Transfer to a rack to cool.

4. When the scones have cooled, drizzle with melted chocolate. Slice and serve with your favorite spread, jam, or jelly.

*Chocolate Raspberry Oat Scones,*
*Almond Chocolate Chip Scones*

**Variation**

CHOCOLATE RASPBERRY OAT SCONES: Reduce the flour to 2 cups. Add 3 tablespoons natural unsweetened cocoa powder and ⅓ cup rolled oats when adding the flour. Replace the chocolate chips with dried raspberries. Replace the melted semisweet chocolate with melted white chocolate.

## Coconut Pecan Topping

¼ cup full-fat coconut milk

1 large egg yolk

2 ounces German sweet chocolate (at least 30% cacao), grated

1 teaspoon vanilla extract

¼ cup granulated sugar

¼ cup unsalted butter

¼ cup fresh or packaged unsweetened shredded coconut

¼ cup chopped pecans

## French Toast

3 large eggs

1 cup whole milk

½ teaspoon vanilla extract

½ tablespoon granulated sugar

¼ teaspoon salt

2 ounces German chocolate (at least 30% cacao), melted and cooled

3 tablespoons unsalted butter

8 (½-inch-thick) slices Chocolate Chip Challah (page 208) or plain challah

2 ounces dark chocolate (at least 65% cacao), finely shaved

8 slices thick-cut, best-quality bacon

4 ounces dark chocolate (at least 65% cacao), melted

## German Chocolate French Toast

*Makes 8 slices*

German chocolate is a sweet baking chocolate that gives this French toast just the right amount of flavor for breakfast. Top with the classic flavor combination of pecans and coconut and serve with maple syrup and Chocolate-Covered Bacon (below).

1. Preheat the oven to 250°F. Place a large baking dish inside to heat it.

2. To make the topping, heat the coconut milk, egg yolk, chocolate, and vanilla in a large saucepan over low heat, stirring until blended. Add the sugar and butter and cook, stirring, for 10–12 minutes, or until thickened. Remove from the heat. Stir in the coconut and pecans and mix well. Refrigerate until ready to use.

3. To make the batter, combine the eggs, milk, vanilla, sugar, and salt in a bowl until the sugar has dissolved. Whisk in the melted chocolate.

4. Grease a griddle with butter. Dip each piece of bread in the batter until fully coated. Cook the toast on each side until lightly browned. Place in the baking dish in the oven to keep warm, and repeat with additional slices.

5. To serve, spoon about 3 tablespoons topping on each slice of toast.

## Chocolate-Covered Bacon

*Makes 8 slices*

Some people like their bacon extra-crisp while others prefer theirs more fatty. Either way, this state fair staple is easy to make at home. It adds a salty boost of protein to a chocolate-filled morning. Serve with German Chocolate French Toast (above).

1. Line a plate with paper towels and set out a cooling rack with a rimmed baking sheet under it. Cook the bacon in a

frying pan until browned on both sides. Set the bacon on the paper towels and pat to degrease.

2. Dip the ends of the bacon into the chocolate and set on the rack to harden.

**Dressing**

¾ teaspoon Dijon mustard

1 teaspoon honey

1 tablespoon apple cider vinegar

2 tablespoons balsamic vinegar

Pinch of salt

Pinch of pepper

3 tablespoons extra-virgin olive oil

**Salad**

2 cups fresh baby arugula

½ cup strawberries, quartered

¼ cup chopped apricot

¼ cup whole walnuts

1 tart Granny Smith apple, cored and thinly sliced in rounds

2 cups mixed spring greens

2 ounces dark chocolate (at least 65% cacao), finely shaved

## Chocolate Apple Salad with Balsamic Cider Dressing

*Makes 1 full-size salad or 2 side salads*

To get my daily intake of chocolate I try it in just about everything I make, and sometimes there are some real surprises—such as this fruity salad with chocolate. This sweet salad can be served as a refreshing dessert, eaten as a full meal, or presented as part of a brunch buffet. The arugula mixes really well with the dark chocolate and the balsamic cider dressing.

1. To make the dressing, whisk together all the ingredients until well incorporated. Set aside.

2. To make the salad, place the arugula, strawberries, apricot, and walnuts in a bowl and toss. Stack the apple slices on a salad plate and add the greens mixture around them. Sprinkle the salad with chocolate shavings. Serve with the dressing on the side.

## Tri-Citrus Marinade

2 cups orange juice

¼ cup freshly squeezed lime juice

¼ cup freshly squeezed lemon juice

1 teaspoon ancho chili powder

2 garlic cloves, minced

8 chicken breasts, cut into cubes

## Mole

2 tablespoons vegetable oil

½ medium Spanish onion, thinly
  sliced

1 celery stalk, sliced

1 carrot, sliced

2 garlic cloves, thinly sliced

1 can (14 ounces) diced tomatoes

2 cups chicken broth

¼ cup raisins

¼ cup ground almonds

2 tablespoons firmly packed light
  brown sugar

2 tablespoons sesame seeds, lightly
  toasted

3–4 chipotle peppers

2 mulato chilies

½ teaspoon ground ginger

¼ teaspoon ground allspice

¾ teaspoon ground cinnamon

¼ teaspoon ground coriander seeds

¼ teaspoon anise seeds

1 jalapeño pepper, ribs and seeds
  removed, chopped

⅛ cup fresh cilantro

⅛ teaspoon ground cloves

½ teaspoon ground pepper

(continued on page 147)

# BARBECUES

I'm lucky enough to live in Southern California, where barbecuing isn't just for summertime—entertaining usually takes place alfresco around a big roaring grill all year round. Chocolate goes so well with many barbecue favorites, whether in the sauces or with the meats, that I could not resist developing some savory chocolate meals. When adding chocolate to a main dish, use natural unsweetened cocoa powder, unsweetened chocolate, or dark chocolate, as their lack of added sugar allows the natural flavors (rather than the sweet side of chocolate) to emerge.

## Chicken Skewers with Sweet Mole Poblano Sauce

*Makes 16 skewers (8 servings)*

Mexican moles come in many different blends, with a variety of spices, depending on the region where they were developed. They are made in large batches, with as many as twenty to thirty different ingredients used to create a blend. This sweet mole includes raisins and almonds as thickeners, as well as the most classic ingredient, chocolate, used to counteract the hotness of the chilies. Prepare the mole at least 6 hours in advance, at the same time you marinate the chicken, to give the spices even more time to blend. (I like to prepare both the evening before and leave them in the refrigerator overnight.) Serve with corn tortillas and fresh lime wedges. Freeze the extra sauce or use it to make enchiladas.

1. To make the marinade, combine the orange juice, lime juice, lemon juice, chili powder, and garlic in a container with a lid. Add the chicken cubes and mix to coat. Cover and refrigerate for at least 6 hours, or overnight.

2. To make the mole, place the oil in a large Dutch oven over medium heat. Add the onion, celery, carrot, and garlic; cook until the onion is browned. Add all the remaining ingredients except the chocolate and stir to combine. Cover and cook for 30–40 minutes. Remove the cover and add the chopped chocolate. Continue to cook uncovered for an

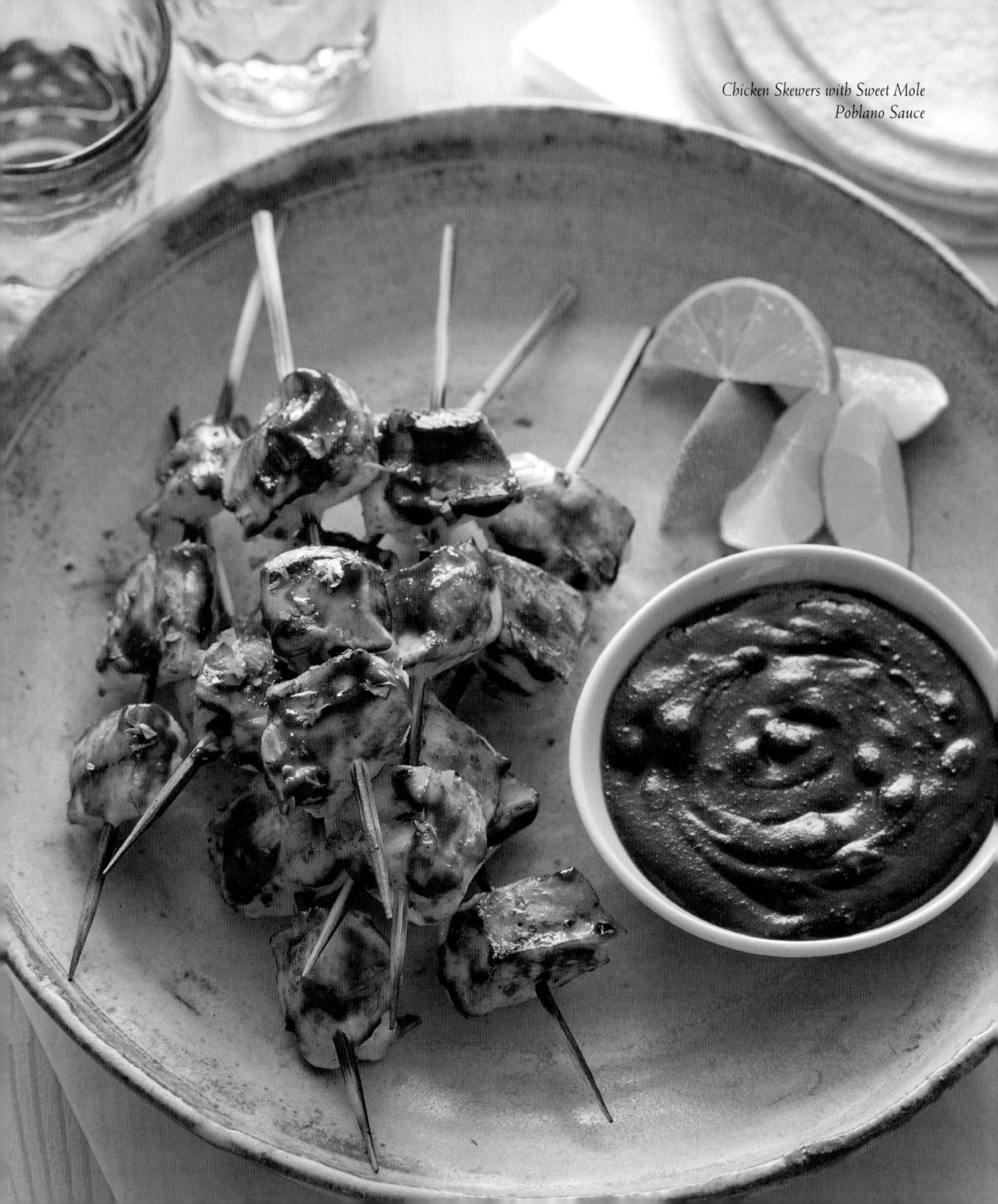

*Chicken Skewers with Sweet Mole Poblano Sauce*

(Mole, continued from page 145)
⅛ teaspoon salt

1½ ounces baking chocolate (100% cacao) or Mexican chocolate, coarsely chopped

## Rub

2 tablespoons olive oil

¼ teaspoon celery salt

¼ teaspoon pepper

## Cocoa Barbecue Sauce

2 tablespoons olive oil

½ yellow onion, diced

4 garlic cloves, minced

2 Roma tomatoes, diced

1 can (6 ounces) tomato paste

2 cups chicken broth

⅓ cup firmly packed dark brown sugar

1½ tablespoons chili powder

2 tablespoons fresh cilantro, chopped

2 tablespoons cider vinegar

¼ cup unsulfured molasses

¼ teaspoon ground cumin

¼ teaspoon ground cinnamon

⅛ teaspoon ground cloves

1 tablespoon Tabasco

½ teaspoon salt

½ teaspoon paprika

(continued on page 148)

additional 10 minutes, until the liquid is reduced and the chocolate is melted. Turn off the heat and let cool. Transfer to a blender and puree.

3. Heat the grill to medium heat. Thread the chicken onto sixteen skewers; set aside.

4. To make the rub, combine the olive oil, celery salt, and pepper in small bowl. Using your fingers, press the mixture onto the chicken and make sure all sides are covered. Grill the chicken skewers over direct heat for 3–4 minutes on each side, or until the chicken is cooked completely and no longer pink. Either spread the mole over the chicken before serving or serve the sauce on the side for dipping.

## Apple-Smoked Ribs with Cocoa Barbecue Sauce

*Makes one 8–10-pound rack pork ribs*

Smoky pork ribs are a favorite in our household. These are flavored with a brown sugar–apple rub and smoked using either apple or hickory wood chips. For tender ribs, cook each side quickly on high heat and then place on indirect heat for slow cooking. Brush the barbecue sauce on at the very end of the cooking process, or it will burn. You can also brush the sauce on after the ribs are removed from the grill.

## Cocoa Barbecue Sauce

*Makes about 3½ cups*

1. Place the oil in a sauté pan over low heat and cook the onion until clear. Add the garlic and continue to cook until golden brown. Add the tomatoes, tomato paste, 1 cup of the chicken broth, sugar, chili powder, and cilantro and cook for 10 minutes. Remove from the heat and let cool for 10 minutes. Blend until smooth in a food processor or blender.

2. Return the sauce to a saucepan and add the remaining 1 cup chicken broth, vinegar, molasses, cumin, cinnamon, cloves, Tabasco, salt, paprika, and cayenne pepper. Stir and reduce the mixture to a sauce consistency. Add the chocolate,

(Cocoa Barbecue Sauce, continued
from page 147)
½ teaspoon freshly ground
cayenne pepper
2 ounces dark chocolate (at least
65% cacao) or Mexican chocolate, chopped into ½-inch pieces

stirring until melted. Simmer for 5 minutes. Store in the
refrigerator for up to 1 week.

## Smoked Ribs

1 cup firmly packed dark brown
sugar
¼ cup coarse salt
2 tablespoons black pepper
¼ cup apple juice
3 tablespoons olive oil
8–10-pound rack pork ribs
2 cups wood chips (preferably
apple wood or hickory), soaked
in water for 1 hour and drained

### Smoked Ribs

1. Combine the sugar, salt, pepper, apple juice, and olive oil in
   a small bowl and mix. Rub the mixture onto both sides of the
   ribs. Cover with plastic wrap and let cure for 4 hours.

2. Set up the grill for indirect grilling and preheat to high. Add
   the wood chips to a smoker box.

3. Scrape the excess rub off of the ribs, leaving a thin coat.
   Place the ribs in the middle of the hot grate and cook for
   3–4 minutes per side to seal in the juices.

4. Lower the heat to medium and place the ribs over indirect
   heat. Cook for 35–40 minutes, turning occasionally. Brush
   on a quarter of the barbecue sauce and continue for cook for
   10–15 minutes, until the meat has shrunk back about ¼ inch
   from the bone and the meat is browned and tender.

5. Brush with additional barbecue sauce before serving. Cut
   the rack into pieces or carve into individual ribs.

## Grilled Corn on the Cob with Milk Chocolate Butter

*Makes twelve ½ ears of corn*

Many Russians enjoy chocolate butter as a sweet indulgence for morning toast. Another way to appreciate its milk chocolaty goodness is on top of sweet and salty corn on the cob. This recipe makes plenty of butter, so use the extra with breads, pancakes, waffles, or anywhere you want a bit more buttery chocolate flavor.

This recipe calls for quickly boiling the corn and then grilling it. Boiling keeps the kernels plump while cooking and grilling adds that smoky flavor. When buying corn, choose cobs with bright green husks that fit snugly around the ear of corn. The kernels should be in tight rows and should look plump and milky. Keep an eye on the corn when barbecuing to make sure you do not char too much on one side.

### Grilled Corn

6 ears corn, husks removed, broken in half

2 tablespoons olive oil

½ teaspoon salt

### Grilled Corn on the Cob

1. Preheat the grill to medium (around 350°F).

2. On the stove top, bring a large pot of water to a boil over high heat. Drop the corn into the boiling water, and when the water starts to boil again, remove the corn with tongs and pat dry.

3. Brush the olive oil on the corn cobs and sprinkle with salt. Place the corn on the grill and cook on one side for 2–3 minutes. Rotate to the other side for an additional 2–3 minutes. Move the corn to indirect heat or to the top shelf, close the cover and cook for another 2–3 minutes, checking periodically to make sure that the corn has not dried out.

4. Serve with Milk Chocolate Butter on the side.

### Milk Chocolate Butter

1 pound (4 sticks) unsalted butter, at room temperature

4 ounces milk chocolate (at least 30% cacao), melted and cooled

2 tablespoons superfine sugar

### Milk Chocolate Butter

*Makes 1½ pounds*

Milk chocolate complements the sweetness of the butter well, although you can substitute semisweet or dark chocolate if you are looking for a richer chocolate taste. I start off with unsalted butter, and I add my own sugar in order to control the sweetness. You can use sweetened butter for extra sugar or salted butter for a sweet-salty taste. Make sure the butter is really soft so you can mix the ingredients well (it should be softer than you would need it if preparing cookies or cakes). Form the butter in candy molds or silicone ice cube molds for an extra-special presentation.

1. Combine the butter, chocolate, and sugar in a bowl. Whip with an electric mixer until the mixture is blended and fluffy.

2. Transfer to a bowl or mold and refrigerate for 30–60 minutes. Serve in the bowl or unmold onto a plate.

## Chocolate Rolls

¼ ounce active dry yeast

¾ cup warm milk

6 tablespoons sugar

4 tablespoons (½ stick) unsalted butter

3 ounces dark chocolate (at least 65% cacao), chopped

1 large egg

½ teaspoon vanilla extract

¼ cup natural unsweetened cocoa powder

¾ teaspoon salt

2½ cups all-purpose or bread flour

¼ cup sesame seeds

## Hamburger Sliders with Sweet Potato Fries and Chocolate Dipping Sauce

*Makes eight ¼-pound burgers*

For a tasty take on a favorite Hawaiian dish, the grilled pineapple burger, the meat is flavored with soy, ginger, and cinnamon. Spread with Cocoa Barbecue Sauce (page 148) and serve on the Chocolate Rolls. Make the rolls first, and then shape the burgers and pineapple to the appropriate size. The rolls also make a great addition to many festive breadbaskets.

## Chocolate Rolls

*Makes 8 rolls*

1. Combine the yeast, warm milk, and 1 tablespoon of the sugar in a small bowl. Let stand for 7–10 minutes, until bubbles form.

2. Combine the butter and chocolate in a small saucepan over medium heat, stirring often, until the chocolate is melted and smooth. Remove from the heat.

3. Add, the egg, vanilla, cocoa powder, the remaining 5 tablespoons of sugar, and salt to a large bowl. Stir to combine.

4. Add 1 cup of the flour and half the chocolate mixture. Stir in the remaining 1½ cups flour, then the remaining chocolate mixture, and continue to stir until just mixed.

5. Knead the dough in a stand mixer with a dough hook attachment or transfer to a floured work surface and knead the dough for 5–8 minutes, until smooth. The dough will be moist.

6. Cover the bowl and let the dough rise for 2 hours, until almost doubled in volume.

7. Knead again for 3–5 minutes; then shape into eight 3-ounce buns. Place on a baking sheet, cover, and let rise for 1 hour.

8. Preheat the oven to 350°F. Scatter the sesame seeds on a plate. Spritz the tops of the buns with water and press into the sesame seeds. Bake for 15 minutes.

### Hamburgers

2½ pounds ground beef

3 tablespoons soy sauce

½ teaspoon ground ginger

¼ teaspoons ground cinnamon

2 garlic cloves, minced

8 (3-inch) pineapple rings, ¾-inch thick

1 tablespoon olive oil

### Hamburgers

1. Set up the grill for indirect heat.

2. Combine the beef, soy sauce, ginger, cinnamon, and garlic in a mixing bowl using your hands or a wooden spoon. Shape the mixture into burgers slightly larger than the rolls, approximately ¼ pound, or 3¼ inches in circumference.

3. Brush the pineapple with olive oil and cook on the hot grill for 3–4 minutes on each side. Place over indirect heat to keep warm.

4. Place the burgers on the grill and cook to taste, 3–4 minutes per side for medium rare. To test doneness, use an instant-read thermometer to check the temperature: 145°F for medium rare, 160°F for medium.

5. Split the chocolate rolls in half, place them on the hot grate, and toast for 1 minute.

6. To assemble the burgers, spread some barbecue sauce on the bottom bun, place the burger on top; add more barbecue sauce, then the pineapple, and finally the top bun.

## Sweet Potato Fries

Vegetable oil for deep-frying
2–3 large sweet potatoes (2–3 lbs)
½ teaspoon salt and ½ teaspoon
    pepper, or 1 teaspoon cinnamon
    sugar (½ teaspoon ground
    cinnamon mixed with ½ tea-
    spoon sugar)

## Chocolate Chipotle Dipping Sauce

6 ounces semisweet chocolate (at
    least 50% cacao), chopped
⅛–¼ teaspoon ground chipotle
    powder
2 tablespoons heavy cream
⅛ teaspoon chili flakes

## Sweet Potato Fries

*Makes three ½ cup servings*

Sweet potato fries are an American icon. Here they are spiced up with a chipotle chocolate dipping sauce. Top with salt or, for a sweeter tone, cinnamon sugar.

1. Place the oil in a large pot over medium heat or deep fryer (see pages 131 and 179) heated to 375°F.

2. Cut the sweet potatoes into 3–4-inch strips and add to the deep fryer. Cook until lightly browned and tender, 5–6 minutes; then transfer to paper towels to drain. Sprinkle with salt and pepper or the cinnamon-sugar mixture.

## Chocolate Chipotle Dipping Sauce

*Makes ¾ cup*

1. Melt the chocolate in the top of a double boiler set over simmering water. Add the chipotle powder to taste.

2. Remove from the heat and stir in the heavy cream. Top with the chili flakes.

---

### SAVORY CHOCOLATE

Smoky and spicy flavors work well with chocolate. Cayenne and chili peppers add heat; cumin adds smokiness; and cinnamon gives chocolate a warm, earthy taste. Chicken, pork, turkey, and beef are the best animal proteins to pair with chocolate.

*Cocoa-Spiced Turkey Chili,*
*Chocolate Chip Corn Muffins*

# DINNER PARTIES

One of the best parts of planning a dinner party is having a reason to venture further than the everyday dinnertime fare and surprising your guests with new tastes of goodness. For example, using a little chocolate to spice up a big pot of chili makes it take center stage. If you want something sweet and special to cap off the meal, individual chocolate desserts are a perfect grand finale.

## Cocoa-Spiced Turkey Chili

*Makes 8 servings*

Cocoa is used as a "grounding" spice in this chili recipe, as it complements the other spices and balances the sweetness of the molasses and the tanginess of the cider vinegar to achieve a subtle cocoa-spice flavor. Use 2 tablespoons of cocoa at first, as suggested in this recipe. If you want a more chocolaty flavor after tasting, add additional cocoa 1 tablespoon at a time. Serve with Chocolate Chip Corn Muffins or Chocolate Honey Corn Bread (page 156).

1½ pounds ground turkey

2 tablespoons olive oil

1 medium onion, chopped

2 celery stalks, chopped

2 jalapeño peppers, ribs and seeds removed, finely chopped

1 medium red bell pepper, ribs and seeds removed, chopped

1 medium yellow bell pepper, ribs and seeds removed, chopped

2 garlic cloves, chopped

1 can (28 ounces) diced tomatoes

1 can (6 ounces) tomato paste

2 cans (14 ounces each) kidney beans

1 can (14 ounces) garbanzo beans

3 cups chicken broth

2 tablespoons natural unsweetened cocoa powder

2 tablespoons chili powder

2 teaspoons ground cumin

½ teaspoon ground ginger

½ teaspoon ground cardamom

½ teaspoon freshly ground black pepper

½ teaspoon celery salt

1½ tablespoons Tabasco

3 tablespoons unsulfured molasses

¼ cup firmly packed dark brown sugar

2 tablespoons cider vinegar

¼ cup chopped fresh cilantro

1. In a Dutch oven, cook the turkey over medium heat, breaking up the meat with a wooden spatula as it cooks, until completely browned. Drain the fat if necessary, and transfer to a large mixing bowl.

2. Wipe the Dutch oven clean, then add the oil over medium heat. Add the onion and celery. Sauté for 3 minutes, or until the vegetables are tender. Add the peppers and garlic and cook for 5 more minutes.

3. Set aside half the cilantro. Add the remaining ingredients and mix well. Bring to a boil, then lower the heat to a simmer. Cover and cook for 30 minutes, stirring occasionally.

4. Add the ground turkey and simmer for an additional 30–40 minutes, or until thick. Add additional chicken broth to thin if necessary. Top with the remaining cilantro and serve.

## Chocolate Chip Corn Muffins

*Makes 24 mini muffins*

These delicious muffins made a great side to any meal. I suggest serving them with Cocoa-Spiced Turkey Chili (page 155).

1. Preheat the oven to 400°F. Line a 24-cup mini muffin tin with paper liners.

2. Mix the flour, cornmeal, sugar, salt, and baking powder in a large bowl.

3. In another large mixing bowl, beat together the eggs, butter, buttermilk, and honey. Gradually add the flour mixture and stir until just combined. Fold in the chocolate chips.

4. Divide the batter among the muffin cups. Each cup should be filled three-quarters full. Bake for 10–15 minutes, or until golden. Cool in the pan on a rack until the muffins are warm. Serve warm.

**Variation**

CHOCOLATE HONEY CORN BREAD: Reduce the flour to ⅔ cup and add ⅔ cup natural cocoa powder to the dry ingredients in step 2. Increase the sugar to ⅔ cup. Bake in an 8 x 8-inch pan for 20–25 minutes, or until the bread springs back in the center when lightly touched.

---

*1 cup all-purpose flour*
*1 cup finely ground yellow cornmeal*
*½ cup granulated sugar*
*½ teaspoon salt*
*1 tablespoon baking powder*
*2 large eggs*
*4 tablespoons (½ stick) unsalted butter, melted*
*1 cup buttermilk, at room temperature*
*¼ cup clover honey*
*1½ cups miniature semisweet chocolate chips (at least 50% cacao)*

---

## Chocolate Fettuccini Pasta

*Makes about 1 pound (4 servings)*

A major advantage to making your own fresh pasta is that you can flavor it any way you like, including with chocolate. Pasta makes a surprisingly good show-stopping dessert. I prefer to serve the pasta hot with a warm sauce, but it is also good chilled. Other interesting toppings include Raspberry Sauce (page 210), Chocolate Sauce (page 242), or just a little fresh Whipped Cream (page 244).

1. Mix the flour, cocoa powder, sugar, and salt with a wire whisk. Pour the mixture onto a flat work surface and build it into a mound. Make a well in the center.

---

*1¾ cups all-purpose flour*
*¼ cup natural unsweetened cocoa*
*2 tablespoons granulated sugar*
*Pinch of salt*
*2 large eggs, beaten*
*1 tablespoon olive oil*
*1 teaspoon vanilla extract*
*Chocolate Sauce (page 242), made using white chocolate*
*1½ cups fresh blueberries*
*1½ cups fresh raspberries*

---

## MAKING PASTA

- When making the dough, mix in the flour a little at a time to achieve the correct smooth consistency.
- Choose the desired attachment for your pasta maker and set up the machine as directed by the manufacturer.
- Dry the pasta a bit before cutting or the strands will stick together and cook too quickly.
- Homemade pasta is softer than the dried store-bought alternative.

2. Add the eggs, olive oil, and vanilla to the well. Set aside about an eighth of the flour mixture, and sprinkle the rest of it over the eggs with a fork, mixing in a little at a time. Note the texture—if it is still moist and sticky, work in a bit more flour mixture.

3. Use your palms to fully integrate the mixture. When you have a soft dough ball, place it on a clean, floured work surface and knead for about 8 minutes, until the dough is soft, smooth, elastic, and uniform in color and texture.

4. Place the dough in a bowl and cover, letting it dry for at least 10 minutes, depending on the humidity. The pasta dough should be pliant but not too soft.

5. Flatten the dough first with your palm and then run it through a pasta machine. Repeat this process 2–3 more times, moving the cylinders closer together after each cycle, to create a thin sheet. Next roll the flattened dough through the broader fettuccini attachment and cut into strips about ¼ inch wide and ¹⁄₁₆ inch thick.

6. Fill a large pot two-thirds full with water. Bring to a boil over medium heat. Cook the pasta in unsalted boiling water for 2–3 minutes. Test a piece to see if it is cooked to your liking, and drain when done. Divide the pasta into bowls and top with warm white chocolate sauce and fresh berries. Serve immediately.

## Pear Risotto in Chocolate Pastry Cups

*Makes 8 servings*

The technique to making a tasty risotto is to infuse the rice with a flavor base. In this recipe, it's a pear wine. Choose firm fruits to poach, since they will soften as they cook. Shape the chocolate piecrust into a free-form edible bowl by draping pastry rounds on the back of muffin pans.

1. To make the edible bowls, first preheat the oven to 350°F. On a floured work surface, roll out the pastry disc to about ¼ inch thick and 12 inches in diameter. Cut out 4-inch circles with round cookie cutters. Drape them over the back of a medium muffin tin to form bowls. Bake for 15–20 minutes, until firm. Remove from the oven and cool to room temperature on the pans.

2. To prepare the risotto, combine the water, wine, sugar, vanilla bean, and cinnamon stick in a large saucepan and bring to a boil.

3. Turn down the heat to a simmer and add the pears and apricots. Cook for 8–10 minutes, stirring occasionally, then cook for an additional 5–8 minutes, until the fruit has softened. Remove from the heat, remove the cinnamon stick and vanilla bean, and strain the fruit from the syrup.

### Edible Bowls

*Chocolate Butter Crust (page 241)*

### Risotto

*3 cups water*

*1 cup red wine (Merlot, Shiraz, or Zinfandel)*

*½ cup granulated sugar*

*1 vanilla bean*

*½ cinnamon stick*

*3 pears, peeled, cored, and cubed*

*3 apricots, pitted and cubed*

*1 tablespoon butter*

*1 cup Arborio rice*

*2 tablespoons natural unsweetened cocoa powder*

*3 ounces dark chocolate (at least 70% cacao), chopped*

*1¼ cups chopped toasted almonds*

*Whipped Cream (page 244)*

*Chocolate shavings*

*½ teaspoon grated orange zest*

*Additional pear and apricot wedges*

*Pear Risotto in Chocolate Pastry Cups*

4. In a large sauté pan over medium heat, melt the butter. Add the rice and sauté for 3–5 minutes, until the rice is golden and translucent.

5. Add ½ cup pear-apricot syrup and stir until the rice has absorbed the liquid. Add more poaching syrup, 1 cup water, and the cocoa powder and stir again. Continue to add syrup whenever the liquid is absorbed, stirring constantly, until the rice is firm and soft. When the rice is done, remove from the heat and stir in the chocolate and almonds. Add the strained fruit.

6. Spoon the risotto into the crust cups. Top with whipped cream, chocolate shavings, orange zest, and fruit wedges.

## Chocolate Marble Cheesecakes

*Makes eight 2¾-inch cakes*

These individual cheesecakes are marbleized with chocolate inside and out. Baking cheesecakes in a water bath keeps the moisture in the oven high and cooks the cheesecake with a gentle heat. These are made in small springform pans, or they can be made in large muffin pans. Seal the outside of the pans with aluminum foil and place directly in the water or, if you're concerned about leakage, place a roasting pan filled with water on the lowest rack and the cheesecake on the middle rack. If you don't have small pans, this recipe will make a 9-inch cheesecake. Bake it for 35–40 minutes.

1. Preheat the oven to 350°F. Butter and flour eight round springform pans (each 2¾ inches in diameter and 3 inches tall) or two large muffin pans.

2. To make the crust, toss the cookie crumbs with the butter in a bowl until well coated. Using your hands, press the crumbs on the bottom of the springform pans or in the cavities of the large muffin tin. Bake for 7 minutes to set. Remove from the oven and cool in the pans on a rack.

### Chocolate Wafer Crust

*2 cups chocolate wafer cookies, crushed*

*¼ cup unsalted butter, melted*

*8 ounces dark chocolate (at least 65% cacao), 3 ounces melted, 5 ounces grated*

*3 ounces white chocolate, melted*

*Chocolate Marble Cheesecake*

## Filling

2 packages (8 ounces each) cream
    cheese, at room temperature

3 tablespoons natural unsweetened
    cocoa powder

1⅓ cups granulated sugar

4 large eggs

4 large egg yolks

1 container (8 ounces) sour cream

⅛ teaspoon salt

1 teaspoon vanilla extract

4 ounces semisweet chocolate (at
    least 50% cacao), melted

24 fresh raspberries

3. Leave the oven on and place a large roasting pan with water on the bottom rack.

4. To make the filling, beat the cream cheese, cocoa powder, and sugar in a large mixing bowl with clean beaters on medium speed until light and fluffy. Add the whole eggs and egg yolks one at a time, beating well after each addition. Beat in the sour cream, salt, and vanilla.

5. Pour the filling over the crusts. Drop spoonfuls of the melted semisweet chocolate over the batter and use a knife to swirl. Place the pans either directly in the water bath or on the middle rack above the water bath and bake for 35–45 minutes, or until firm. Turn off the oven, open the door

slightly, and cool in the oven for 1 hour. Transfer the pans to a rack to cool completely. Cover in plastic wrap and chill for 3 hours.

6. Remove the cakes from the pans. If using a muffin pan, run a knife around the edge and lift carefully. Place on a cooling rack with a baking pan underneath.

7. Pour the melted dark chocolate over the cakes. Transfer the melted white chocolate to a piping bag fitted with a small round tip and drizzle over the still-wet dark chocolate. With a toothpick or small pastry brush, drag the white chocolate into the dark chocolate to create a feathering pattern. When the chocolate has partially but not completely set, press grated chocolate into the sides with your hands. Use a spatula to transfer to a clean baking sheet and chill for at least 10 minutes to set the chocolate completely. Refrigerate until ready to serve. Serve with fresh raspberries.

### Mousse

1 packet (¼ ounce) unflavored gelatin

¼ cup granulated sugar

2 tablespoons water

1 teaspoon vanilla

5 large egg yolks

⅛ teaspoon salt

½ cup warm milk

4 ounces milk chocolate (at least 30% cacao), chopped

⅓ cup ground pistachios

½ cup heavy cream

## Chocolate Pistachio Mousse Cakes

*Makes nine 3-inch cakes*

One of the glories of eating chocolate is savoring the smooth textures. These personal dinner party delights contain a spongy layer of white chocolate cake topped with a layer of creamy pistachio mousse and then coated with a melt-in-your-mouth chocolate ganache. The mousse can set in a shaped silicone mold (such as the hexagonal one pictured on page 163), with the cake cut to fit the bottom. If you have an ovenproof flexible mold, you can bake the cake and set the mousse in the same mold. If you don't have a shaped mold, or if you prefer a quicker method, set the mousse on top of the baked cake in the baking pan and cut the layers as squares before covering with ganache.

1. To make the mousse, combine the gelatin, sugar, and water in a small saucepan, stirring over low heat until the gelatin and sugar are dissolved. Remove from the heat and add the vanilla. Set aside to cool completely.

## Chocolate Leaves

3 ounces white chocolate, melted
　and tempered (page 29)
4 x 8-inch transfer sheet

## White Chocolate Cake

3 ounces white chocolate, chopped
1¾ cups all-purpose flour
¼ teaspoon baking soda
¼ teaspoon baking powder
¼ teaspoon salt
½ cup (1 stick) unsalted butter, at
　room temperature
1 cup granulated sugar
¼ cup firmly packed light brown
　sugar
1 tablespoon vanilla extract
3 large eggs
½ cup buttermilk

## Chocolate Ganache

*Makes 2⅔ cups*
12½ ounces dark chocolate (at
　least 65% cacao), chopped
1½ cups heavy cream
3 tablespoons butter, cut into small
　cubes

## Topping

1 cup pistachios, chopped
9 Maraschino cherries
9 Chocolate Leaves

2. Beat the egg yolks and salt together in the top of a double boiler over low heat. Gradually add the milk. Add the chopped chocolate and stir until melted. Remove from the heat and let cool, then stir in the gelatin mixture and ground pistachios.

3. In a medium bowl, beat the heavy cream with an electric mixer on medium speed until soft peaks form. Gently fold into the batter with a rubber spatula.

4. Add the mousse to 2½–3-inch silicone hexagonal molds. Cover with plastic and freeze for 2–3 hours, until hard.

5. To make the chocolate leaves, spread the white chocolate over the transfer sheet and let set to dry. Cut the hardened sheet into leaf shapes with a utility knife. Set aside.

6. Preheat the oven to 350°F. Butter and flour a 9 x 9-inch square pan.

7. To make the cake, melt the chocolate in the top of a double boiler set over simmering water, stirring constantly. Set aside to cool.

8. Combine the flour, baking soda, baking powder, and salt in a mixing bowl; set aside.

9. In a large mixing bowl, beat the butter, both sugars, and vanilla with an electric mixer on medium speed until creamy. Add the eggs one at a time, beating well after each addition. Blend in the chocolate.

10. Gradually add the flour mixture, alternating with the buttermilk, mixing on low speed until blended. Spread the batter in the pan. Bake for 18–22 minutes, or until a knife inserted in the center comes out clean. Once the cake has cooled, cut with a knife to the size and shape of the bottoms of the molds and place some mousse on top of each cake.

11. To make the chocolate ganache, place the chocolate in a heatproof bowl. Bring the cream to a boil over low heat and pour over the chocolate. Stir gently to blend. Add the butter and stir until blended. Allow the mixture to cool to room temperature.

*Chocolate Pistachio Mousse Cake*

12. Line a rimmed baking sheet with parchment paper and set a wire rack on top. Set the cakes on the rack and pour the ganache over them. Repeat with the ganache that has settled in the tray. Continue pouring until the cakes are completely coated. Gather some chopped pistachios in your cupped hands and press onto the sides of the cakes. Transfer the cakes to dessert plates. Top with cherries and chocolate leaves. Let sit on the counter, or refrigerate to harden the ganache. Serve at room temperature.

# COCKTAIL PARTIES

You could consider chocolate and spirits to be family, or at least very close friends. Most liquors, wine, and beer taste great with chocolate. I highly recommend hosting a cocktail party with chocolate drinks and desserts that can be enjoyed while working the crowd.

### Chocolate Martinis

*Makes 2 martinis*

Say cheers with these indulgent drinks made with dark or white chocolate. Spiral the chocolate sauce on the inside of the glasses and dip the rims in grated chocolate. Top with berries or cherries.

¼ cup dark or white Chocolate Sauce (page 242)

2 tablespoons white chocolate or dark chocolate (at least 65% cacao), grated

4 ounces chocolate liqueur

3 ounces vodka

3–4 fresh raspberries

1. Brush the rims of the martini glasses with chocolate sauce and dip in grated chocolate.

2. Fill a large shaker with ice cubes. Pour in the chocolate liqueur and vodka and shake until the container starts to look frosty.

3. Drizzle the remaining chocolate sauce into the glasses in a spiral or splash pattern. Add the martini mixture.

4. Slide the raspberries onto a skewer and add to the drink or serve on the rim of the glass.

### White Chocolate Martinis

*Makes 2 martinis*

¼ cup dark or white Chocolate Sauce (page 242)

2 tablespoons white chocolate or dark chocolate (at least 65% cacao), grated

½ teaspoon vanilla

2 ounces vodka

1 ounce white crème de cacao

2 ounces white chocolate liqueur

2 ounces half-and-half

2 Bing cherries, pitted

1. Brush the rims of two martini glasses with chocolate sauce and dip in grated chocolate.

2. Fill a large shaker with ice cubes. Add the vanilla, vodka, crème de cacao, and liqueur. Shake until the container starts to look frosty.

3. Add the half-and-half to the shaker and swirl it gently to combine. Strain into the martini glass.

4. Slide the Bing cherries onto a skewer and add to the drink, or serve them on the rim of the glass.

4 cups whole milk

2 cups water

⅓ cup granulated sugar

⅛ teaspoon salt

6 ounces dark chocolate (at least 65% cacao), grated

1½ teaspoons vanilla extract

⅓–½ cup bourbon, or more to taste

2 cups Bourbon Whipped Cream (page 244)

¼ cup dark and white striped chocolate curls (page 34)

*Chocolate Hot Toddies, Chocolate Madeleines*

## Chocolate Hot Toddies

*Makes eight 8-ounce toddies*

Think of this drink as hot chocolate all grown up. Serve on a cool night with warm Chocolate Madeleines (page 72) or tea cakes to feel sweet, warm, and cozy.

1. Combine the milk, water, sugar, and salt in a medium saucepan. Heat over medium heat, stirring occasionally, until the sugar has dissolved.

2. Reduce the heat to low, add the chocolate, and stir until the chocolate has melted. Do not let the mixture boil. Remove from the heat and stir in the vanilla and bourbon.

3. Ladle the hot toddies into eight heatproof glasses or mugs and top each with ¼ cup whipped cream and chocolate curls.

## Chocolate Marshmallows

3 tablespoons unflavored gelatin

1½ cups granulated sugar

¾ cup light corn syrup

½ cup honey

1 tablespoon amaretto liqueur, or more to taste

⅓ cup natural unsweetened cocoa powder

½ cup confectioners' sugar

½ cup cornstarch

## Chocolate Amaretto Marshmallows with Amaretto Orange Fondue

*Makes sixteen 2-inch marshmallows*

Dipping homemade chocolate marshmallows in chocolate fondue at a party is bound to spur some interesting conversation. Both the marshmallows and fondue are spiked with amaretto, a sweet Italian almond liqueur. For a kid-friendly treat, replace the amaretto with 1 teaspoon vanilla. To prevent sticking when making the marshmallows, make sure the pan and tools are well greased.

1. Grease an 8-inch baking pan, rubber spatula, and offset palette knife with vegetable oil and set aside.

# CHOCOLATE BEER

Chocolate works very well with the yeasty flavors of beer, with stouts being the most popular variety for micro-brewers and home brewers to experiment with. Directions for home brewing beer are beyond the scope of this book, but I have come up with some tips and suggestions for adding chocolate to beer for those who are interested.

- Use cocoa, baking chocolate, or cacao nibs (found in baker's supply shops or some supermarkets). Always choose chocolate with little or no cocoa butter. A little sugar is okay. White chocolate is not good for brewing.
- Add cocoa, baking chocolate, and cacao nibs in the final 15 minutes of the boiling stage.
- Since unsweetened chocolate is bitter, cut back on the hops and dark grains, which add bitterness.
- Chocolate is most loved when paired with sweet flavors. Choose a sweet beer when experimenting with including chocolate.
- Add ½–1 pound lactose (milk sugar) per 5-gallon batch during the boiling step (brewer's yeast cannot ferment lactose) to sweeten the beer. Add a little vanilla extract or vanilla beans for a milk chocolate flavor.
- Add ⅔–1 pound chocolate malt to the grain bill. This will give you more chocolate flavor without adding excess cocoa butter.

2. To make the marshmallows, combine the gelatin with ½ cup cold water and set aside.

3. Combine the granulated sugar, corn syrup, honey, and ½ cup water in a medium heavy-bottomed saucepan. Stir over medium heat until the temperature reaches 250°F on a candy thermometer. Transfer the syrup to a large mixing bowl and let it cool to 210°F.

4. Melt the gelatin-water mixture in the top of a double boiler set over simmering water. Add to the syrup and whip with a mixer until the mixture is light and fluffy, about 6 minutes. Whip in the amaretto and cocoa powder.

*Chocolate Amaretto Marshmallow with Amaretto Orange Fondue*

### Amaretto Orange Fondue

*12 ounces dark chocolate (at least 65% cacao), chopped*

*1½ tablespoons unsalted butter*

*1 teaspoon grated orange zest*

*¾ teaspoon cornstarch*

*3 tablespoons amaretto liqueur*

5. Use the oiled spatula to spread the marshmallow in the baking pan. Use the oiled offset palette knife to smooth out the top. Cover with plastic wrap and allow to set at room temperature for at least 3 hours, or overnight.

6. When you're ready to cut the marshmallows, combine the confectioners' sugar and cornstarch in a small bowl. Dust a work surface with a third of the mixture. Turn the marshmallow slab out onto the surface. Cut into 2-inch cubes with kitchen shears. Dredge each piece in the remaining sugar-cornstarch mixture to prevent sticking.

7. To make the fondue, combine the chocolate, butter, and orange zest in a fondue pot and stir until the chocolate has melted. In a separate small bowl, stir the cornstarch into the amaretto until it dissolves, and then add to the fondue pot, stirring until the mixture has thickened. Transfer the fondue to a bowl or leave in the pot. Use skewers to dip the marshmallows into the fondue.

## Black Forest Brownie Bites

*Makes twenty-four 2-inch brownies*

3 ounces semisweet chocolate (at
   least 50% cacao), cut into
   pieces
12 tablespoons (1½ sticks) butter
1 teaspoon vanilla extract
1 tablespoon Kirsch or cherry
   brandy
¾ cup all-purpose flour
¾ teaspoon baking powder
¾ cup granulated sugar
½ cup firmly packed dark brown
   sugar
3 large eggs
½ cup finely chopped fresh cherries
   or ⅓ cup chopped dried cherries
Kirsch Whipped Cream (page
   244)
24 fresh cherries

This dessert receives its name from the Black Forest, a region in Germany from which the sour cherries used to make both the Kirsch and the cake in this recipe come. A Black Forest is also a chocolaty alcoholic beverage named after the cake and the same deep, dark woods. These brownie bites combine the best of the cake and the drink, but with the chewiness of brownies. For a selection of desserts, prepare the Irish cream and coffee liqueur variations, too. Make the brownies in mini muffin pans for bite-size entertaining.

1. Preheat the oven to 350°F. Butter and flour two mini cupcake pans.

2. Melt the chocolate and butter in the top of a double boiler set over simmering water. Remove from the heat and add the vanilla and Kirsch; set aside to cool.

3. Combine the flour and baking powder in a bowl and set aside.

4. Beat the sugars and eggs until blended. Add the flour mixture, alternating with the chocolate mixture, until well mixed. Fold in the chopped cherries. Add by the tablespoon to the muffin pans. Bake for 15–18 minutes, or until a toothpick inserted in the center comes out clean. Remove from the oven and cool the brownies in the pans.

5. Place the whipped cream in a pastry bag fitted with a large round tip. Pipe the whipped cream on top and then add whole cherries.

### Variations

IRISH CREAM BROWNIE BITES: Omit the cherries and Kirsch. Add 2 tablespoons Irish cream liquor (or more to taste) with the vanilla. Top with Irish Cream Whipped Cream (page 244) and grated chocolate.

COFFEE LIQUEUR BROWNIE BITES: Omit the cherries and Kirsch. Add 2 tablespoons coffee liqueur (or more to taste) with the vanilla. Top each brownie with 1 teaspoon melted chocolate and chocolate-covered espresso beans to taste. Place in the refrigerator for 30 minutes to allow the chocolate to harden.

*Black Forest, Coffee Liqueur, and Irish Cream Brownie Bits*

## Rum Balls

1¼ cups chocolate cookies

1 cup walnuts, toasted

½ cup confectioners' sugar

4 tablespoons natural unsweetened
  cocoa powder

2 tablespoons light corn syrup

¼ cup golden rum

½ gallon chocolate ice cream

Chocolate Ganache (page 104)

1½ cups chocolate sprinkles

Chocolate Buttercream (page 243)

12 Maraschino cherries with stems

12 fresh pineapple wedges

## Chocolate Truffle Ice Cream Rum Balls

*Makes 12 rum balls*

Dress up these ice cream rum balls for a cocktail party. If you have 3-inch hemisphere silicone molds, it is easy to place a special surprise rum ball in the center of the two halves and then shape the ice cream into perfect spheres. If you don't have the molds, place the rum ball in the scoop and scoop the ice cream around it. Shape the ice cream into a ball by rotating it in the scoop.

1. Grind the cookies and walnuts in a food processor until fine. Add the confectioners' sugar and cocoa powder and pulse until blended. Add the corn syrup and rum and mix well. If necessary, add either more corn syrup or more cookies to make the batter a consistency that will allow you to form it into a ball. Place in a bowl, cover, and chill for 30 minutes. When ready, remove from the refrigerator, shape into 1-inch balls, cover, and chill on a baking sheet for 1 hour.

2. Line two rimmed baking sheets with parchment paper. Freeze for 10 minutes. Remove 1 sheet.

3. Thaw the ice cream for 5 minutes (it should be soft but not melting). If you don't have a mold, place a rum ball in your ice cream scoop and drag the scoop across the top of the ice cream, rolling the ice cream around the rum ball into a 3-inch ball (about 5–6 ounces) made by rotating the scoop. Release the ball from the scoop and shape by hand if necessary. Place on the cold sheet. Freeze the balls for 1 hour. To form in a silicone mold, press the ice cream into the cavities, leaving a 1-inch indention in the center of each hemisphere. Place a rum ball in one of each pair of hemispheres. Put the halves back together and shape into a sphere. Freeze the balls for 1 hour.

4. Prepare the chocolate ganache and let sit at room temperature. Dip the ice cream balls into the ganache and roll them in the sprinkles. Add the buttercream to a piping bag fitted with a star tip and pipe on top of the balls. Freeze for 2 hours. When ready to serve, top with a cherry and a pineapple wedge.

# Chapter 5

# Holiday Chocolate

## NEW YEAR'S

At the beginning of a new year, people around the world get together with their pals to celebrate with special foods. Here I highlight a few of my favorite international recipes, all with a twist of added chocolate. Chinese New Year and Rosh Hashanah change dates each year, so check a calendar to find out the dates.

### Mochi with Chocolate Ganache Filling

*Makes 12 rice cakes*

Mochi—steamed rice cakes—are *the* New Year's treat in Japan. Mochi are traditionally filled with red beans, but today you can find mochi with fillings that range from strawberry to peanut butter. For this recipe I have filled them with a rich chocolate ganache. The rice flour used for the dough can be found in most Asian markets or in the ethnic section of many supermarkets. You will know it's done steaming when the dough is sticky and semi-translucent. You may need to repeat the steaming and assembly process several times depending on the size of your steamer.

1. Place the chocolate in a heatproof bowl. Heat the cream in a saucepan over low heat until almost boiling. Pour the cream over the chocolate and let sit for 1 minute. Stir with a whisk until smooth. Let cool to room temperature, stirring occasionally to keep smooth. Add the vanilla. Cover and refrigerate for 45–60 minutes, until thick but not hard.

**Filling**

½ *pound dark chocolate (at least 65% cacao), chopped*

¾ *cup heavy cream*

1 *teaspoon vanilla extract*

**Cakes**

2¼ *cups sweet rice flour*

¾ *cup granulated sugar*

2¼ *cups water*

¼ *cup tapioca or potato starch*

⅓ *cup confectioners' sugar*

173

2. Line a baking sheet with parchment paper. When the chocolate mixture is ready, shape it into twelve 1-inch spheres. Set on the baking sheet, cover with plastic wrap, and refrigerate for 1 hour.

3. Place water in a steamer pot over medium heat. Line a round pan that fits in the steamer with parchment paper. Grease the paper with cooking spray.

4. Combine the rice flour, sugar, and water in a medium bowl and mix until smooth. Pour into the round pan to ⅜ inch thickness. Cover with foil. Cover and steam for 15 minutes, until the dough is semi-translucent and tacky to the touch. Remove the foil. Let cool for 5 minutes.

5. Dust a work surface with starch. Remove the parchment, place the dough on the starch, and dust additional starch on top. Dust a rolling pin with starch and roll out the dough to ⅜ inch thick.

6. Cut out 3-inch circles with a cookie cutter. Add a ganache ball to the center of each and bring the dough around the filling, pinching together the ends to seal. Sprinkle with confectioners' sugar. Serve immediately or store in an airtight container in the refrigerator for up to 24 hours. Bring to room temperature to serve.

## Pineapple Filling

*Makes about 1¾ cups*

1 tablespoon cornstarch

¾ cups water

1 cup sugar

1½ cups pineapple chunks

4 ounces milk chocolate (at least 30% cacao), melted and cooled

6 ounces milk chocolate (at least 30% cacao), melted and tempered (page 29)

## Chocolate Pineapple Moon Cakes

*Makes 15 cakes*

Moon cakes are a traditional Chinese treat, and these pineapple moon cakes are a Taiwanese take on this specialty. For this recipe I added chocolate to the pineapple filling.

1. To make the pineapple filling, dissolve the cornstarch in ¼ cup of the water; set aside.

2. Combine the remaining ½ cup water with the sugar in a large saucepan over medium heat, and cook, stirring, until the sugar dissolves. Add the pineapple and cook for 4–5 minutes, until

*Clockwise from top left: Chocolate-Dipped Fortune Cookies, Chocolate-Dipped Almond Cookies, Chocolate Pineapple Moon Cakes, Chocolate-Dipped Sesame Brittle, Caramel Chocolate Sesame Candy*

## Dough

2¼ cups all-purpose flour

1 teaspoon baking powder

¾ pound (3 sticks) unsalted butter, at room temperature

¼ cup granulated sugar

2 large eggs

1 teaspoon vanilla extract

¼ cup whole milk

softened. Raise the heat to high, mix in the cornstarch-water, and cook, stirring, for 3–4 minutes, until the filling is thick and much of the liquid has evaporated. Remove from the heat and let cool.

3. Preheat the oven to 350°F. Butter two baking sheets.

4. To make the crust, combine the flour and baking powder; set aside. In a separate large bowl, cream the butter and sugar with a mixer until fluffy. Add the eggs and vanilla and beat until combined. Add the flour mixture to the butter mixture, alternating with the milk; add additional milk or flour as necessary to yield a pie-dough consistency.

5. Pinch off about 2½ tablespoons of the dough and shape into a ball. Make a ¾-inch-deep indention in the center of the ball with your finger. Fill the cavity with pineapple and melted milk chocolate. Pinch off a teaspoon of dough, press it down over the filling to cover it completely, and smooth the seams. Shape the package into a square by pressing it into a square mold or the corners of a square pan. Set on a baking sheet. Repeat until you have used up all the dough.

6. Bake the cakes for 15–20 minutes, until golden brown. Transfer the cakes to a rack and let cool. Once cooled, spoon the melted, tempered milk chocolate on top. Let set for 1 hour before serving.

## Chocolate-Dipped Fortune and Almond Cookies

Baking and dipping cookies in chocolate is a great way to celebrate Chinese New Year. Both of these cookies are common desserts at Chinese restaurants, but the homemade versions are fresher and much more flavorful. The best part is that you can create your own fortunes. Prepare your fortunes on paper that is cut to 3½ x ½ inches. Either write on the paper by hand or print them out on a computer and cut to size.

### Fortune Cookies

*Makes 12 fortune cookies*

1. Preheat the oven to 225°F. Draw twelve 5-inch circles on parchment paper and place the paper on cookie sheets. Set out a bowl with a wide mouth.

2. Combine the flour and salt in a bowl; set aside.

3. Beat the egg whites and sugar for about 30 seconds, until blended. Mix in the butter, cream, and vanilla. Gradually add the flour mixture until well mixed.

4. Spoon ½–2 tablespoons batter into one of the circles on the parchment paper and use the back of the spoon to spread the batter. It will have a crepe-like consistency.

---

**Fortune Cookies**

1⅛ cups all-purpose flour

⅛ teaspoon salt

4 large egg whites

1 cup confectioners' sugar

5 tablespoons unsalted butter, melted and cooled

3 tablespoons heavy cream

1 teaspoon vanilla extract

Repeat with the other circles. Bake for 17–20 minutes. Remove from the oven.

5. Working quickly, use a spatula to lift the cookie from the sheet. Place a fortune in the center and fold the cookie in half, pinching together to form a semicircle. Bend the semicircle in the center over the ends of a bowl; then lay flat on a plate to set. Let cool completely before dipping.

## Almond Cookies

*Makes 24 cookies*

1. Preheat the oven to 325°F. Line a baking sheet with parchment paper.

2. Combine the flour, baking powder, baking soda, and salt in a medium bowl; set aside.

3. Beat the butter, shortening, and sugar until creamy. Add the unbeaten egg, food coloring, and almond and vanilla extracts. Beat until blended.

4. Gradually add to the flour mixture and stir until blended but a little crumbly. Using your hands, bring the dough together to form a ball. Divide in half and form two 10-inch logs. Cover in plastic wrap and refrigerate for 2 hours.

5. Cut the logs into ¾-inch-thick pieces and place 1½ inches apart on a cookie sheet. Press an almond into the center of each cookie.

6. Brush the cookies with the beaten egg. Bake for 15–18 minutes, until golden brown. Cool before dipping.

## Chocolate Dipping Sauce

*Makes 16 ounces*

1. Set out a cooling rack with a baking sheet underneath.

2. Dip half a cookie into the dark or white chocolate and shake it over the pot several times to remove excess chocolate. Place it on a cooling rack. Repeat with remaining cookies. Let dry for

---

### Almond Cookies

2 cups all-purpose flour

½ teaspoon baking powder

½ teaspoon baking soda

⅛ teaspoon salt

½ cup (1 stick) unsalted butter, at room temperature

½ cup shortening

¾ cup granulated sugar (plus up to 2 more tablespoons, if desired)

2 large eggs, 1 lightly beaten

1 drop orange food coloring

1 ½ teaspoons almond extract

1 teaspoon vanilla extract

24 whole, blanched almonds

---

### Chocolate Dipping Sauce

8 ounces dark chocolate (at least 65% cacao), melted and tempered (page 29)

8 ounces white chocolate, melted and tempered (page 29)

1 hour. Peel the cookies off the cooling rack and serve. To store, layer between sheets of waxed paper in an airtight container.

## Caramel Chocolate Sesame Candy

*Makes 18 candies*

1 cup toasted sesame seeds

14 ounces chocolate caramel squares or vanilla caramel squares

1 tablespoon natural unsweetened cocoa powder

3 tablespoons heavy cream

3 ounces milk chocolate (at least 30% cacao), melted

1. Butter a baking sheet. Sprinkle ½ cup sesame seeds on the baking sheet, making three circles, each about 7¼ inches in diameter.

2. Combine the caramels, cocoa powder, and cream in a small saucepan over medium-low heat, stirring occasionally, until melted and smooth. Spoon the caramel in a circle over the seeds. Sprinkle the remaining seeds on top. Drizzle with melted chocolate. Let set for 1 hour.

3. Using a 7-inch plate as a template, cut the candy into a clean circle. Cut into six wedges with a pizza cutter, or pull apart with your fingers to eat.

## Chocolate-Dipped Sesame Brittle

*Makes 24 pieces*

1 cup granulated sugar

½ cup light corn syrup

½ cup water

1 tablespoon unsalted butter

1 teaspoon vanilla extract

1 cup toasted sesame seeds

6 ounces dark chocolate (at least 65% cacao), melted and tempered (page 29)

1. Butter a large baking sheet.

2. Combine the sugar, corn syrup, and water in a heavy saucepan over medium heat and stir until the sugar is dissolved and the syrup boils. Raise the heat and continue to cook until the mixture reaches 290°F on a candy thermometer, just short of the hard crack stage (page 9). Remove the pan from the heat.

3. Stir in the butter, vanilla extract, and all but 2 tablespoons of sesame seeds. Continue to stir until the butter is melted. Spoon the candy onto the baking sheet in 1½–2-inch circles. After a few minutes, run a small offset metal spatula under the candies to lift them and prevent sticking. Let the candies harden and cool.

4. Set out a cooling rack with a rimmed baking sheet underneath. Melt the chocolate in the top of a double boiler

set over simmering water and remove from the heat. Dip the brittle halfway into the chocolate and set on a rack. Sprinkle with the remaining sesame seeds while the chocolate is still wet. Let dry for 1 hour.

## Sesame Balls with Honey Chocolate Ganache
*Makes fifteen 1¾-inch balls*

Sweet rice cakes are the dessert of choice in many Asian cultures. When I'm out at a dim sum restaurant, I'm always really happy when the cart with fried sesame balls turns the corner and heads my way. Traditionally, they are filled with red bean or lotus seed paste, but here I broke with tradition and filled them with chocolate honey ganache. Make sure you serve these immediately after they are made, when the dough and the melted chocolate are at their best.

### Filling
2 tablespoons unsalted butter

2 tablespoons clover honey

4 ounces semisweet chocolate chips
  (at least 50% cacao)

1 teaspoon vanilla extract

### Dough
1¾ cups water

½ cup firmly packed light brown
  sugar

2 cups glutinous rice flour

3 ounces sesame seeds

Vegetable oil for frying

1. To make the filling, melt the butter and honey in a small saucepan over medium heat. Remove from the heat and add the chocolate chips, stirring until melted. Mix in the vanilla, cover, and place in the refrigerator. Let chill for 30 minutes.

2. To make the dough, place the water and sugar in a small saucepan over medium heat and stir to dissolve. Set aside to cool.

3. Pour the rice flour into a medium bowl and make a well in the center. Add the sugar syrup to the well and stir until it gathers into a ball. Transfer to a rice flour–covered work surface, dust your hands with rice flour, and knead for 5 minutes, until the dough is stretchy and firm.

4. Shape the dough into fifteen 1½-inch balls. Cover with a slightly damp towel while working to prevent them from drying out.

5. Pull off a piece of dough to save as a test piece. Then pull off enough dough to make a 1½-inch ball. Using your thumb, press an indentation in the center of the ball.

*Chocolate Bubble Tea, Sesame Balls with Honey Chocolate Ganache*

2 cups water

1½ tablespoons granulated sugar

⅓ cup pearl tapioca

1 cup tea brewed with 1 black teabags or equivalent loose tea, chilled

½ cup whole milk

1 tablespoon sweetened condensed milk, or more to taste

3 tablespoons firmly packed light brown sugar or peen tong cut from slab

1½ cups ice cubes

6. Spoon the filling into the ball and pull the dough around the filling. Pinch together the ends to seal it; then smooth into a ball.

7. Scatter the sesame seeds on a plate. Roll the balls in the seeds one at a time, pressing them into the dough as you roll.

8. Set out a baking tray with paper towels on top. Heat the oil to 350°F in a wok or deep fryer. Add the test piece to the oil to see if it browns quickly (it should take 15–20 seconds).

9. Place 4 or 5 balls at a time in the oil and let cook until the sesame seeds and dough brown. The balls may also begin to float to the top. Transfer to the towel-lined sheet to drain. Complete the remaining batches and serve warm.

## Chocolate Bubble Tea

*Makes 2 cups of tea*

Invented in Taiwan in the 1980s, "bubble tea" has taken the world by storm. Any sweet, chewy tapioca pearls can be used for this chocolate tea recipe, although I like the large black ones that contain brown sugar. The pearls will expand to the size of marbles, so be sure pick up straws that are wide enough for the pearls to pass through. This recipe calls for light brown sugar, but use *peen tong*, a Chinese brown sugar candy, if you can find it, as it provides a more authentic caramel taste.

1. Boil the water and granulated sugar in a small saucepan over medium heat. Add the pearl tapioca. Cook for 30 minutes, stirring occasionally to prevent the tapioca from sticking. Remove from the heat, cover, and let sit for an additional 30 minutes, until the pearls are translucent. Drain, rinse, and pour the pearls into a serving glass. Refrigerate for 1 hour.

2. Pour the tea, milk, condensed milk, and sugar into a cocktail shaker. Shake until the sugar has dissolved and the milk and tea are well mixed.

3. Add the ice cubes and shake again to chill. Add the drink to the glass of pearls. Serve with a thick straw.

## Dough

1 tablespoon active dry yeast

1 cup warm water

½ cup whole milk, warmed

¾ cup granulated sugar

4¼ cups all-purpose flour

¾ cup Dutch-process cocoa
   powder

2 teaspoons salt

1 teaspoon grated nutmeg

1 teaspoon ground cinnamon

1 teaspoon grated lemon zest

10 tablespoons (1¼ sticks) unsalted butter, at room temperature

5 large egg yolks

## Chocolate Cream Cheese King Cake

*Makes 1 cake (serves 6–8)*

This New Orleans cake is commonly associated with the season that runs from Three Kings' Day in early January to Fat Tuesday in early February and is the official cake of Mardis Gras. King cakes have a small ceramic or plastic baby baked into them, said to represent the baby Jesus. Chocolate cake and chocolate cream cheese frosting are a nice change from the traditional vanilla or citrus cake.

1. To make the dough, dissolve the yeast in the water. Add the milk and 1 tablespoon of the sugar. Let sit for 10 minutes.

2. Combine the flour, cocoa powder, salt, nutmeg, cinnamon and lemon zest in a food processor or blender. Pulse 3–5 times to mix.

3. In a separate bowl, cream the butter and the remaining sugar until fluffy. Beat

## Cream Cheese Chocolate Chip Filling

1 package (8 ounces) cream cheese, at room temperature

¼ cup granulated sugar

3 tablespoons all-purpose flour

1 large egg yolk

1 teaspoon freshly squeezed lemon juice

1 teaspoon vanilla extract

1½ cups mini semisweet chocolate chips (at least 50% cacao)

1 tiny (1-inch) plastic baby

1 large egg white

1 tablespoon whole milk

## Almond Icing

¼ cup water

½ teaspoon almond extract

1 teaspoon vanilla extract

⅛ teaspoon salt

2½ cups confectioners' sugar

1 tablespoon each red, green, and gold colored sugars

in the egg yolks. Gradually add the butter mixture to the flour mixture and process until coarse crumbs form. Add the yeast mixture. Pulse 8–10 times, until the dough forms an elastic ball. If the dough is too sticky (it should not stick to your hands), add more flour, 1 tablespoon at a time. If it is too dry (it should have a satiny shine), add more water, 1 tablespoon at a time. Place the dough in an oiled bowl and cover. Let sit in a warm, dry place for at least 2 hours, until the dough doubles in volume.

4. To make the filling, combine the cream cheese, sugar, flour, egg yolk, lemon juice, and vanilla in a bowl and blend until smooth. Fold in the chocolate chips. Refrigerate until ready to use.

5. Butter a large baking sheet.

6. When the dough is ready, punch it down a few times to get the air bubbles out and flatten it a bit. On a floured work surface, roll out the dough to about 24 inches long and ⅜ inch thick.

7. Spread the cream cheese filling over the dough, leaving 1 inch bare on all sides. Roll up the long side of the dough, forming a long cylinder, and pinch the edges to seal. Wrap the log into a circle. Where the ends come together, insert the plastic baby and pinch the ends together to seal, smoothing the dough to hide the seam. Transfer the ring to the prepared baking sheet and cover with plastic wrap. Let sit for 45 minutes, or until the dough doubles in volume.

8. Preheat the oven to 350°F. Beat the egg white with the milk. When the dough has risen, brush it with the egg white mixture. Bake for 35–40 minutes, until golden, or until a thermometer inserted into the center reads 200–210°F. Let cool.

9. To make the almond icing, combine the water, almond extract, vanilla, and salt. Mix in the confectioners' sugar gradually, until the icing reaches a thin piping consistency. Pour or pipe almond icing over the cake and allow it to drip slowly over the sides. Sprinkle immediately with colored sugars if desired. Let the topping set before serving.

# VALENTINE'S DAY

I am a big fan of this holiday for several good reasons—I met my husband on Valentine's Day—but there is one major reason to love it: This is *the* chocolate holiday. For traditional Valentine's Day treats, you can prepare homemade molded candies, although if you want to try something different, give your friends and family some chocolate cherry pie.

## Chocolate Cherry Hand Pies

*Makes six 4 x 3½-inch pies*

Break from the traditional cherry candy cordials this year and give your cutie-pie a cute hand pie. With chocolate crusts and cherry fillings, these offer the cherry-chocolate flavor combination associated with the holiday. These pies can be prepared using one batch of chocolate crust. The words on your pies will add a three-dimensional effect, or mix up the crust colors with contrasting doughs (see sidebar below).

1. Line two baking sheets with parchment paper.

2. To make the cherry filling, combine the flour and sugar in a large bowl. Add the cherries and butter to the flour-sugar mixture and stir to coat.

3. On a floured work surface, roll out each half of the chilled pastry into a circle about ⅛ inch thick and 14 inches in diameter. Using cookie cutters or a knife, cut out twelve 4 x 3½-inch hearts. Place the bottom crusts (six of the twelve shapes) on the prepared baking sheets.

4. Using ¾–1-inch alphabet cookie cutters (or cutting freehand with a utility knife) cut out loving words, symbols, and phrases. Place on a baking sheet covered with waxed paper and refrigerate until ready to use.

5. Spoon ⅓ cup cherry filling into the bottom crusts, leaving a ½-inch border. Brush the egg white around the border. Place the top heart over the filling and press the edges together

---

## Cherry Filling

3 tablespoons all-purpose flour

⅓ cup granulated sugar

2½ cups Bing or other fresh sweet cherries, stemmed and pitted

½ tablespoon cold unsalted butter, cut into cubes

## Crust

Chocolate Butter Crust (page 241), made into three rounds

2 large egg whites, beaten

---

## CONTRASTING DOUGHS

Make two similar doughs in contrasting colors or textures—for example, a butter crust and a chocolate butter crust, or a plain crust and an herb crust. Just make sure they have similar ingredients and the same baking time. Cut out shapes in both crusts with cookie cutters and inlay the cutouts of one on top of the other to create a contrasting pattern.

## Vanilla Buttercream Centers

*7 ounces white chocolate, chopped*

*¼ cup heavy cream*

*2 teaspoons vanilla extract*

*1½ tablespoons butter*

*8 ounces white chocolate for shells*

## Dark Chocolate Centers

*12 ounces dark chocolate (at least 65% cacao), chopped*

*2 tablespoons light corn syrup*

*½ cup heavy cream*

*1 tablespoon unsalted butter*

*1 teaspoon vanilla extract*

*8 ounces dark chocolate (at least 65% cacao) for shells*

to seal. Use a fork or the tip of a knife to create a patterned edge. Cut vents in the top pieces.

6. Brush egg white on the top of the pies and attach words and designs using the letters and symbols you cut out. Freeze the pies for 1 hour before baking.

7. Preheat the oven to 375°F. Bake for 18–23 minutes, or until crisp. Cool on a baking sheet on a rack.

## Filled Molded Chocolates

*Makes 24 chocolates*

Indulge in the sweet sophistication and luxury of molded chocolate. One of the advantages of molding chocolate is that you can choose from an infinite number of fillings and mold shapes. The chocolates are easy to fill; just stock up on a few assorted molds and basic ingredients, and experiment with some of the recipes here—or create your own. See page 187 for how to create the chocolate shells to go around the fillings.

## Centers

1. Place the chopped chocolate in a heatproof bowl.

2. Place the heavy cream and corn syrup (if working with dark or milk chocolate) in a saucepan over low heat, stirring occasionally, until it comes to a boil. Remove from the heat, stir in the vanilla, and pour over the chocolate. Let sit for 2–3 minutes. Stir until blended.

3. Add the butter and blend until melted. Let cool to room temperature.

4. Add the mixture to a piping bag fitted with a medium round tip and pipe in the center of the chocolate shell.

### White Chocolate Shell Variations

LIME BUTTERCREAM CENTERS: Replace the vanilla with the juice and zest of 1 lime.

PUMPKIN BUTTERCREAM CENTERS: Add 3 tablespoons canned pumpkin puree, ¼ teaspoon ground cinnamon, ⅛ teaspoon ground ginger, ¼ teaspoon grated nutmeg, a pinch of ground cloves, and a pinch of ground cardamom.

MATCHA BUTTERCREAM CENTERS: Add 2 teaspoons matcha powder.

COCONUT BUTTERCREAM CENTERS: Replace half the cream with thick coconut milk and add ½ cup unsweetened desiccated coconut.

BOURBON BUTTERCREAM CENTERS: Replace the vanilla with 3 tablespoons bourbon.

### Dark Chocolate Shell Variations

APRICOT CENTERS: Replace the vanilla with 2 tablespoons apricot liqueur. Add a few pieces of chopped dried apricots to each shell before sealing.

ORANGE CENTERS: Replace the vanilla with the juice of half an orange and 1 teaspoon grated orange zest.

### Milk Chocolate Shell Variations

MILK CHOCOLATE CURRY CENTERS: Replace the cream with coconut milk. Omit the vanilla and add 1 teaspoon orange curry powder.

MILK CHOCOLATE CASHEW CENTERS: Add ½ cup ground cashews to the filling.

## Chocolate Molds

Following are the directions for making molded chocolate. Once tempered, chocolate is easy to mold. For solid chocolate pieces, pour the chocolate directly into the mold with a ladle, filling the mold to the top. Tap the mold on the countertop to allow air bubbles to rise to the surface. Chocolates that are filled or have centers are made by creating an outer shell that is allowed to harden and that is then filled with a center and sealed with a chocolate bottom. Always temper more chocolate than you think you will need so that you don't run out in the middle of working. Tap the molds on the countertop after pouring chocolate into them to allow air bubbles to rise to the surface.

1. If you're working with a colored finish, such as luster dust, scatter or brush the dust into the mold to cover the surface

of the cavities before adding the chocolate. If you're working with a patterned decal finish, add the decal to the mold before pouring in the chocolate.

2. Use a ladle to fill the mold halfway with tempered chocolate, gently shake the chocolate around so that it coats every surface, then pour the excess chocolate back into the bowl.

3. Let the chocolate set on the countertop for about 5 minutes. When it has begun to set, use a knife to scrape off any excess chocolate on the top of the mold (not in the cavities). Allow the chocolate to set completely. For solid chocolate, demold the chocolate and clean off any excess chocolate on the bottom with a sharp paring knife.

4. Add the filling to a piping bag and pipe it about ³⁄₁₆ inch from the top. If it is a solid filling, allow it to set. Next, ladle or pipe tempered chocolate to the top of the mold to create bottoms. Scrape off the excess with a knife.

5. Place the mold in the refrigerator for about 15 minutes to harden. Allow the chocolate return to room temperature. Invert the mold over a piece of parchment paper and tap to release.

1 cup heavy cream

2 tablespoons unsalted butter

⅛–¼ cup Frangelico, Grand Marnier, Kirsch, amaretto liqueur, or golden rum

8 ounces dark chocolate (at least 65% cacao), melted

1 teaspoon luster dust

12 ounces dark chocolate (at least 65% cacao), melted and tempered (page 29)

2 sheets vark

Almond Dragée Eggs (page 193)

4 sheets gold leaf

## Chocolate Liqueur–Filled Gems

*Makes twenty-four to thirty ¼–1-ounce pieces*

These gem-shaped chocolates are filled with a selection of liqueur ganache fillings. Add ¼–½ cup of your favorite flavors to suite your taste. I get good use out of my gem molds, especially for Valentine's Day. The flexible silicone molds allow the gems to pop right out, but to achieve a two-sided gem using plastic molds, I attach two of the pieces together using melted chocolate and allow them to set.

1. To make the filling, scald the cream in a saucepan over medium heat. Remove from the heat and cool to room temperature. Add the butter and whisk until melted. Stir in the liqueur; let cool to room temperature.

*Filled Molded Chocolates*

2. Add the melted dark chocolate and beat with an electric mixer until light and fluffy. Cover and chill for 30–60 minutes, or until the filling has cooled to a good piping consistency.

3. Next, brush the luster dust into the mold cavities with a pastry brush, coating the surface. Reserve 1 ounce of the tempered chocolate to use as an adhesive. Use a ladle to fill the molds halfway with tempered chocolate. Shake the molds so that every surface of the indention is coated. Let set on a countertop for about 5 minutes. When it has begun to set, use a knife to scrape off any excess chocolate that is not in the cavities. Allow the chocolate to set completely for about 10 minutes. Repeat if the shell layer is too thin.

## WINE AND CHOCOLATE PAIRINGS

A wine and chocolate tasting is a must-try for those whole love those two great tastes. When pairing chocolate and wine, the general rule is that light chocolates work better with light wines and dark chocolates go well with more full-bodied wines. You are looking for a rich, buttery blended flavor. The wine should not overwhelm the chocolate or vice versa, and you should be able to taste the subtle flavor variations.

Keep in mind that winemakers and chocolate makers embed their own flavor nuances in their products, so all wines of the same type will not always pair well with the same piece of chocolate. Following I have included some general tasting guidelines to help you get started. To start the pairing test, take a bite of the chocolate first. Let it slowly melt in your mouth until it has completely dissolved. Sip the wine and allow it to swirl around your taste buds. An unbelievable taste means you have a good match. A bitter, sour, or bad taste means the flavors aren't compatible.

• White chocolate (no cacao content) has a creamy, buttery flavor with a strong dairy undertone. It goes well with sweeter wines, such as dry sherry, Moscato d'Asti, Orange Muscat, white Zinfandel, and Champagne.

Sour white and red wines do not go well with white chocolate.

• Milk chocolate (above 30% cacao) has less cacao content and more sugar than darker chocolates. Its sugary, milky taste calls for a sweet wine, so pair it with Pinot Noir, Merlot, sweet Riesling, dessert wine, rosé, Champagne, or muscatel.

• Semisweet chocolate (above 50% cacao) has nutty, spicy, peppery, and fruity nuances that many wines can pick up beautifully. In addition to the wines suggested for bittersweet chocolate, try semisweet chocolate with red Zinfandel, dry Riesling, or ruby port.

• Dark chocolate (above 65% cacao) has a bold, bitter flavor that needs a strong wine with fruity notes. Serve with Cabernet Sauvignon, tawny vintage port, Shiraz, Bordeaux, or Beaujolais. Acidic wines don't work well with acidic dark chocolate.

• Filled chocolates require a bit more complicated thought when pairing them with wine. First you need to consider the types of chocolates used, then the type of filling. Fruity chocolates go well with red wines that have peppery flavors, such as Zinfandel or Pinot Noir. Sweeter white wines, such as Chardonnay, tawny port, and sherry, work with nut- or butter-based centers.

4. Spoon the filling into a pastry bag set with a medium round tip. Pipe the filling into the center to about ⅛ inch from the top of the mold. Fit a clean pastry bag with another medium round tip. Reheat the tempered chocolate and then let it cool enough to add to the pastry bag. Pipe the tempered chocolate to the top of the mold to create the candy bottoms. Scrape off excess chocolate with a knife. Place the mold in the refrigerator for about 15 minutes to let the chocolate harden. Let the chocolate return to room temperature. Invert the mold over a piece of parchment paper and tap to release the candies. Clean off any excess chocolate with a sharp paring knife.

5. Remelt the reserved chocolate and use it to attach two candies together to make double-sided gems. Wrap smaller candy gems in vark or attach to the tops of a few gems. Cover the dragée almonds in gold leaf and serve with the gems.

*Top left: Chocolate Coconut Nests with Almond Dragée Eggs; top right: Candy Lollipops; center: Marshmallow-Filled Chocolate Fish; bottom left: Chocolate Lollipops; bottom right: Chocolate-Coated Almond-Flavored Easter Egg*

# EASTER

Happy Easter! Although Easter is an important Christian holiday, these days Easter is celebrated by people of diverse faiths as a symbol of spring. Baskets of chocolate, eggs, and bunnies (as well as their "favorite" food—carrots) are the flavors and symbols of the season. The Chocolate Easter Cookies in this section provide an opportunity to decorate with natural ingredients in dozens of ways.

## Almond Dragée Eggs

1 cup whole almonds

6 ounces milk chocolate (at least 30% cacao), melted and tempered (page 29)

2 tablespoons natural unsweetened cocoa powder

## Nests

12 ounces milk chocolate (at least 30% cacao)

2½ cups shredded unsweetened coconut

½ cup unsweetened coconut flakes

## Chocolate Coconut Nests with Almond Dragée Eggs

*Makes 8 nests, each with 3 almond eggs*

Using two types of coconut—coconut flakes and shredded coconut—makes these candy nests look realistic, although using just shredded coconut will work just fine. To make the dragées, dip the nuts individually into the melted chocolate to make a smooth surface or, if you don't mind a rougher surface, stir the almonds together in a bowl with the chocolate to coat.

1. Preheat the oven to 325°F. Toast the nuts for 7–10 minutes, or until golden. Stir a few times to brown all sides. Allow the nuts to cool completely.

2. Either individually dip the nuts into the chocolate using a dipping tool and place on a baking sheet, or add all the nuts to a medium bowl, stir in the melted chocolate, and mix to coat. Separate the nuts and place on a baking sheet. Chill for 10 minutes. Dust the nuts with cocoa powder and shake off any excess.

3. To make the nests, grease a muffin pan with butter. Melt the chocolate in the top of a double boiler set over simmering water and stir in the coconut a little at a time, mixing until well coated.

4. Distribute the mixture among 8 cups in the muffin pan. Form into nests with your hands, making a cavity large enough to hold 3 almonds in the center. Leave the top edges rough to resemble twigs. Lift each nest from the pan and round the bottom to give it a natural look. Place the nests back in the pan and refrigerate for 1 hour, until solid. Add the almond dragée eggs to serve.

**Variation**

GOLD LEAF ALMOND DRAGÉES: After the chocolate has dried, individually wrap each almond in gold leaf.

## Chocolate Lollipops

*Makes twenty-four 1-ounce pops*

You can tell which candy molds are for lollipops because they have places for the sticks to go. Lollipop molds come in all shapes and sizes, as well as different materials. Plastic, silicone, or metal will do for these pops. Since sticks also come in a variety of sizes, make sure you have the correct stick for your mold. For this Easter chocolate buffet, I created bunnies, chicks, and playful stars.

*8 ounces milk chocolate (at least 30% cacao), melted and tempered (page 29)*

*8 ounces white chocolate*

*8 ounces green- or pastel-colored chocolate*

1. Melt one of the chocolates in the top of a double boiler set over simmering water and stir until it reaches 86–88°F. Remove from the heat.

2. Using a ladle, pour the chocolate almost to the top of the molds, leaving the slot for the stick empty. Lay the stick in the mold, with at least ¾ inch covered in chocolate. Place the mold on a baking sheet and place in the refrigerator for 30 minutes.

3. Clean out the double boiler and make sure it's completely dry. Repeat steps 1 and 2 with the other two chocolates.

4. Scrape off any chocolate overflow with the tip of a knife, creating a clean edge around your lollipop. Press the pops out of the mold, wrap in candy bags, and tie with a ribbon.

**Variations**

LIME CHOCOLATE LOLLIPOPS: Add ¼ teaspoon grated lime zest to the chocolate after it has melted.

MILK CHOCOLATE MINT LOLLIPOPS: Add ½ teaspoon chopped mint leaves to the milk chocolate after it has melted.

## Candy Lollipops

*Makes twelve 3-inch lollipops*

When making hard candy lollipops, as opposed to melted chocolate lollipops, it's best to stick to molds of simple shapes, like these round pops, as pops with more detailed shapes are harder to get out of the mold. Choose a silicone mold or metal molds specifically for shaping hard candy. Plastic molds are hit or miss when it comes to removing the pops from the molds. You can also make these rounds free-form by spooning the candy into rounds on a baking sheet lined with a silicon mat or parchment paper. The naturally transparent candy color works well with the natural nuts with or without food coloring, but if you want more of a chocolate look, use a few drops of brown food coloring.

¼ cup slivered almonds

12 whole hazelnuts

1 cup plus 2 tablespoons granulated sugar

2 tablespoons light corn syrup

¼ cup water

¼ teaspoon cream of tartar

1 tablespoon chocolate flavoring

Brown food coloring, optional

1. Arrange flower shapes on a cutting board, using 7–8 slivered almonds for the petals and a whole hazelnut as the center.

2. Combine the sugar, corn syrup, water, and cream of tartar in a small saucepan over medium heat. Bring to a boil. Continue to heat until a candy thermometer reads 300°F. Remove from the heat and let the mixture cool until the bubbling subsides. Add the flavoring and the food coloring, if desired.

3. Pour the mixture into the molds to three-quarters full. Quickly add the flower shapes, being careful that the molds don't overflow. Add the lollipop sticks. Allow the pops to harden for 15 minutes, until they are still slightly warm but almost cooled. Remove the lollipops from the molds and cool completely. If you have trouble removing the lollipops from the molds, use the tip of a knife to pry them out. Place in candy bags and close with a ribbon.

## Chocolate Shell

16 ounces milk chocolate (at least
   30% cacao) or dark chocolate
   (at least 65% cacao), melted
   and tempered (page 29)

## Marshmallow Filling

1 cup marshmallow cream

3 tablespoons unsalted butter

¼ cup confectioners' sugar

# Marshmallow-Filled Chocolate Fish

*Makes 12 marshmallow-filled fish*

Fish are commonly associated with Christianity because they were used as a secret symbol by early Christians, making them a welcome addition to an Easter basket or candy buffet, especially since fish candy molds are easy to find. You can prepare them as solid fish or fill them with marshmallow cream for extra fun. If you choose to fill them, use large molds—these are 4 x 1¾ inches, which provides more room for the filling. Here the outer layer of chocolate is painted into the mold, but it can also be added with a ladle and swirled around to evenly coat the mold (see page 37).

1. Paint the melted chocolate on the insides of the fish molds using a large pastry brush. Place the molds in the refrigerator for 10 minutes. Remove and paint on a second coat, building the surface to ⅛ inch thickness. Chill for 10 minutes to harden.

2. Stir the marshmallow cream in the top of a double boiler set over simmering water to soften it. Add the butter and stir until melted and blended. Transfer to a bowl and beat in the confectioners' sugar with an electric mixer for 1–2 minutes. Add the mixture to a piping bag and let cool.

3. Pipe the marshmallow cream into the molds, leaving about ¼ inch on top. Seal the molds with the remaining melted chocolate. Let sit for 20 minutes to cool. Chill in the refrigerator for 1 hour before demolding. Serve at room temperature so the marshmallow filling is soft.

## Almond Paste

*Makes 1¼ cups*

*¼ cup granulated sugar*

*¼ cup clover honey*

*2 tablespoons water*

*¾ cup ground almonds*

*2 tablespoons unsalted butter, at room temperature*

## Shell

*12 ounces dark chocolate (at least 65% cacao), melted and tempered (page 29)*

*Candy dots, flowers*

*3 tablespoons melted green chocolate*

## Chocolate-Coated Almond-Flavored Easter Eggs

*Makes 18 egg candies*

These hand-formed and dipped eggs are filled with almond paste and decorated with spring flowers. Use homemade or store-bought almond paste. Pipe the flowers yourself or purchase premade flowers at a cake-decorating store.

1. To make the almond paste, combine the sugar, honey, and water in a small saucepan over medium heat, stirring until the sugar has dissolved. Blend the ground almonds with the sugar mixture in a food processor until they form a smooth paste. Cover with plastic wrap and chill for 30 minutes. Line a baking sheet with parchment paper.

2. After the filling has chilled, knead in the butter using your hands. Shape the almond paste into rounded egg shapes that are 1¼ inches wide, 1½ inches tall and ¾ inch high, pressing the bottom on a table to flatten. Place on a greased baking sheet and chill for 30 minutes.

3. To prepare the shells, add the melted and tempered chocolate to a bowl. Allow it to cool for about 10 minutes, until it starts to thicken. Insert a dipping fork or large dinner fork into the almond paste center and submerge it in the chocolate. Repeat this a few times to coat the center completely, and then tap it against the edge of the bowl to remove excess chocolate. Transfer to the baking sheet. Repeat with the remaining eggs. Let dry completely for about 30 minutes.

4. Using a bamboo skewer or toothpick, draw on the stems, leaves, and a candy dot on top of each piece of candy to create the flowers. Place a dot of melted chocolate on the egg to use as an adhesive base for the flowers, and quickly attach the candy dots and flowers. Let dry 30 minutes to harden.

## Cupcakes

1½ cups grated carrots

¾ cup firmly packed light brown
  sugar

⅓ cup vegetable oil

½ cup crushed pineapple

½ cup unsweetened shredded
  coconut

1 teaspoon grated orange zest

1 cup apple juice

1½ cups all-purpose flour

1½ teaspoons baking powder

½ teaspoon salt

1¾ teaspoons ground cinnamon

¼ teaspoon ground cardamom

¼ teaspoon grated nutmeg

½ cup natural unsweetened cocoa
  powder

½ cup semisweet chocolate chips
  (at least 50% cacao)

## Chocolate Cream Cheese Frosting

1 package (8 ounces) cream
  cheese, at room temperature

6 tablespoons (¾ stick) unsalted
  butter, at room temperature

3½ cups confectioners' sugar

1 teaspoon vanilla extract

1 ounce dark chocolate (at least
  65% cacao), melted and cooled

## Topping

½ cup walnuts, chopped

¼ cup grated chocolate

⅛ cup grated orange zest

# Chocolate Carrot Cupcakes with Chocolate Cream Cheese Frosting

*Makes 18 medium (2¾-inch) cupcakes*

The chocolate in this recipe draws out the natural sweetness of the carrots. When the cupcakes are topped with chocolate cream cheese frosting, you have a taste reminiscent of a classic carrot cake.

1. Preheat the oven to 350°F. Line medium muffin tin with liners.

2. Combine the carrots, sugar, oil, pineapple, coconut, orange zest, and apple juice in a large bowl.

3. In a separate bowl, combine the flour, baking powder, salt, cinnamon, cardamom, nutmeg, and cocoa powder.

4. Add the flour mixture to the carrot mixture. Mix well. Fold in the chocolate chips.

5. Fill the cupcake liners three-quarters full. Bake for about 20 minutes, or until a knife inserted in the center of a cupcake comes out clean. Cool the cupcakes in the pan.

6. To make the frosting, beat the cream cheese and butter with a mixer until smooth. Slowly sift in the confectioners' sugar, and beat until all lumps are gone. Add the vanilla and melted chocolate. Mix until fully blended and smooth.

7. Place the frosting in a pastry bag with a large star tip and pipe it onto the tops of the cupcakes. Add the chopped nuts around the edge where the frosting meets the cupcake, and sprinkle grated chocolate and orange zest on top.

## Cookies

1¾ cups all-purpose flour

1 teaspoon baking soda

½ cup Dutch-process cocoa

½ cup (1 stick) unsalted butter, at
room temperature

1 cup granulated sugar

2 large eggs

1½ teaspoons vanilla extract

3 ounces dark chocolate (at least
65% cacao), melted and cooled

## Milk Chocolate Glaze

3 ounces milk chocolate (at least
30% cacao)

3 tablespoons unsalted butter

1½ cups confectioners' sugar

¼ teaspoon salt

## Toppings

Sesame seeds

Chocolate-covered sunflower seeds

Nuts (whole almonds, slivered
almonds, almond slices, pecan
halves)

# Chocolate Easter Cookies

*Makes twelve 3½-inch cookies*

Inspired by mazureks, traditional Polish Easter cakes that are decorated with seeds and nuts and are made to celebrate new beginnings,
these extra-large cookies have plenty of room for decorating. Make
smaller flower-shaped cookies to place on top and add dimension.

1. Preheat the oven to 325°F. Line two cookie sheets with
   parchment paper.

2. Combine the flour, baking soda, and cocoa in a bowl; set
   aside.

3. Cream the butter and sugar until fluffy. Beat in the eggs and
   vanilla. Mix in the melted chocolate. Gradually add the flour
   mixture until blended.

4. Cover in plastic wrap and refrigerate for 30 minutes. When
   the dough has chilled, roll out on a cutting board to ¼ inch
   thickness. Refrigerate for 1 hour.

5. Cut the chilled dough into 3½–4-inch circles and 1½-inch
   flower shapes. Transfer to the cookie sheets and bake for 8–10
   minutes, until lightly browned. Transfer to a rack to cool.

6. To make the milk chocolate glaze, melt the chocolate and
   butter in the top of a double boiler set over simmering water.
   Stir in the confectioners' sugar and salt.

7. Spread the glaze on top of the cookies and attach the
   smaller cookies, seeds, nuts, and other toppings. Let dry.

# JEWISH HOLIDAYS

I love having so many Jewish friends—each of their holiday meals is filled with traditional foods, some homemade the old-fashioned way and others boasting modern flavors. Here you will find a selection of treats that are all made with chocolate.

## Chocolate Chip Raisin Rugelach

*Makes 20 cookies*

Rugelach is prepared for several Jewish holidays including Rosh Hashanah (the Jewish New Year) and Hanukkah. Make one batch topped with coarse sugar and the other topped with chocolate chips.

1. Soak the raisins in ¼ cup hot water for 15 minutes. Drain the water and puree the soaked raisins in a food processor with ¼ cup of the granulated sugar and the walnuts. Melt 1½ cups of the chocolate chips and fold into the raisin mixture. Set aside.

2. Preheat the oven to 375°F. Line two baking sheets with parchment paper and grease the paper with butter.

3. Combine the remaining 1¼ cups of granulated sugar with the cinnamon in a small bowl and set aside.

4. Cream the butter, confectioners' sugar, and vanilla until fluffy. Add the cream cheese and blend until smooth. Add the flour and mix until the dough comes together into a ball. Divide the dough into three batches, cover in plastic wrap, and refrigerate for 2 hours.

5. After the dough is chilled, roll out one batch on a lightly floured work surface into a 12 x 16-inch rectangle that is ⅛ inch thick. Spread with a third of the raisin-chip filling. Roll the dough into a long log about 2 ½ inches wide and 1 inch tall and refrigerate for 20 minutes. Prepare the other two logs in the same manner.

6. When the dough is ready, mix the egg with 1 tablespoon of water and brush on the logs. Sprinkle the logs with coarse

---

2 cups raisins

1½ cups granulated sugar

½ cups walnuts, toasted and chopped

2 cups chocolate chips

1 tablespoon ground cinnamon

¾ pound (3 sticks) unsalted butter, at room temperature

¾ cup confectioners' sugar

1 teaspoon vanilla extract

1½ packages (12 ounces) cream cheese, at room temperature

3½ cups all-purpose flour

1 large egg, beaten

4 tablespoons coarse sugar

---

*Opposite, clockwise from top left: Hamantaschen, Chocolate Chip Raisin Rugulach topped with chocolate chips, Chocolate Chip Raisin Rugelach topped with coarse sugar*

sugar. Press the remaining chips into the surface of one log. Cut the logs into 1-inch slices and place on baking sheets 1 inch apart. Bake for 20–30 minutes, until light brown. Remove from the oven and transfer to a rack to cool.

## Chocolate Filling

1 cup semisweet chocolate (at least 50% cacao), melted and cooled

¼ cup granulated sugar

1 tablespoon unsalted butter, melted and cooled

1¼ cups whole milk

1 teaspoon vanilla extract

1 large egg

## Cookies

3 cups all-purpose flour

1½ teaspoons baking powder

⅛ teaspoon salt

½ cup (1 stick) unsalted butter, at room temperature

6 ounces (¾ package) cream cheese, at room temperature

1 teaspoon vanilla extract

2 teaspoons freshly squeezed lemon juice

Zest of 1 lemon

1 cup granulated sugar

2 large eggs

## Decoratation

½ cup semisweet chocolate chips, melted

# Hamantaschen

*Makes fifteen 3½-inch cookies*

These filled cookies with a cream cheese base are traditionally prepared for the Jewish holiday of Purim. The shape of the pastry represents the three-pointed hat that Haman the villain wears in the Purim story. Many types of filling are used for hamantaschen, and chocolate is one of the most popular.

1. Preheat the oven to 350°F. Butter two cookie sheets.

2. To make the filling, combine the chocolate, sugar, butter, milk, and vanilla in a medium bowl. Stir in the egg until combined. Transfer to a saucepan and stir over medium heat for 4–5 minutes, until thick. Remove from the heat and let cool.

3. To make the dough, combine the flour, baking powder, and salt in a medium bowl, and set aside.

4. With a mixer, cream the butter, cream cheese, vanilla, lemon juice, and zest until combined. Beat in the sugar and eggs. Add the flour mixture to the butter mixture until incorporated. Do not overmix. Form the dough into a flat disc, cover in plastic wrap, and chill for 30 minutes.

5. After the dough has chilled, roll it out on a floured work surface to ⅛ inch thickness. Cut the dough into 5-inch rounds using a cookie cutter. Use cold water to wet the edges of the circle halfway around.

6. Score a triangle on the dough without cutting all the way through. Add 1½ tablespoons of filling to the center of each triangle, leaving a clean border around the edges. Using the scored triangle as a guide, fold ¾ inch of the edge of the

dough over toward the middle in three sections, leaving the filling exposed. Pinch the edges together where the dough meets. Transfer to cookie sheets and bake for 30–35 minutes, until golden. Let cool for 5 minutes. Transfer to a rack to cool completely.

7. Place the melted chocolate in a piping bag with a small round tip. Pipe patterns around the cookie. Let set for 20 minutes; then serve.

### Variation

CHOCOLATE HAMANTASCHEN DOUGH WITH PRUNE CHOCOLATE FILLING: For the dough, reduce the flour to 1¾ cups and add ⅓ cup natural unsweetened cocoa powder and 2 additional tablespoons of sugar. Reduce the chocolate in the filling to ¾ cup and add ½ cup pureed prunes.

## Hazelnut Meringues

*Makes 24 cookies*

Since they don't contain any leavening, meringues are Passover-friendly cookies. These are crunchy on the outside and chewy in the middle.

4 large egg whites

2 cups confectioners' sugar

¼ teaspoon salt

½ cup superfine sugar

3 tablespoons natural unsweetened cocoa powder

¾ cup ground hazelnuts

½ cup whole hazelnuts

1. Preheat the oven to 350°F. Line two cookie sheets with parchment paper.

2. Combine the egg whites, confectioners' sugar, and salt in the top of a double boiler set over simmering water and heat, continually stirring, for about 3 minutes, until the mixture is warm to the touch. Transfer to a bowl and beat for 3 more minutes, until thick and glossy. Gradually add the superfine sugar, beating until stiff, glossy peaks form.

3. Sift in the cocoa powder. Fold in the ground hazelnuts and whole hazelnuts.

4. Spoon 2½-inch rounds of dough 2 inches apart on the cookie sheet. Bake for 18–22 minutes, until the meringues are dry and cracked on the top. Turn off the oven and open the door slightly. Leave the pans in the oven for 2 hours to finish drying out the cookies.

5. If after 2 hours they are still warm, transfer the parchment paper and cookies to racks to cool. Peel the cookies off the paper when ready to serve.

## Filling

¼ *cup water*

¾ *cup granulated sugar*

1 *cup light corn syrup*

4½ *cups unsweetened shredded coconut*

¾ *cup marshmallow cream*

1 *teaspoon vanilla extract*

18 *Almond Dragée Eggs (page 193)*

12 *ounces dark chocolate (at least 65% cacao), melted and tempered (page 29)*

2 *ounces milk chocolate (at least 30% cacao), melted and tempered (page 29)*

## Coconut Almond Truffles

*Makes eighteen 2-inch balls*

I use this filling to make chewy coconut truffles as well as coconut patties, although the size, method, and shaping process are different. These truffles have a hidden surprise—a dark chocolate–covered almond—in the center.

1. Line two baking sheets with parchment paper.

2. Combine the water, sugar, and corn syrup in a saucepan. Cook over medium heat until the sugar syrup reaches 245°F.

3. Remove from the heat and stir in the coconut, marshmallow cream, and vanilla. Allow the filling to cool to room temperature.

4. Form the filling into 2-inch spheres using either an ice cream scoop or your hands. Add an almond in the center of each and reshape into a ball. Place on baking sheets.

5. Set out a cooling rack with a rimmed baking sheet underneath. Dip the balls completely into the dark chocolate to coat. If the coating is thin, repeat a second time. Set on the rack and let harden for 2 hours. Drizzle milk chocolate over the balls.

### Variation

COCONUT PATTIES: Once the coconut mixture has cooled, form it into four logs 1½–2 inches high and 8 inches long. Cut into 1-inch pieces. First dip the pieces a third of the way into the dark chocolate, then dip the sides and the bottom. Press a white chocolate chip into the chocolate. Set on a rack to harden.

*Opposite, clockwise from top left: Coconut Almond Truffles, Chocolate Matzo, Hazelnut Meringues, Coconut Patties*

## Chocolate Matzo

*Makes 2¼ pounds*

This Passover favorite tastes even better dipped in chocolate and smothered in almonds. For perfect squares, break the matzo on the perforated seams. For a more handmade feel, break the matzo with a rough edge.

- 1 box (1 pound) square matzo, broken into pieces
- 1 pound semisweet chocolate (at least 50% cacao), melted and tempered (page 29)
- 1 cup slivered almonds

1. Set out a cooling rack with a rimmed baking sheet underneath. Break the matzo into 3-inch squares or 3 x 4-inch rectangles.

2. Hold the matzo by one end and dip it in the chocolate, leaving an inch uncoated. Lie on a cooling rack and top one side with almonds. Let it harden for 30 minutes.

## Chocolate Chip Challah

*Makes one 14-inch loaf*

Challah is a braided egg bread eaten on the Sabbath and Jewish holidays. Here semisweet chocolate chips further sweeten the loaf. It's tasty eaten warm with fruit jam (raspberry is my favorite), or it makes the perfect leftover sweet bread for making German Chocolate French Toast (page 142) or Chocolate Pear Raisin Bread Pudding (page 93). On Rosh Hashanah, shape the braid into a ring and add 1 tablespoon honey (a food that symbolizes new beginnings) to the egg wash.

- ¾ cup warm milk
- ½ cup granulated sugar
- 2 teaspoons active dry yeast
- 4 cups bread flour
- 1 teaspoon kosher salt
- 4 tablespoons (½ stick) unsalted butter, melted
- 2 large eggs
- 1½ cups semisweet chocolate chips
- 1 large egg yolk

1. Combine the milk, 1 teaspoon of the sugar, and the yeast in a small bowl. Let sit until foamy, about 10 minutes.

2. Combine the flour, salt, and remaining sugar in a large bowl and set aside.

3. Whisk the butter and eggs in a large bowl. Add the yeast mixture. Gradually add the flour mixture and stir with a wooden spoon until a dough forms.

4. Transfer the dough to a lightly floured work surface and knead for 6–8 minutes, until smooth. In the last minute, knead in the chocolate chips. Transfer to a lightly greased bowl and cover. Place in a warm place for about 1 hour, until doubled in size. Punch down, cover again, and let rise for 30 minutes.

5. Line a baking sheet with parchment paper. Divide the dough into four equal portions and roll each one into a 16-inch-long rope. Place the ropes on the baking sheet, placing them parallel to one another, and pinch them all together at one end. Braid the ropes, making sure to keep the tension from getting too tight or too loose. Pinch the ends of the braid together to seal. Cover and let rise for 1 hour.

6. Preheat the oven to 375°F. Brush the egg yolk on the surface of the loaf. Bake for 30–35 minutes, until the loaf is dark golden brown. Transfer to a wire rack to let cool.

## Holiday Star Bark

*Makes one 7-inch star*

Once candy is formed into bark, it can be cut into any shape you like. This Star of David can be packaged as a gift or served on a tray at a family gathering. This recipe yields one star; increase the ingredient volumes to make multiples.

1. Draw two diamond shapes that are 3¾ inches in length by 2¼ inches in width on parchment paper. Cut them out to create a template. Draw 6 smaller diamonds on the paper, then flip over the parchment paper and make sure you can see the lines through the paper. Set aside.

2. Line a baking sheet with the larger diamond template and butter the parchment paper.

3. Pour the chocolate onto the buttered parchment paper, spreading it ¼ inch thick over the diamonds. Smooth the surface with an offset spatula. Press dried fruits, nuts, and candies into the surface. Let the chocolate set for 2 hours.

4. To cut the bark into diamond shapes, place the smaller diamond templates over the candy. Use a chef's knife or utility knife to score lines in the chocolate halfway to three-quarters of the way through. Break the chocolate along the lines using your hands. Arrange in a star shape.

*3 ounces milk chocolate (at least 30% cacao), melted and tempered (page 29), with ½ teaspoon shortening added*

*3 ounces dark chocolate (at least 65% cacao), melted and tempered (page 29), with ½ teaspoon shortening added*

*3 ounces white chocolate, melted and tempered (page 29), with ½ teaspoon shortening added*

*1 cup total nuts, dried fruit, and candies: toasted almond slivers, candied orange peel, large coconut chips, dried banana chips, white chocolate candy stars, dried cranberries*

# FOURTH OF JULY

If you're tired of putting American flags on food to make it festive for this holiday, these recipes give you some creative new ideas. Host a chocolaty breakfast featuring the colors of the season, take a hike with some red, white, and blue treats, or enjoy all the fresh seasonal berries in a pie.

## Blueberry Chocolate Chip Buttermilk Pancakes with Raspberry Sauce

*Makes 18 pancakes*

Red, white, and blue berry-and-chocolate pancakes make a festive brunch for the Fourth of July. Serve them with Red Velvet Waffles (page 212) and their respective toppings for an unexpected and colorful chocolate spread.

1½ cups all-purpose flour

3 tablespoons natural unsweetened cocoa powder

½ cup granulated sugar

1½ teaspoons baking powder

½ teaspoon baking soda

½ teaspoon salt

1½ cups buttermilk or whole milk

4 tablespoons (½ stick) unsalted butter, melted and cooled

2 large eggs, separated

1 teaspoon vanilla extract

1 cup fresh or frozen blueberries

1 cup semisweet chocolate chips (at least 50% cacao)

3 tablespoons unsalted butter, for greasing the pan

Raspberry Sauce (page 243)

1. Place a covered baking dish on the middle rack of the oven and preheat to 225°F.

2. Combine the flour, cocoa powder, sugar, baking powder, baking soda, and salt in a large mixing bowl. Make a well in the center and set aside.

3. Whisk together the buttermilk, butter, egg yolks, and vanilla.

4. Pour the buttermilk mixture into the well of the flour mixture and mix with a wooden spoon until combined.

5. Beat the egg whites until they form stiff peaks but are still moist. Gently fold the whites into the batter. Fold in the blueberries and chocolate chips.

6. Heat a large griddle over medium-high heat. Melt some butter on the griddle. Spoon about ⅓ cup batter onto the griddle for each pancake. Cook until the top of each pancake begins to bubble. Turn the pancakes over and cook them on the other side until golden brown. Transfer the cooked pancakes to the covered baking dish to keep warm. Melt more butter on the griddle and repeat with the remaining batter.

7. Place three warm pancakes on each of 6 serving plates, top with raspberry sauce, and serve immediately.

*Opposite: Red Velvet Waffles with Cream Cheese Topping, Blueberry Chocolate Chip Buttermilk Pancakes with Raspberry Sauce*

## Waffles

2½ cups all-purpose flour

¼ teaspoon salt

1 teaspoon baking powder

4 tablespoons natural unsweetened cocoa

3 large eggs, separated

¼ cup granulated sugar

4 tablespoons (½ stick) unsalted butter, melted and cooled

1 cup buttermilk

½ cup whole milk

1 teaspoon vanilla extract

2 tablespoons red food coloring

½ cup chopped pecans

½ cup unsweetened coconut flakes

## Cream Cheese Topping

*Makes 2½ cups*

½ package (4 ounces) cream cheese, at room temperature

4 tablespoons (½ stick) unsalted butter, at room temperature

3 tablespoons confectioners' sugar

1½ cups whole milk, at room temperature

## Garnish

½ cup unsweetened coconut flakes or fresh coconut curls

½ cup chopped pecans

# Red Velvet Waffles with Cream Cheese Topping

*Makes eight 3½ x 5-inch waffles*

The flavors of chocolaty red velvet, tangy cream cheese, and nutty pecans are traditionally paired in a Southern-style layer cake, but in these very special celebratory waffles I have taken those addictive flavors, as well as the lovely colors, and applied them to waffles for a Fourth of July brunch. To complete the spread, prepare them with Blueberry Chocolate Chip Buttermilk Pancakes (page 210).

1. Preheat a waffle iron and lightly grease the surface. Place a covered baking dish on the middle rack of the oven and preheat the oven to 225°F.

2. To make the waffles, combine the flour, salt, baking powder, and cocoa in a large mixing bowl; set aside.

3. Using an electric mixer on high speed, beat the egg whites until soft peaks form. Sprinkle in the sugar and beat until the egg whites are stiff and glossy. Set aside.

4. Using an electric mixer, beat the egg yolks in a medium bowl until frothy. Stir in the butter, buttermilk, whole milk, vanilla extract, and food coloring.

5. Gradually add the yolk mixture to the flour mixture, beating with the electric mixer until smooth. Fold in the egg whites, pecans, and coconut.

6. Spoon about ⅔ cup batter into the waffle iron for each batch, and cook until the waffles are crisp. Remove them from the iron and place in the covered baking dish in the oven to keep warm. Repeat with the remaining batter.

7. To make the topping, combine the cream cheese, butter, sugar, and milk in a medium mixing bowl. Beat with an electric mixer on medium speed until smooth and well blended. If the topping is too thick, add a bit more milk. Drizzle over the warm waffles and top with coconut and pecans.

2 cups rolled oats

1 cup whole wheat flour

¼ cup natural unsweetened cocoa powder

1 cup chopped golden raisins

1 cup chopped dried cherries

½ cup roasted almonds

1 large egg, beaten

½ cup apple juice

½ cup agave nectar

¼ cup firmly packed light brown sugar

1 cup semisweet chocolate chips (at least 50% cacao)

# Chewy Chocolate Fruit Bars

*Makes 16 bars*

For most Americans, the Fourth of July is a get-out-of-town holiday. For my family, it's a day to hit the trails for a day hike. Along the way we snack on these chocolaty, fruity, chewy granola bars and the Red, White, and Blue Berry Chocolate Trail Mix (page 214).

1. Preheat the oven to 325°F. Line a 7 x 12-inch baking pan with parchment paper.

2. Combine the oats, flour, and cocoa powder in a bowl and set aside.

3. Mix the raisins, cherries, and almonds in a bowl. Stir in the oat mixture. Add the egg, apple juice, agave nectar, and sugar. Mix until blended. Fold in the chocolate chips. Spread the mixture in the prepared baking pan and bake for 25–30 minutes. Cool in the pan on a rack. Cut the 7-inch length in half. Cut into 1½ x 3½-inch bars.

*Red, White, and Blue Berry Chocolate Trail Mix, Chewy Chocolate Fruit Bars*

## Red, White, and Blue Berry Chocolate Trail Mix

*Make 3¼ cups*

½ cup dried cherries

½ cup dried cranberries

½ cup dried blueberries

¾ cup whole almonds

½ cup chocolate-covered almonds

½ cup yogurt-covered almonds

This trail mix is a simple recipe for kids to make—all it requires is good measuring skill to perfectly balance the ingredients. Serve in small bowls or pack in plastic bags for travel.

1. Stir all the ingredients together in a large bowl.

## Berry Pie with Chocolate Crust

*Makes one 12-inch pie*

1½ cups raspberries

1½ cups blackberries

2 cups blueberries

2 cups strawberries

1 teaspoon freshly squeezed lemon juice

½ cup granulated sugar

3 tablespoons instant tapioca or ½ cup granola

¼ teaspoon salt

1 tablespoon cold unsalted butter, cut into cubes

Chocolate Butter Crust (page 241)

Nothing says "homemade" more than berry pie. Berries and chocolate make a tasty combination, and this pie is especially good with a drizzle of Chocolate Sauce (page 242). Use 7 cups of any berries—I choose the works: strawberries, raspberries, blackberries, and blueberries. Tapioca is a light thickener, so for an earthier taste replace with ½ cup granola. The dough can be rolled directly on a work surface or between two pieces of plastic wrap or waxed paper.

1. Preheat the oven to 450°F. Butter and flour a 12-inch pie pan.

2. To make the filling, combine the berries and lemon juice in a large bowl and toss to coat. Combine the sugar, tapioca, and salt in a small bowl. Sprinkle over the berries and toss to coat. Gently toss with the butter.

3. To make the bottom crust, roll out the larger disk on a floured work surface, forming a circle about ⅛ inch thick and 14 inches in diameter. Drape the dough over the pie pan, allowing the excess to hang over the rim. Fill the cooled bottom crust with filling.

4. To make the top crust, roll out the smaller disk into a circle about ⅛ inch thick and 13 inches in diameter. Using a pastry wheel or a knife, cut the dough into 12 strips, each just over 1 inch wide. Lay half the strips over the fruit filling, leaving space between the strips. Lay the other half of the strips on top, placing them perpendicular to the bottom strips. You

## MAKING A LATTICE CRUST

Roll out the top crust to a size slightly larger than the diameter of your pie pan. Cut the dough into strips with a knife or a pastry or pizza cutter. Lay half the strips on top of the pie in one direction, leaving space between them, then lay the other half on top of and perpendicular to the bottom strips. You can also weave the strips over and under each other to create a grid. Press the ends of the strips into the bottom crust to seal before crimping the edge with a fork.

can also weave the strips in a basketweave pattern. Press the ends of the strips into the edge of the bottom crust. Fold the bottom crust's overhang over the rim to conceal the edges of the lattice. Seal by pressing together the top and bottom crusts with the tines of a fork.

5. Bake for 15 minutes. Lower the temperature to 375°F and bake for an additional 25–30 minutes, or until the juices are shiny and bubbly. If the edges begin to darken, cover them with a pie shield (page 76). Remove from the oven and cool on a rack.

*Berry Pie with Chocolate Crust, Chocolate Sauce*

# HALLOWEEN AND DAY OF THE DEAD

Chocolate treats are a must-have for a Halloween party. Everyone who's skilled at trick-or-treating ends up with way too many packaged chocolates. Why not make them into bark? Or try creating your own from scratch instead. To celebrate the Day of the Dead, I have included skull-shaped candies and Mexican hot chocolate in honor of the Aztecs and Mayans—the inventors of drinkable chocolate.

## Spicy Hot Chocolate

*Makes 1 cup*

To me, Halloween and the Day of the Dead kick off the fall holiday season perfectly. Even in Southern California, where I live, those holidays mark the start of sweater season and what I think of as hot-chocolate time. This Mexican hot chocolate, created in honor of the Day of the Dead, is spiced with cayenne and chili flakes. Everyone enjoys a different level of hotness, so make it with ¼ teaspoon cayenne first and add more if you like it hotter.

1 cup whole milk

2 tablespoons granulated sugar

¼–½ teaspoon cayenne pepper

½ teaspoon ground cinnamon

½ teaspoon vanilla

4 ounces semisweet chocolate (at least 50% cacao) or Mexican chocolate, melted

2 tablespoons Whipped Cream

Chili flakes to garnish

1. In a small saucepan over medium-low heat, stir the milk, sugar, cayenne pepper, cinnamon, and vanilla together and heat slowly to just below a boil. Remove from the heat, blend in the chocolate, cover, and let sit for 10 minutes.

2. Return to the stove top and reheat over low heat to just below a boil; then pour into a heatproof mug. Top with whipped cream and chili flakes. Serve with Skull Candy with Dulce de Leche Filling (below).

## Skull Candy with Chocolate Dulce de Leche Filling

*Makes twenty-four 1-inch candies*

These chocolate skulls are filled with dulce de leche, a caramel milk candy commonly used in Latin American sweets. Make your own and flavor it with chocolate, or use store-bought vanilla-caramel-flavored dulce de leche and add the chocolate at home. Serve with Spicy Hot Chocolate (page 217).

*Opposite: Spicy Hot Chocolate, Skull Candy with Chocolate Dulce de Leche Filling*

## Chocolate Dulce de Leche

1 vanilla bean

4 cups milk

1¼ cups sugar

½ teaspoon sea salt

1 ounce semisweet chocolate (at least 50% cacao), chopped

1 pound white chocolate, dark chocolate (at least 65% cacao), or milk chocolate (at least 30% cacao), melted and tempered (page 29)

1. To make the chocolate dulce de leche, slice the vanilla bean and scrape the seeds into a large saucepan. Add the milk, sugar, and salt to the saucepan. Whisk the mixture over medium heat until it comes to a full boil. Reduce the heat to a low simmer and cook, stirring occasionally, for 2–2½ hours, until reduced to 1–1½ cups, with a caramel-like thickness. Remove from the heat and stir in the semisweet chocolate. Let cool in the refrigerator for 1 hour.

2. To make the skull shells, use a ladle to fill the mold halfway full with tempered chocolate. Shake the mold around so that the chocolate coats every surface of the cavity. Pour the excess back into the bowl. Let the chocolate set on the countertop for about 5 minutes. When it has begun to set, use a knife to scrape off any excess chocolate that is on the top of the mold (not in the cavities). Allow the chocolate to set completely.

3. Add the dulce de leche to a piping bag fitted with a small round tip. Pipe the filling into molds, leaving ³⁄₁₆ inch at the top. Refrigerate for 15 minutes.

4. Pour additional chocolate on top to seal the bottoms of the candies. Let set on the countertop for 30 minutes, place in the refrigerator for 30 minutes, then return to room temperature before releasing from the mold. Invert the mold over a piece of parchment paper and tap to release.

1 pound milk chocolate (at least 30% cacao), melted and tempered (page 29)

1½ teaspoons vegetable shortening

2 cups candy corn

## Candy Corn Bark

*Makes 1½ pounds*

Wondering what to do with all that leftover candy from trick-or-treating or looking for a novel way to use pumpkin seeds? Make it into candy bark! Any type of candy, seed, or nut can be prepared into bark. Use the same types of candies in one bark or mix various ones together to create novel flavors.

1. Line a baking sheet with parchment paper and butter the parchment.

*Pumpkin Seed, Milk Chocolate and White Chocolate Almond, and Candy Corn Barks*

4 medium sweet-tart apples, such as Braeburn, Fuji, or Gala, rinsed, dried, and stems removed

4 wooden pop sticks, chopsticks, or 6-inch-long wooden dowels

1 bag (14 ounces) individually wrapped caramels, unwrapped

1 tablespoon heavy cream or whole milk

1 cup miniature marshmallows

1 tablespoon water

12 ounces dark chocolate (at least 65% cacao), milk chocolate (at least 30% cacao), or white chocolate, chopped

1 tablespoon shortening

1 cup chopped salted almonds, pecans, or peanuts

2. After tempering the chocolate, add the shortening and stir until melted.

3. Pour the chocolate onto the parchment, spreading it into a rectangle that is ¼ inch thick. Smooth the surface with an offset spatula. Press the candy corn into the surface. Let set for 3 hours to cool, and then break the candy into bark.

**Variations**

PUMPKIN SEED BARK: Replace the candy corn with 1 cup shelled pepitas (pumpkin seeds).

MILK CHOCOLATE AND WHITE CHOCOLATE ALMOND BARK: Replace the candy corn with 1 cup white chocolate chips and 1 cup white Almond Dragée Eggs, either store-bought or homemade (page 193).

## Chocolate Caramel Marshmallow Apples

*Makes 4 candied apples*

These double-dipped apples—dunked first in caramel, then in chocolate—are a twist on the classic Halloween favorite. If you're lucky, the caramel and chocolate will flow onto the parchment paper a bit, giving you even more candy-coated goodness. This recipe calls for medium-size apples for a hearty dessert or snack, but if you are looking for a bite-size dessert, try using the small Lady apples that appear in markets in the fall. If you're looking for another variation, replace the apples with firm but slightly soft pears. Remember to push the stick all the way into the center of the apple and to chill the apples before dipping to ensure that the apple doesn't fall off the stick and that the coating adheres securely to the fruit.

1. Line a baking sheet with parchment paper. Press a pop stick into the center of each apple until it reaches halfway through. Arrange the apples on the baking sheet and refrigerate for 1 hour.

2. Combine the caramels, cream, marshmallows, and water in the top of a double boiler set over simmering water. Stir until the caramels are almost melted. Remove from the heat and stir until smooth. Dip each apple into the caramel

mixture, coating it thoroughly. Allow the excess to drip back into the pan. Place the coated apples on the baking sheet and refrigerate for 1 hour, or until the coating has hardened.

3. Line a second baking sheet with another piece of parchment paper. Combine the chocolate and shortening in the top of a double boiler set over simmering water and stir until the ingredients are just melted. Turn off the heat. Dip each coated apple a quarter of the way into the chocolate and return it to the baking sheet. Sprinkle with nuts toward the bottom of the apple and on the caramel chocolate that has flowed onto the parchment paper. Refrigerate until hardened, about 1 hour.

## Chocolate Cream Cheese Dough

1¾ cups all-purpose flour

1 teaspoon baking powder

2 tablespoons Dutch-process cocoa powder

¼ teaspoon salt

⅓ cup (⅔ stick) unsalted butter, at room temperature

3 ounces cream cheese, at room temperature

⅔ cup granulated sugar

1 large egg

½ teaspoon vanilla extract

### Filling

Chocolate Dulce de Leche (page 217)

## Thumbprint Cookies with Dulce de Leche Filling

*Makes 20 cookies*

Thumbprints are very simple drop cookies—to make them, just press your finger in the middle of one of the dough drops to create a cavity that will hold the filling. These are filled with chocolate dulce de leche. If you like a fluid caramel candy, do not refrigerate these cookies; for a thicker filling, place the cookies in the refrigerator for 30 minutes before serving, or keep stored in the refrigerator.

1. Preheat the oven to 350°F. Line two baking sheets with parchment paper.

2. Combine the flour, baking powder, cocoa powder, and salt in a bowl and set aside.

3. Beat the butter, cream cheese, and sugar until blended; then add the egg and vanilla and mix. Gradually add the flour mixture until blended. Form the dough into 1½-inch balls. Flatten them slightly; then press into the center with your thumb to leave an indentation. Place them 2 inches apart on the cookie sheets and bake for 10–12 minutes, until set. Set on a rack to cool.

4. Spoon the filling into the indentions in the center of the cookies. Refrigerate for 30 minutes before serving.

### Variation

THUMBPRINTS WITH CHOCOLATE FILLING: Use Chocolate Filling (page 81) instead of Dulce de Leche Filling.

# THANKSGIVING

Although chocolate is not usually associated with Thanksgiving, it complements some of the most anticipated tastes of the holiday: pecan, pumpkin, and cranberry. Since Thanksgiving is also known as the pie holiday, chocolate makes an appearance here in many family favorites.

## Crust

*Chocolate Butter Crust (page 241)*

## Chocolate Pecan Filling

3 large eggs, beaten
¾ cup firmly packed dark brown sugar
¼ cup maple syrup
¼ teaspoon salt
3 tablespoons unsalted butter, melted
2 tablespoons bourbon
1 teaspoon vanilla extract
3 ounces dark chocolate (at least 65% cacao), melted
3 cups chopped pecan halves
¼ cup whole pecan halves

## Chocolate Bourbon Pecan Pie

*Makes one 9-inch pie*

The pecan is the only major nut tree that grows wild in North America, making pecans a favorite of indigenous people in the central, eastern, and southern United States. Today, some residents can still forage for nuts to bake into their traditional Thanksgiving pies. Chocolate adds a fudgy taste and gooey texture; the bourbon adds a subtle touch of the South.

1. Butter and flour a 9-inch pie pan. Preheat the oven to 325°F.

2. On a floured work surface, roll out the chilled pastry disc to form a circle about ⅛ inch thick and 12 inches in diameter. Drape the dough over the pie pan, allowing the excess to hang over the rim. Press the dough into the bottom edges, then fold the top edges onto the rim and crimp decoratively.

3. To make the filling, combine the eggs, sugar, maple syrup, salt, butter, bourbon, vanilla, and melted chocolate in large bowl. Stir in the chopped pecans and pour the filling into the crust. Arrange the pecan halves on top in a decorative pattern.

4. Bake for 45–50 minutes, or until set. Cool on a rack to room temperature.

### Variations

CHOCOLATE ORANGE PECAN PIE: Omit the bourbon and add 1 teaspoon grated orange zest in step 3.

CHOCOLATE RUM PECAN PIE: Replace the bourbon with ¼ cup golden rum.

## Crust

4 ounces dark chocolate (at least
   65% cacao), melted and tempered (page 29)

Sweet Chocolate Tart Crust
   (page 241)

## Pumpkin Filling

4 large eggs

⅓ cup granulated sugar

⅓ cup firmly packed dark brown
   sugar

2 cups canned pumpkin puree

1 teaspoon ground ginger

1¾ teaspoons ground cinnamon

½ teaspoon ground cloves

½ teaspoon ground allspice

½ teaspoon ground cardamom

⅛ teaspoon salt

1 cup heavy cream

½ cup half-and-half

1½ cups Whipped Cream
   (page 244)

## Pumpkin Tart

*Makes one 11-inch tart*

It's my belief that Thanksgiving cannot be called a celebration without a pumpkin recipe. The smooth texture of this tart showcases the spices in the pumpkin filling, and the delicate chocolate crust makes this a good choice for chocolate lovers. The chocolate leaves provide a hint to the hidden surprise—the layer of dark chocolate that lines the crust. Pile a tall batch of whipped cream in the center of the pie, or serve individual slices with Whipped Cream (page 244) and chocolate pieces.

1. Using half the melted and tempered chocolate, fill leaf molds to the top and tap on a countertop to allow bubbles to rise to the surface. Set aside on the countertop or in the refrigerator to set. Keep the remaining chocolate warm in the double boiler.

2. Preheat the oven to 450°F. Butter and flour an 11-inch tart pan.

3. On a floured work surface, roll out the large pastry disc to about ¼ inch thick and 13 inches in diameter. Place it over the pie pan, allowing any excess to hang over the rim. Press into the bottom of the pan, making the crust flush with the

rim of the pan. Prick the bottom of the crust with a fork. Line with parchment paper and fill with pie weights. Blind-bake for 7–10 minutes. Remove from the oven and transfer to a rack. Reduce the oven temperature to 350°F.

4. Pour the remaining melted chocolate into the shell, covering the bottom and sides.

5. To make the filling, beat the eggs and sugars in a large bowl. Beat in the pumpkin, ginger, 1½ teaspoons of the cinnamon, cloves, allspice, cardamom, and salt until blended. Stir in the cream and the half-and-half until smooth. Set aside.

6. Pour the filling into the piecrust and bake the pie for 10 minutes. Reduce the heat to 325°F and bake for another 40–50 minutes, until a knife inserted in the center comes out clean. Cool on a rack to room temperature. Top with chocolate leaves and whipped cream. Sprinkle the whipped cream with cinnamon.

**Variation**

BANANA RUM PUMPKIN PIE: Reduce the pumpkin puree to 1½ cups. Add 2 mashed ripe bananas and 3 tablespoons dark rum to the filling.

---

### Cranberry Filling

2¼ cups fresh whole cranberries

1 cup granulated sugar

1 cup water

½ teaspoon grated orange zest

---

## Cranberry Chocolate Crostata

*Makes one 9-inch crostata*

When cranberries are in season I add them to all my chocolate recipes. Some of my favorites are cranberry chocolate chip cookies, chocolate cake with cranberry filling, cranberry gingerbread tarts, and this Cranberry Chocolate Crostata. A crostata is a traditional Italian dessert tart, usually filled with cherry, peach, apricot, or berry jam. It makes an excellent choice to encase cranberry filling, which gets very juicy while baking. The large opening in the center allows the extra juice to evaporate. Crostatas are meant to look rustic, so there's no need to worry about creating picture-perfect edges. Just make sure that the rim is folded over enough to contain the filling during baking and that there is enough cranberry filling exposed and not covered with crust in order for the moisture to escape. Crostatas are baked directly on a

## Pastry

1¾ cups all-purpose flour

½ cup natural unsweetened cocoa
   powder

¼ cup granulated sugar

¼ teaspoon salt

¾ cup (1½ sticks) cold unsalted
   butter, cut into cubes

3 tablespoons ice water

1½ teaspoons vanilla extract

3 tablespoons cornmeal

## Topping

1 large egg white, beaten

2 tablespoons sifted confectioners'
   sugar

baking stone to brown the bottom nicely. If you don't have a baking stone, use a baking sheet lined with parchment paper.

1. To make the cranberry filling, combine 2 cups of the cranberries, the sugar, water, and orange zest in a medium saucepan and bring to a boil over medium heat. Lower the heat and cook for 10 minutes, stirring occasionally, until thickened. Remove from the heat and stir in the remaining ¼ cup cranberries. Cover and chill in the refrigerator until ready to use.

2. To make the dough, combine the flour, cocoa powder, sugar, and salt. With a pastry blender or your fingertips, mix in the butter until the mixture resembles coarse meal.

3. Combine the ice water and vanilla in a small bowl, then add to the dough and stir until the dough forms a ball. Add a little more water if necessary. Flatten into a disk, cover with plastic wrap, and chill for 1 hour.

4. Dust a baking stone with cornmeal and preheat the oven to 400°F.

5. On a floured work surface, roll the dough into a circle 14 inches in diameter. Use a large plate as a template if necessary. Place the dough on the baking stone.

6. Drain the excess liquid from the filling and spread the filling over the dough, leaving a 2½-inch border. Fold the border of the dough up and around the filling, creasing and pressing down to hold the dough in place. Brush the border with the beaten egg white.

7. Bake for 45–50 minutes, until the crust is browned and the juices are bubbling. Cool for 30 minutes on a rack. Sprinkle the crust with confectioners' sugar. Serve warm.

**Variation**

PEAR CROSTATA WITH CHOCOLATE CRUST: Replace the cranberry filling with pear filling. To make the filling, gently combine 4 peeled, cored, and sliced Bosc pears, ½ cup brown sugar, 3 tablespoons freshly squeezed lemon juice, ½ teaspoon vanilla, ½ teaspoon ground cinnamon, 1½ tablespoons flour, and 1½ teaspoons cornstarch.

## Marbled Chocolate Pumpkin Bread

*Makes one 4½ x 8½-inch loaf*

A light breakfast is a good way to kick off the Thanksgiving holiday, leaving plenty of room for the large holiday meal. This bread adds a nice holiday flavor to the beginning of the day, so indulge in a slice.

1½ cups all-purpose flour

1 teaspoon baking soda

¼ teaspoon baking powder

1 teaspoon salt

1½ teaspoons ground cinnamon

1 teaspoon ground ginger

½ teaspoon grated nutmeg

¼ teaspoon ground cloves

6 tablespoons (¾ stick) butter, at room temperature

¾ cup granulated sugar

¾ cup firmly packed light brown sugar

2 large eggs

⅓ cup whole milk

½ teaspoon vanilla extract

1 cup pumpkin puree

½ cup chopped walnuts

3 ounces semisweet chocolate (at least 50% cacao), melted

1. Preheat the oven to 350°F. Butter and flour a 4½ x 8½-inch loaf pan.

2. Combine the flour, baking soda, baking powder, salt, cinnamon, ginger, nutmeg, and cloves in a mixing bowl.

3. Beat the butter and sugars in a large mixing bowl with an electric mixer on medium speed until creamy. Add the eggs one at a time, beating well after each addition. Beat in the milk, vanilla, pumpkin puree, and walnuts. Gradually add the flour mixture on low speed until blended. Divide the batter in half and add the melted chocolate to one batch.

4. Transfer the batters to the pan and swirl together with a knife. Bake for 55–60 minutes, or until a knife inserted in the center comes out clean. Cool in the pan for 10 minutes. Transfer to a rack to cool completely.

# CHRISTMAS

Gifting chocolate in all forms—from candy to cookies—is more thoughtful and gratifying for both the giver and the recipient than giving store-bought gifts. Sometimes a traditional chocolate candy treat is just what is needed; at other times you want a new recipe that includes the flavors that have become synonymous with seasonal holidays. After all, chocolate is sometimes a bit naughty—but always nice.

## Chocolate-Covered Gingerbread Men

*Makes twelve 5-inch cookies*

Molasses and cider vinegar give this gingerbread cookie its classic flavor. The chocolate coating helps keep the decorations attached. These cookies are coated with chocolate on both the bottom and the top, but to save some time you can always coat just the top.

4¾ cups all-purpose flour

⅓ cup natural unsweetened cocoa powder

½ teaspoon salt

1 teaspoon baking powder

1 teaspoon ground cinnamon

1 teaspoon grated nutmeg

¼ teaspoon ground cloves

2 teaspoons ground ginger

½ pound (2 sticks) unsalted butter, at room temperature

1 cup firmly packed dark brown sugar

⅔ cup unsulfured molasses

1 large egg

1 teaspoon cider vinegar

12 ounces milk chocolate (at least 30% cacao), melted and tempered (page 29)

1 tablespoon shortening

½ cup assorted candies for decorating (sprinkles, grated chocolate, chocolate chips)

*Opposite, top: Chocolate-Covered Gingerbread Men; bottom: Chocolate Gingerbread Cake*

1. Combine the flour, cocoa powder, salt, baking powder, cinnamon, nutmeg, cloves, and ginger; set aside.

2. Cream the butter and sugar until light and fluffy. Add the molasses, egg, and vinegar. Gradually add the flour mixture until combined. Divide the batch in two and flatten into disks. Cover the disks in plastic wrap and chill for 1 hour.

3. Preheat the oven to 350°F. Line two cookie sheets with parchment paper. On a floured work surface, roll out the dough until ¼ inch thick. Cut gingerbread men using a 5-inch cookie cutter or a utility knife and place 1½ inches apart on cookie sheets. Bake for 12–14 minutes, until the cookies are light brown around the edges. Remove from the oven and transfer to a rack with a rimmed baking sheet underneath to cool.

4. Combine the melted chocolate with the shortening and stir until smooth. Invert the cookies so the bottoms are facing up. Pour the melted chocolate-shortening mixture over the cookies and let the excess chocolate drip onto the baking sheet. Return the extra chocolate to a double boiler.

5. Let the cookies harden for 2 hours on the rack. Flip them over, remelt the chocolate, and cover the tops. Decorate with candies while still wet. Let sit for 2 hours to dry.

## Chocolate Gingerbread Cake

*Makes eighty-one 1-inch cubes*

This cake is cut into small cubes and left un-iced to bring out the subtle flavors, although it also tastes great coated in chocolate. Try it with Chocolate-Amaretto Fondue (page 166).

1¾ cups all-purpose flour

⅓ cup Dutch-process cocoa powder

½ teaspoon baking soda

1 teaspoon baking powder

1 tablespoon ground ginger

1 teaspoon ground cinnamon

½ teaspoon ground allspice

¼ teaspoon grated nutmeg

¼ teaspoon ground cloves

¼ teaspoon salt

1 cup firmly packed light brown sugar

6 tablespoons (¾ stick) unsalted butter, melted

⅓ cup unsulfured molasses

2 large eggs

1 tablespoon grated peeled fresh ginger

1¼ cups warm whole milk

1. Preheat the oven to 350°F. Butter a square 9-inch baking pan.

2. Combine the flour, cocoa powder, baking soda, baking powder, ginger, cinnamon, allspice, nutmeg, cloves, and salt; set aside.

3. In a medium bowl, combine the sugar, butter, molasses, eggs, and fresh ginger and beat until blended. Add the flour mixture in three rounds, alternating with the milk. Pour the batter into the prepared pan. Bake for 25–30 minutes, or until a tester comes out clean. Cool on the rack for 20 minutes. Invert the cake onto a rack and cool completely. Cut into 1-inch cubes to serve.

1 cup light corn syrup

⅓ cup clover honey

¾ cup granulated sugar

⅓ cup water

2 large egg whites

2 teaspoons vanilla extract

2 cups whole hazelnuts, pistachios, almonds, or dried fruit

1 teaspoon cornstarch

16 ounces dark chocolate (at least 65% cacao), melted and tempered (page 29)

## Torrone Candy Bars

*Makes 24 small (1½ x 2-inch) bars or 8 large (1½ x 6-inch) bars*

Instead of spending time out on the town, frazzled by the Christmas frenzy, I find it more comforting to carry out my Italian family traditions at home during the holiday season. Torrone, a honey nougat filled with nuts or dried fruit or both, has been a welcome surprise in Christmas stockings throughout Italy since the fifteenth century. I love making it for friends as gifts. Today, many regions of the world have their own version of this chewy candy. This recipe calls for the torrone to be covered in dark chocolate, making it similar to the torrones often included in boxed assortments of chocolates. To achieve the candy's signature chewy texture, incorporate part of the sugar syrup at 240°F and part at 275°F. Work quickly when you're beating the eggs, since you want to add the first batch of syrup at temperature. In addition, you can use this method of pouring chocolate over caramel, caramel-and-peanut mixtures, or nougat-and-peanut mixtures to make some of your other favorite candy bars. To make the candy easier to handle, dust it with cornstarch and wrap it in waxed paper. You can also wrap it in edible rice paper, found in Asian grocery stores—that way you can eat your candy and the wrapper, too!

1. Set out a cooling rack with a rimmed baking sheet underneath. Butter a 9 x 9-inch baking dish and dust it with cornstarch.

2. In a heavy medium saucepan over medium heat, combine the corn syrup, honey, sugar, and water, stirring until the sugar is dissolved and the mixture begins to boil. Stop stirring and cook until the mixture reaches the soft ball stage, 236–240°F. Pour 1 cup of the mixture into a heatproof measuring cup. Leave the remaining syrup in the saucepan with the heat on low.

3. In a clean medium bowl, using an electric mixer with clean beaters, beat the egg whites until soft peaks form. From a height, slowly pour the hot syrup from the measuring cup into the egg whites in a thin stream, beating with the mixer at medium speed. Continue beating until the remaining syrup in the saucepan reaches the soft crack stage (275°F); then pour it into the heatproof measuring cup and, using

the same technique, gradually add it to the egg mixture. Continue beating for about 10 minutes, or until the mixture has cooled. Stir in the vanilla and 1 cup of the nuts or fruit.

4. Dip a metal spatula in cold water and use it to spread the torrone in the baking dish, smoothing the top as you go. Top with the remaining nuts or fruit. Dust the cornstarch on top. Cover with plastic wrap and let set for 2 hours.

5. Dust a cutting board with cornstarch. Run a knife along the edge of the baking dish to loosen the candy. Invert the pan onto the cutting board and unmold. Cut the candy into small (1½ x 2-inch) bars or large (1½ x 6-inch) bars. Transfer to the cooling rack.

6. Divide the chocolate in half into two bowls. Dip the bottom of the bars into one half of the melted and tempered chocolate and set on the rack for 30 minutes. When the chocolate has hardened, turn the bars over, chocolate-side down, and pour the remaining melted and tempered chocolate over them. Let the bars harden for 1 hour. Store in an airtight container with waxed paper between the layers, or wrap the bars individually in waxed paper. Store at room temperature for up to 2 weeks.

### Variations

PEANUT NOUGAT BARS: Omit the honey and increase the granulated sugar to 1 cup. Substitute peanuts for the other nuts and dried fruit.
CHOCOLATE NOUGAT TORRONE: Add 3 ounces melted dark chocolate (at least 65% cacao) with the vanilla.

## Chocolate-Cherry Almond Panforte de Sienna
*Makes one 8-inch cake*
This rich, fruit-filled, candy-like Italian cake (the name actually means "strong bread") is the perfect note to end a holiday meal. It is traditionally served in small slices along with a digestive drink such as grappa, port, or dessert wine, or with a wedge of well-aged Parmesan cheese. This recipe uses French Valrhona cocoa powder for a very intense chocolate flavor and mahogany color. If you can't find it, substitute natural

*Chocolate-Cherry Almond Panforte de Sienna*

## Panforte

1½ cups whole almonds, toasted (page 28)

1½ cups all-purpose flour

2 tablespoons bread crumbs

½ cup chopped candied citrus peel

1 cup dried cherries

½ cup dried mission figs

⅓ cup Valrhona cocoa powder or natural unsweetened cocoa powder

½ teaspoon ground cinnamon

¼ teaspoon ground cloves

¼ teaspoon ground ginger

¼ teaspoon grated nutmeg

¾ cup granulated sugar

¾ cup clover honey

3 ounces dark chocolate (at least 65% cacao), chopped

¼ cup unsalted butter

### Chocolate Spice Topping

1 tablespoon confectioners' sugar

1 teaspoon natural unsweetened cocoa powder

1 teaspoon ground cinnamon

½ teaspoon ground cardamom

unsweetened cocoa powder. For gifting, wrap in waxed paper first; then add a decorative patterned paper around that. Seal with string or sticker.

1. Preheat the oven to 300°F. Line an 8-inch round springform pan with parchment paper.

2. Grind ½ cup of the almonds in a food processor and coarsely chop the remaining 1 cup with a knife. Combine 2 tablespoons of the ground almonds, 1 tablespoon of the flour, and the bread crumbs in a small bowl. Sprinkle the mixture on the bottom of the pan.

3. Combine the remaining ground and chopped nuts, remaining flour, candied citrus peel, dried cherries, dried figs, cocoa powder, cinnamon, cloves, ginger, and nutmeg. Stir to mix and set aside.

4. Combine the granulated sugar, honey, chocolate, and butter in a small saucepan over low heat, and stir until the sugar is dissolved and the chocolate and butter are melted. Continue cooking, stirring constantly, for 3 minutes, until the butter is bubbly. Add the melted butter mixture to the nut mixture and stir to combine.

5. When the mixture has cooled enough to touch, press it into the prepared pan. Bake for 50–60 minutes, until firm and a knife inserted in the center comes out clean. Let cool in the pan for at least 30 minutes.

6. To make the chocolate spice topping, combine the confectioners' sugar, cocoa powder, cinnamon, and cardamom in a small bowl. Sprinkle on top of the cooled cake. Cut the cake in thin slices to serve.

**Variations**

CRANBERRY PISTACHIO PANFORTE: Replace the dried cherries with dried cranberries and the almonds with pistachios.

APRICOT HAZELNUT PANFORTE: Replace the dried cherries with chopped dried apricots. Replace the almonds with hazelnuts. Add 2 tablespoons orange juice to the dough.

½ cup granulated sugar

½ cup water

1 tablespoon light corn syrup

Peel of 2 oranges, cut into thin strips

Peel of 3 lemons, cut into thin strips

2 unpeeled oranges, sliced into thin rings

24 ounces chopped dark chocolate (at least 65% cacao), melted and tempered (page 29)

⅓ pound crystallized ginger

⅓ pound dried mission figs

⅓ pound dried plums

¼ pound dried kiwifruit

¼ pound dried cherries

½ pound dried apricots

## Chocolate-Dipped Dried and Candied Fruit

*Makes 4½ pounds*

Although dried and candied fruits get a bad rap when made into fruitcake, they take on a beautiful elegance worthy of contemporary gifting when they're dipped in chocolate. Dipping is as easy as can be, as is creating homemade candied orange and lemon peels. Make the candied fruits the day before so they will be rigid when it's time for dipping. To supplement the orange and lemon, choose 2 pounds of additional varieties of moist, plump dried fruit in flavor combinations that suit your taste. Place a sheet of waxed paper between the layers when packaging for gifting or storing.

1. Set out a cooling rack with a rimmed baking sheet underneath to catch drippings.

2. Bring the sugar, water, and corn syrup to a boil in a medium saucepan over medium heat. Add the orange peel, lemon peel, and orange slices and boil for 20 minutes, stirring occasionally. Using tongs, remove the fruit from the liquid and place the pieces on the wire rack. Let dry uncovered overnight.

3. After the fruit has dried, set out a second wire cooling rack with a rimmed baking sheet underneath. Hold each piece of dried fruit by the stem or the side. Dip the fruit halfway into the chocolate and set on the rack to dry. To coat the fruit fully, use a fork to dip the whole piece into the chocolate. Remove the fruit from the chocolate, shake over the pot several times to remove excess chocolate, then place on the cooling rack. Repeat until all the fruit is dipped or coated. Return the excess chocolate from the baking sheet to the pot and remelt if needed.

4. Let the fruit sit on the cooling rack for about 1 hour, or until the chocolate hardens. Peel the fruit off the cooling rack and serve. To store, place in an airtight container with waxed paper between the layers. Store in a cool, dry place for up to 2 weeks.

1 pound dark chocolate (at least 65% cacao), melted and tempered (page 29)

1 pound white chocolate, melted and tempered (page 29)

1 tablespoon vegetable shortening

½ cup coarsely crushed peppermint candies

## White and Dark Chocolate Peppermint Bark

*Makes 2¼ pounds*

Peppermint bark is one of the easiest and most impressive homemade gifts to make. Layering dark, white, and peppermint chocolate gives this candy a true holiday flavor. Eat it with a warm glass of Spicy Hot Chocolate (page 217). This bark can also be used to decorate cakes, or to top pudding or ice cream—just break it into small pieces and adorn each serving with a piece.

1. Line a baking sheet with parchment paper and butter the parchment.

2. Combine the melted, tempered dark chocolate and 1½ teaspoons of the shortening in the top of a double boiler set over simmering water. Stir until melted and combined.

3. Pour the chocolate onto the parchment paper, spreading into a rectangular shape to ¼ inch thickness. Smooth the surface with an offset spatula. Let set undisturbed for 1 hour.

4. Combine the melted, tempered white chocolate and the remaining 1½ teaspoons of shortening in the top of a double boiler set over simmering water and stir until melted. Pour the white chocolate over the dark chocolate rectangle. Smooth the surface with an offset spatula. Sprinkle with peppermint candies. Let set for 2 hours to harden, then break the candy into bark.

### Chocolate Ladyfingers

5 large egg yolks

¾ cup granulated sugar

6 large egg whites

1 cup all-purpose flour

¼ cup natural unsweetened cocoa powder

¼ cup confectioners' sugar

## Milk Chocolate Eggnog Cream Trifle with Red Currants

*Makes six 8-ounce servings*

Trifles are sponge cakes or cookies soaked in liquor or coffee, interspersed with layers of cream or pudding. In this recipe I take one of the most popular drinks of the season, eggnog, and make it into a chocolate pudding. The trifle features ladyfingers around the edge of each glass. Fresh currants, hard to find most of the year, are most readily available and at their tastiest in the Christmas season.

1. To make the ladyfingers, preheat the oven to 425°F. Fit a ½-inch tip onto a pastry bag. Cut parchment paper to the

## Eggnog Pudding

⅓ cup cornstarch

¾ cup granulated sugar

3 large egg yolks

3 cups eggnog

6 ounces milk chocolate (at least
    30% cacao), melted

1 teaspoon vanilla extract

1 tablespoon golden rum

## For Finishing

2 tablespoons golden rum for
    soaking

½ cup fresh red currants

2 cups Chocolate Whipped Cream
    (page 244)

size of the cookie sheets and draw parallel lines across the paper lengthwise, 2½ inches apart. Flip the paper over and put it on cookie sheets. You should see the lines through the paper; if you don't, darken them until you can.

2. Beat the egg yolks with 2 tablespoons of the sugar for 2 minutes, until well blended.

3. Beat the egg whites until they form stiff peaks. Gradually add the remaining ½ cup plus 2 tablespoons sugar and beat until firm. Fold the egg whites into the egg yolk mixture. Gradually fold in the flour and cocoa powder.

4. Place half the batter into the pastry bag and pipe the ladyfingers in strips along the lines you drew on the parchment paper, making them 1 inch wide, 4 inches long, and ¾ inch high. Continue until you use all the batter. Dust with the confectioners' sugar.

5. Bake for 8–10 minutes. Remove from the oven, slide the parchment paper onto racks, and let cool.

6. To make the eggnog pudding, mix the cornstarch and ¼ cup of the sugar in a medium heatproof bowl. Add the egg yolks and stir to form a paste. Stir in ½ cup of the eggnog.

7. Combine the remaining 2½ cups eggnog and the remaining ½ cup sugar in a saucepan and bring to a boil over medium heat. Pour into the paste mixture and beat well.

8. Pour the mixture back into the saucepan and cook over medium heat for 7–10 minutes, or until thick and smooth. Remove from the heat, stir in the melted chocolate, vanilla, and rum, and continue to stir for an additional minute.

9. To assemble the trifle, brush the ladyfingers with rum. Add a few currants to each serving dish. Place the ladyfingers standing up around the sides of each dish. Fill each dish halfway with eggnog pudding and a little whipped cream. Add more currants. Top again with eggnog pudding and whipped cream. Add currants on top. Cover in plastic wrap and chill for 3 hours before serving.

## Green Tea Cupcakes

1½ cups (3 sticks) unsalted butter, at room temperature

1¼ cups granulated sugar

6 large eggs, separated

1 teaspoon vanilla extract

3 cups self-rising flour

3 tbsp matcha powder (optional)

¼ teaspoon cream of tartar

## Dark Chocolate Pudding Filling

¼ teaspoon salt

2½ tablespoons cornstarch

3 ounces Dutch-processed cocoa powder

1 large egg

2 egg yolks

2½ cups whole milk, divided

⅓ cup granulated sugar

2 tablespoons unsalted butter

1 teaspoon vanilla extract

6 ounces dark chocolate (at least 65% cacao), melted

## Toppings

12 strawberries

¼ cup Vanilla Icing (page 243)

24 semisweet chocolate chips

# Matcha Green Tea Sponge Cupcakes with Chocolate Pudding Filling

*Makes 12 large 3½-inch cupcakes*

These delightfully cute, strawberry-adorned green and red cupcakes were inspired by Chinese, Japanese, and Korean Christmas cakes. I love the airy, light sponge cakes found in Asian bakeries, and they're even better when flavored with green tea. The chocolate pudding in the center of the cupcakes complements the taste of the green tea nicely. If you beat enough air into the sponge cake batter, you just might get cupcakes so fluffy they almost pop out of the pan.

1. Preheat the oven to 350°F. Arrange the oven racks so that one of them is at the highest possible position. Line twelve large 3½-inch muffin cups with paper liners.

2. Beat the butter and sugar in a large mixing bowl with an electric mixer on medium speed until pale and creamy.

3. Beat in the egg yolks and vanilla, then gradually beat in the flour on low speed. Mix in the matcha powder. Set aside.

4. In a clean bowl with clean beaters, beat the egg whites and cream of tartar until stiff peaks form. Gradually fold the egg whites into the batter with a rubber spatula.

5. Divide the batter among the liners and bake on the top rack for 15–20 minutes, or until golden brown and a knife inserted in the center comes out clean. Cool in the pans for 10 minutes, then transfer to a rack to cool completely.

6. To make the pudding, combine the salt, cornstarch, and cocoa in a small bowl and set aside.

7. In a medium bowl, beat the whole egg and two yolks with ½ cup milk for about 1 minute, until blended and foamy.

8. Bring the remaining milk and sugar to a boil in a heavy saucepan over medium-high heat, making sure not to scald the milk. Lower the heat to medium. Add the dry ingredients that you set aside in step 6 and stir until

blended. Gradually add the egg mixture and stir until the pudding thickens. Remove from the heat and add the butter, vanilla, and melted chocolate. Cool for 15 minutes, until thick but not set.

9. Use a knife to remove some of the center of each cupcake to make a well for the filling. Transfer the pudding to a piping bag set with a large round tip and pipe into the well. Cover and refrigerator for 2 hours to set the pudding.

10. To make the strawberry topping, cut two grooves in the lower half of the strawberry and remove a wedge piece. Pipe two dots of vanilla frosting on the strawberry and top with chocolate chips to create eyes. Place one strawberry on the top of each cupcake and serve.

### Variation

LAYERED SPONGE CAKE: Instead of using muffin tins, bake the cake in two buttered and floured 8-inch cake pans for 25–30 minutes. Cut each of the cakes in half lengthwise, making four layers. Add the pudding between the layers and top with Chocolate Buttercream (page 243) and strawberries.

# Chapter 6
# Crusts, Sauces, and Toppings

## CRUSTS

2⅓ cups all-purpose flour

¼ cup Dutch-process cocoa powder

2 tablespoons granulated sugar

½ teaspoon salt

½ pound (2 sticks) cold unsalted butter, cut into cubes

6 tablespoons cold water

### Chocolate Butter Crust

*Makes one 9-inch single-crust pie with appliqué border or one 9-inch double-crust pie*

1. Combine the flour, cocoa powder, sugar, and salt in a bowl.

2. Using a pastry blender or your fingertips, cut in the butter until the mixture resembles coarse meal. Add the water a little at a time, tossing with a fork until the dough sticks together, adding more in small amounts if necessary. Pat the dough into 2 flattened disks, one slightly larger than the other, cover in plastic wrap, and chill for 30 minutes.

3 large eggs

2 teaspoons vanilla extract

2½ tablespoons cold water

2¼ cups all-purpose flour

½ cup Dutch-process cocoa powder

⅔ cup confectioners' sugar

¼ teaspoon salt

½ pound (2 sticks) cold unsalted butter, cut into cubes

2 ounces semisweet chocolate (at least 50% cacao), melted and cooled

### Sweet Chocolate Tart Crust

*Makes one 12 x 6-inch tart*

This tart crust can be rolled if it is chilled for 1–2 hours or pressed into the pan if it is chilled for 30 minutes. Bake in a tart pan with a removable bottom.

1. Combine the eggs, vanilla, and water in a small bowl; set aside.

2. Combine the flour, cocoa powder, sugar, and salt in a large mixing bowl. Using a pastry blender or your fingertips, cut in the butter until the mixture resembles coarse meal. Add the egg yolk mixture, tossing with a fork until the dough sticks together. Mix in the chocolate.

3. Using your hands, form the dough into a ball; then press it on a floured surface, kneading it a few times to make sure all the butter pieces are worked in. Form the dough into one or more flattened disks (whatever is called for in the recipe), cover with plastic wrap, and chill for 1–2 hours before proceeding as directed in the recipe.

## PASTRY BLENDER

A pastry blender is a tool that is used to work fat (butter, shortening, or lard) into dough. It has several parallel U-shaped wires attached to a handle. The fat should be cut into the flour until the mixture forms pea-size crumbs, usually about the size of coarsely ground meal. This is a critical step when making a tender crust by hand. To use the pastry blender, press it into the fat and butter and rotate both the tool and the bowl with a slight twist. You can also use two butter knives (holding one in each hand) by starting in a "crossed swords" position and moving the knives away from each other, cutting the fat into little pieces and mixing it with the flour in the process.

# SAUCES

## Chocolate Sauce
*Makes 2⅛ cups*

4 ounces unsweetened chocolate (any variety)
2 tablespoons unsalted butter
¼ cup granulated sugar
1¼ cups heavy cream

1. Melt the chocolate and butter in the top of a double boiler set over simmering water.

2. Stir in the sugar and cream and lower the heat. Continue to cook, stirring occasionally, for about 10 minutes, or until thick.

## Hot Fudge
*Makes 2¾ cups*

About 4 ounces (⅔ cup) unsweet-ened chocolate, coarsely chopped
½ cup (1 stick) unsalted butter
½ teaspoon salt
3 cups granulated sugar
1 can (12 ounces) evaporated milk

1. In the top pan of a double boiler, combine the chocolate, butter, and salt.

2. Stir until the chocolate is melted. Add ½ cup sugar at a time, stirring until dissolved after each addition. Slowly add the evaporated milk until fully integrated. Store extra sauce in the refrigerator for up to 1 week.

## Raspberry Sauce

*Makes 2 cups*

2 cups fresh raspberries

1 tablespoon freshly squeezed
  lemon juice

½ cup water

½–¾ cup confectioners' sugar

Everyone knows how well chocolate and raspberries complement each other. This tangy sauce is made with confectioners' sugar, which contains cornstarch and acts as a thickener. You can add more water to achieve your desired thickness. Serve hot or cold. For a seedless raspberry sauce, strain the puree through a fine-mesh sieve into a bowl. Transfer to the saucepan to cook.

1. In a food processor, puree the raspberries.

2. Place the raspberry puree, lemon juice, and water in a medium saucepan over low heat. Stir in ½ cup of the sugar until it has dissolved and the mixture has thickened. Add additional sugar to taste.

# TOPPINGS

## Chocolate Buttercream

*Makes 2¼ cups*

2 tablespoons hot milk

2 teaspoons natural unsweetened
  cocoa powder

4 ounces semisweet chocolate (at
  least 50% cacao), melted and
  cooled

6 tablespoons (¾ stick) unsalted
  butter, at room temperature

2¼ cups confectioners' sugar

1 teaspoon vanilla extract

1. Combine the milk and cocoa powder in a medium bowl, stirring until smooth. Let cool.

2. Add the chocolate, butter, confectioners' sugar, and vanilla, and beat until smooth and fluffy.

### Variation

COFFEE BUTTERCREAM: Replace the cocoa powder with 2 teaspoons instant coffee granules dissolved in water.

## Vanilla Icing

*Makes 1½ cups*

3 cups confectioners' sugar, plus
  more if necessary

3 tablespoons warm water

2 teaspoons vanilla extract

1. Place the sugar in a medium bowl and gradually beat in the water until the mixture is smooth.

2. Blend in the vanilla. If necessary, add more sugar to stiffen the mixture.

**Variation**

LEMON ICING: Replace the vanilla with freshly squeezed lemon juice.

## Whipped Cream
*Makes 3½–4 cups*

Beat the cream only until soft peaks form if you want to dollop it on top of or alongside your pie; beat it until medium peaks form if you want to transfer it to a pastry bag and use it for piping.

2 cups heavy cream
1½ teaspoons vanilla extract
2 tablespoons granulated sugar

1. Combine all ingredients in a large mixing bowl. Beat with an electric mixer on medium speed until the cream reaches the desired consistency.

**Variations**

CHOCOLATE WHIPPED CREAM: Add 3 tablespoons Dutch-process cocoa powder and 3 additional tablespoons sugar to the mixture before beating.
WHITE CHOCOLATE WHIPPED CREAM: Beat 6 ounces finely chopped white chocolate into the cream after it has stiffened.
KIRSCH WHIPPED CREAM: Replace the vanilla with 1½ tablespoons Kirsch.
IRISH CREAM WHIPPED CREAM: Replace the vanilla with 2 tablespoons Irish cream.
BOURBON WHIPPED CREAM: Replace the vanilla with 3 tablespoons bourbon.

# Metric Equivalents

## LIQUID INGREDIENTS

This chart can also be used for small amounts of dry ingredients, such as salt and baking powder.

| U.S. Quantity | Metric Equivalent |
| --- | --- |
| ¼ teaspoon | 1 ml |
| ½ teaspoon | 2.5 ml |
| ¾ teaspoon | 4 ml |
| 1 teaspoon | 5 ml |
| 1¼ teaspoons | 6 ml |
| 1½ teaspoons | 7.5 ml |
| 1¾ teaspoons | 8.5 ml |
| 2 teaspoons | 10 ml |
| 1 tablespoon | 15 ml |
| 2 tablespoons | 30 ml |
| ⅛ cup | 30 ml |
| ¼ cup (2 fluid ounces) | 60 ml |
| ⅓ cup | 80 ml |
| ½ cup (4 fluid ounces) | 120 ml |
| ⅔ cup | 160 ml |
| ¾ cup (6 fluid ounces) | 180 ml |
| 1 cup (8 fluid ounces) | 240 ml |
| 1½ cups (12 fluid ounces) | 350 ml |
| 2 cups (1 pint, or 16 fluid ounces) | 475 ml |
| 3 cups | 700 ml |
| 4 cups (1 quart) | 950 ml (.95 liter) |

## DRY INGREDIENTS

| Ingredient | 1 cup | ¾ cup | ⅔ cup | ½ cup | ⅓ cup | ¼ cup | 2 tablespoons |
|---|---|---|---|---|---|---|---|
| All-purpose flour | 120 g | 90 g | 80 g | 60 g | 40 g | 30 g | 15 g |
| Granulated sugar | 200 g | 150 g | 130 g | 100 g | 65 g | 50 g | 25 g |
| Confectioners' sugar | 100 g | 75 g | 70 g | 50 g | 35 g | 25 g | 13 g |
| Brown sugar, firmly packed | 180 g | 135 g | 120 g | 90 g | 60 g | 45 g | 23 g |
| Cornmeal | 160 g | 120 g | 100 g | 80 g | 50 g | 40 g | 20 g |
| Cornstarch | 120 g | 90 g | 80 g | 60 g | 40 g | 30 g | 15 g |
| Butter | 240 g | 180 g | 160 g | 120 g | 80 g | 60 g | 30 g |
| Shortening | 190 g | 140 g | 125 g | 95 g | 65 g | 48 g | 24 g |
| Chopped fruits and vegetables | 150 g | 110 g | 100 g | 75 g | 50 g | 40 g | 20 g |
| Chopped nuts | 150 g | 110 g | 100 g | 75 g | 50 g | 40 g | 20 g |
| Ground nuts | 120 g | 90 g | 80 g | 60 g | 40 g | 30 g | 15 g |

# Index

Note: Page numbers in *italics* indicate photographs. (Page ranges with one page number in *italics* include at least one photograph.)